Research Methods in Service Innovation

SERVICES, ECONOMY AND INNOVATION

Series Editor: John R. Bryson, *Professor of Enterprise and Economic Geography, School of Geography, Earth and Environmental Sciences, The University of Birmingham, UK and Distinguished Research Fellow, Foundation for Research in Economics and Business Administration (SNF), Bergen, Norway*

An ever-increasing proportion of the world's business involves some type of service function and employment. Manufacturing is being transformed into hybrid production systems that combine production and service functions both within manufacturing processes as well as in final products. Manufacturing employment continues to decline while employment in a range of services activities continues to grow. The shift towards service dominated economies presents a series of challenges for academics as well as policy makers. The focus of much academic work has been on manufacturing and until recently services have been relatively neglected. This is the first series to bring together a range of different perspectives that explore different aspects of services, economy and innovation. The series will include titles that explore:

- The economics of services.
- Service-led economies or enterprises.
- Service work and employment.
- Innovation and services.
- Services and the wider process of production.
- Services and globalization.

This series is essential reading for academics and researchers in economics, economic geography and business.

Titles in the series include:

Research Methods in Service Innovation

Edited by

Flemming Sørensen

*Department of Social Sciences and Business, Roskilde
University, Denmark*

Francesco Lapenta

*Department of Communication and Humanities, Roskilde
University, Denmark*

SERVICES, ECONOMY AND INNOVATION

Edward Elgar
PUBLISHING

Cheltenham, UK • Northampton, MA, USA

Published by
Edward Elgar Publishing Limited
The Lypiatts
15 Lansdown Road
Cheltenham
Glos GL50 2JA
UK

Edward Elgar Publishing, Inc.
William Pratt House
9 Dewey Court
Northampton
Massachusetts 01060
USA

A catalogue record for this book
is available from the British Library

Library of Congress Control Number: 2016949987

This book is available electronically in the **Elgar**online
Business subject collection
DOI 10.4337/9781785364860

ISBN 978 1 78536 485 3 (cased)
ISBN 978 1 78536 486 0 (eBook)

Typeset by Servis Filmsetting Ltd, Stockport, Cheshire
Printed and bound by CPI Group (UK) Ltd, Croydon, CR0 4YY

Contents

Figures

Tables

Contributors

Claire Esther Staddon Forder, Department of Social Sciences and Business, Roskilde University, Denmark

Lars Fuglsang, Department of Social Sciences and Business, Roskilde University, Denmark

Niels Nolsøe Grünbaum, Department of Social Sciences and Business, Roskilde University, Denmark

Anne Vorre Hansen, Department of Social Sciences and Business, Roskilde University, Denmark

Francesco Lapenta, Department of Communication and Humanities, Roskilde University, Denmark

Jørn Kjølseth Møller, Department of Social Sciences and Business, Roskilde University, Denmark

Anne Rørbæk Olesen, Department of Communication and Humanities, Roskilde University, Denmark

Ada Scupola, Department of Social Sciences and Business, Roskilde University, Denmark

Flemming Sørensen, Department of Social Sciences and Business, Roskilde University, Denmark

Jon Sundbo, Department of Social Sciences and Business, Roskilde University, Denmark

1. Service innovation research methods

Flemming Sørensen and Francesco Lapenta

1.1 THE CONTEXT AND PURPOSE OF THE BOOK

This book aims to discuss, exemplify and broaden the horizon of methods applied in service innovation research. Supported by applied research examples and contemporary theories, the book offers a structured overview of a number of innovative research methods that can help to approach the investigation of different aspects of service innovation within an eclectic range of theoretical and methodological traditions.

Services, service innovation and service innovation processes have gained increasing socioeconomic importance in the past decades and are receiving growing interest from the research community (Drejer, 2004; Miles, 2005; Bitner et al., 2008; Carlborg et al., 2013). Services not only play a fundamental role in well-established economic sectors, they also have an increasingly broad impact on a wide range of developments related to interpersonal and social relations that affect society as a whole (Miles, 2005; Bryson and Daniels, 2015).

Despite this growing interest in service innovation and service innovation research, there is an apparent void of methodological literature on this topic. Furthermore there has been little or no systematized effort in offering an overview of all the available or developing methods in service innovation research. Quantitative surveys, qualitative case studies and semi-structured interviews seem to dominate the landscape of service innovation research literature. This book with its exploration of alternative methodological approaches offers to move towards a more inclusive and organized account of developing and available methods. This book aims to present service innovation research methods that are particularly relevant to the contemporary socioeconomic context. To that end, the chapters in this book are based on a number of studies that we believe to be representative of areas of growing relevance for contemporary service innovation studies (Chapter 1, section 1.2.2). The chapters also make a case for the specificity of the processes underlying service innovation and the unique dimensions of service innovation (Chapter 1, section 1.2.1). Together they arrive at and are based on the conclusions that: The knowledge and application of new research methods developed for the study of service innovation need to become part of the common toolset of the service innovation researcher and practitioner. Additionally, it is the responsibility of the research community to develop new theoretical models and specific methodological frameworks that can support practitioners and businesses in their efforts to innovate in an ever-changing environment (Chapter 1, section 1.2.3).

This book seeks to be a first step in that direction and offers an overview of innovative methods that the research community and students in the field can explore. Additionally it is an organized and creative methods toolbox that service innovation practitioners can exploit and use to reflect upon, initiate and conduct sustained innovation efforts in service companies and organizations.

1.2 THE THEORETICAL AND METHODOLOGICAL FRAMEWORK OF THE BOOK

How can we define service innovation? How do we observe, capture and influence often complex service innovation processes? What theoretical interpretation may we use to interpret them? How can we detect and collect data about unplanned innovation processes lacking systematization in order to analyse and understand them? How can dynamic service innovation processes involving many different types of actors be grasped? What methods can researchers and practitioners apply to optimize collaboration in service innovation research and development? And how can different methodological approaches to all these different aspects lead to practical solutions that result in improved innovation processes and innovation capacities in service companies? How do we identify, quantify, or estimate the effects of service innovation? To what extent can quantitative approaches explain the nature and complexity of service innovation and service innovation processes? And in what instances and in what research issues are phenomenological, hermeneutic, interpretive and qualitative approaches relevant? This introductory chapter offers an overview of the theoretical and methodological framework that undergirds the answers given to these and other questions in the chapters of the book. It contextualizes these different questions and answers by identifying what we believe to be the three unique dimensions and dynamics that characterize and influence service innovation research today. One dimension is theoretical and methodological. There are a number of interpretations and theories that deal with service innovation research; two representative ones appear to be in apparent juxtaposition. In this chapter we contextualize the different contributions of the book under one theoretical umbrella and approach that positions it within these established traditions. Two other dimensions that are perhaps not immediately discussed in service innovation literature are those of the forces that are influencing its very own evolution and development. In this chapter we identify trends that have at times a problematic programmatic influence on service innovation studies and research. We believe that these influences, of which we are also subject, need to be known and problematized to understand both the contribution of this book and the challenges of the books that will hopefully follow on these subjects. We conclude the introduction with a short presentation of the individual chapters and their specific methodological subjects and contribution.

1.2.1 The Unique Theoretical and Methodological Dimensions of Service Innovation

The term 'innovation' is normally used in service studies to refer to new service 'products' introduced in an established service sector. These innovations include, for example, new services, new production processes, new organizational structures or new marketing strategies. In the context of service innovation analyses, however, the term 'innovation' is often used as a synonym for the term 'innovation processes', more specifically related to the activities that lead to the development of these new products. These alternative uses of the term 'innovation' as either a service *product* or service *product development process* can create confusion and are part of a definition of service innovation that remains fuzzy (Snyder et al., 2016; Witell et al., 2016). Their juxtaposition, however, offers the opportunity to position this book and its chapters within an ongoing theoretical debate that emphasizes different interpretations of what innovation in services is, what it entails, how it can be studied and how it can be elicited.

The main aim of the research methods analysed in this book is to focus on service innovation processes rather than innovations. Innovation research methods, as applied in this book, comprise methods that are, of course, related to the study of innovations; they are, however, focused on the processes that lead to such innovations, the drivers and barriers to such processes as well as the complex dynamics that exist among actors, activities, resources and other elements and factors that may impact such processes. This theoretical and methodological position can be contextualized within the two above-mentioned areas of debate. One looks at the definition of what constitutes innovation in services. The other investigates the underlying dynamics that lead to innovation in services and their specificity (as opposed to other processes of innovation).

Traditionally, innovation is defined as new products, production processes, organizational structures, or marketing strategies that have already gained acceptance in an organization, in the market or in society (Amabile et al., 1996; Kanter, 1996; Sundbo, 1998; Mulgan and Albury, 2003; OECD, 2005). Certain criteria and conditions are emphasized that need to characterize these products to define them as innovations. These new products need to be intentional (part of a specific process of research and not part of accidental evolution). They must represent significant or radical changes in products or practice. Furthermore, they must have a recognizable benefit (especially economic) and be possible to replicate and put into systematic production (Drejer, 2004; Koch et al., 2005; OECD, 2005; Toivonen et al., 2007; Fuglsang and Sørensen, 2011).

While the above-mentioned perceptions of innovation have also been applied in services, especially in the more recent service innovation research, these definitions and limitations have been contested (e.g. Toivonen et al., 2007; Fuglsang and Sørensen, 2011; Sørensen et al., 2013; Kallio, 2015). It has been argued that, because of the nature of services and because of the way services are often produced and consumed, the typical delimitations discussed above do not always represent innovative services well, the processes that lead to their development, how they may occur and how they may be organized (Gallouj and Weinstein, 1997; Sundbo, 1997; Edvardsson et al., 2000; Miles, 2005; Nijssen et al., 2006; Toivonen et al., 2007; Toivonen and Tuominen, 2009; Fuglsang and Sørensen, 2011; Sundbo et al., 2013).

The authors of this book share the latter critical perspective, but accept some considerations of the former. The focus of the book and the majority of its individual chapters is on qualitative and interpretive approaches for the study of service innovation processes. This is the result of our understanding of service innovation and innovation processes as complex, iterative, interactive and dynamic processes that can be better captured and explored by qualitative and interpretive research approaches. We acknowledge, but do not investigate specifically, other quantitative tools and methods that can be developed and can be complementary or necessary to assess, for example, innovation impact and business performance (however, see Chapter 2 for a discussion about innovation measurements). We do, however, focus on innovative qualitative research methods that can elicit an understanding of service innovation processes and foster these processes of service innovation.

At a general level, three different approaches have been suggested regarding how to understand service innovation processes: 1) an assimilation approach that considers service innovation processes to be similar to innovation processes in manufacturing; 2) a demarcation approach that argues that service innovation processes are different from those of manufacturing and that they have features that require new theories and instruments; and 3) a synthesis approach, which suggests that service innovation processes have intrinsic characteristics but these can also be of relevance for manufacturing (Coombs and Miles, 2000; Carlborg et al., 2013). As service innovation research has developed during the last three or so decades the demarcation approach, and later the synthesis approach, have gained support instead of the assimilation approach (Carlborg et al., 2015).

Based on the individual investigations and experience of its contributing authors, this book follows the assumption that specific characteristics do exist that set innovation processes in services apart from other areas of innovation (for example, industrial product innovation) thus supporting the demarcation approach (though without neglecting the relevance of the synthesis approach). These peculiarities of service innovation research processes have consequences that affect not only the perception of service innovation but also how this specific form of innovation can be theoretically understood and methodologically studied.

The authors accept Schumpeter's notion that ideas are not in themselves valuable. Ideas, Schumpeter stated, must be turned into actual new products or services, or result in actual organizational changes or changed practices, to really be interpreted as innovation (Schumpeter, 1969). New marketing practices, for example, must have an economic impact or contribute to reshaping an organization, a company and/or society to be considered actual innovation. However, we also acknowledge that services are, among other things, intangible and perishable, and their processes of production and consumption are inseparable (Vargo and Lusch, 2004) often relying on unstructured employee–user interactions (or service encounters) (Carlzon, 1989; Bitner et al., 1990; Nickson et al., 2005; Sørensen et al., 2013). This intangibility and immediacy often lead to innovation processes in services that occur as ad hoc innovation (Gallouj and Weinstein, 1997) based on bricolage combining resources at hand (Fuglsang, 2010), or in specific project-oriented efforts (Salunke et al., 2013), or during daily interactions with users resulting in changes over time (Fuglsang and Sørensen, 2011) that may be recognized and acknowledged as innovations only in hindsight (Toivonen et al., 2007).

It is our opinion that to grasp service innovation it is necessary to consider these and other characteristics of services. When production and consumption are inseparable, innovation and innovation processes are also conceptually and practically integrated. Acknowledging these dynamics also means refusing the otherwise often cited requirement of service innovations to necessarily arise as a consequence of a conscious managerial strategy (Fuglsang and Sørensen, 2011). Many service organizations do not have innovation or R&D departments, and while some or most might have established procedures designed to take care of innovation within the business, it is also common for innovation processes in services to occur as spontaneous (Sundbo and Sørensen, 2014) or invisible (Fuglsang, 2010) processes lacking systematization (Sundbo, 2010).

The recognition of these complex interactions, the fact that service innovation can be characterized by both top-down- and bottom-up-based innovation processes (Sundbo, 1997, 2010; Rubalcaba et al., 2012; Sørensen et al., 2013; Kallio, 2015), systematic or spontaneous efforts, leads us to understand service innovation as a form of innovation that requires methods apt to interact and integrate with service innovation specific dynamics. For example, understanding the origin of service innovations that result from unsystematic processes, and understanding the drivers and barriers of such processes, can benefit from certain ad hoc types of data collection techniques. Similarly innovations evolving gradually during daily routines and/or on the basis of employees' interactions with users may not be detected and understood through traditional methods of measuring innovativeness. But their understanding can benefit from alternative methods, for example, by observing innovation processes 'in action'. Chapters in this book will discuss, for example, how mapping methods, critical incident techniques and narrative methods can be applied to capture complex and partly invisible service innovation processes and how the inputs to and outputs from such processes (and thus their profitability) may be measured. Others will indicate how innovative methods can integrate in established practices of idea generation that can be later transformed, via practice and experimentation, into innovation in services.

1.2.2 Trends in Service Innovation Research and Themes Reflected in the Book

Departing from the general theoretical and methodological aspects of services and service innovation processes discussed above, we also contend that a number of specific social trends that characterize contemporary service industries influence the development of identifiable types of innovation processes in service organizations and affect the methodological possibilities for investigating such service innovation processes.

These contemporary developments create a hierarchy of relevance among a number of possible methodological approaches to the study of innovation and innovation processes in services. They also remind us that such methods need to be in constant development and problematized. Relevant developments for the book include, for example, the contemporary role of experience (Boswijk et al., 2007; Pine and Gilmore,

2013; Sundbo and Sørensen, 2013), individualization (as well as 'trib-alization') and self-actualization of consumers (Cova, 1997; Boswijk et al., 2012), the role of co-creation of value (Prahalad and Ramaswamy, 2004; Kristensson et al., 2008; Payne et al., 2008; Melton and Hartline, 2015), and the role of value in use (Sandström et al., 2008; Grönroos and Voima, 2013) or well-being (Anderson et al., 2013). They also include the development of hybrid production systems (Bryson and Daniels, 2015) or new business models (Chesbrough, 2010) that have increased the awareness of the value-creating potential of services in traditional industrial sectors resulting in product-service systems (Baines et al., 2007; Beuren et al., 2013) and servitization processes (Baines et al., 2009; Neely, 2009). User-based (Alam, 2002; Magnusson et al., 2003; Sundbo and Toivonen, 2011; Kallio, 2015), employee-driven (Rubalcaba et al., 2012) and service encounter-based innovation processes (Sørensen et al., 2013; Sundbo et al., 2015), co-creation (Kristensson et al., 2008; Grissemann and Stokburger-Sauer, 2012) and other types of interactive innovation processes, including networking (Gilsing and Duysters, 2008; Ahuja et al., 2012; Eide and Fuglsang, 2013; Rusanen et al., 2014; Sørensen and Fuglsang, 2014; Sørensen and Mattsson, 2016), public–private (Link, 2006) and open innovation processes (Chesbrough, 2003; Huizingh, 2011; Mina et al., 2014), are all examples of aspects of innovation processes in services that have gained increasing importance because of the mentioned societal trends among others. However, these trends also raise new questions about perceptions of the elements that constitute service innovation. For example, the value in use perspective refers to customer-created value (Grönroos and Voima, 2013) but innovation definitions have failed to include aspects of the user value of innovations (Snyder et al., 2016).

In this already complex scenario, we cannot forget to account for the role of communication and information technologies in service production and consumption and its potential role in service innovation (Gago and Rubalcaba, 2007; Cabiddu et al., 2013; Della Corte et al., 2015; Nicolaisen et al., 2016). The disruptive and almost endless potential and affordances offered by these technologies have the potential to constantly renegotiate not only innovation and innovation processes in services but also the data collection and methods of analysis they create and entail.

The above-mentioned concepts are part of some of the key trends that influence how we can investigate service innovation processes and what we can choose to investigate about such processes. In relation to the above-mentioned aspects, different chapters in the book will, for example, discuss methods that use social media or discuss the possible use of developing technologies and information technologies. Other chapters investigate co-creation processes, the services' deeper values for users and the methods that study open service innovation processes occurring between companies and their users.

1.2.3   The Role of Service Innovation Research

The above-mentioned societal and academic trends exert significant influence on contemporary understandings of service innovation. As we have seen, these trends are important to understand what theoretical and methodological approaches might be used to investigate and confront service innovation. However, current developments in service innovation research cannot be fully understood without a larger contextualization in the changing dynamics that exist between business and academia as well as the changing demands posed by governments and society on the service innovation research community.

These trends include growing governmental, institutional and civil society demands concerning evident benefits, practical applicability and specific societal and business value of research results (Bornmann, 2013). A kind of Mode 2 research (Novotny et al., 2001) is being advocated, that results, for example, in an increased focus on more collaborative research methods (Van de Ven, 2007) involving close collaboration between researchers and service companies and organizations. These forces have methodological consequences and are favouring specific methods and approaches, such as action research methods (Stringer, 2013) and field experiments, in which researchers are encouraged to develop and implement new innovation procedures in close collaboration with companies (Sørensen et al., 2010).

Furthermore the growing governmental and intergovernmental interest in (often) large-scale research projects that involve a number of different research institutions as well as other public and private stakeholders is another factor that currently influences service innovation research. This has resulted in the creation of increasingly complex collaborative innovation research projects and set-ups that include a multitude of actors in, for example, Triple Helix (Leydesdorff, 2013) or Quadruple Helix projects and in subsequent Mode 3 knowledge production (Carayannis and Campbell, 2012). This results in new methodological challenges as well as challenges concerning the organization and collaboration in such projects, challenges which need scrutiny and investigation.

The relevance of the mentioned expectations for service innovation research methods will be emphasized in various chapters in this book. It will be discussed, for example, how action research, Future Workshops, Future-Oriented Technology Analysis, and experiments can be applied as collaborative service innovation research methods. Additionally, how public–private and university–company collaboration may be developed and organized in large triple helix service innovation research projects to overcome some of the obstacles of research collaboration will be discussed. Such challenges are posed, for example, by the different ontologies, practices and objectives of actors participating in the projects.

1.3   FRAMEWORK AND CHAPTERS OF THE BOOK

The three unique dimensions of service innovation research explored above form the framework upon which the book is based. These dimensions suggest that complex social dynamics, societal changes, research trends, and evolving theoretical models have an influence on relevant service innovation processes and studies. Social changes and research trends have an impact on relevant service innovation processes and on the different actors' participation in these evolutions. As our discussions above have evidenced, these actors include not only service practitioners, but also service innovation research that is equally affected by social trends and evolution. This framework forcefully describes a dynamic environment in which, in a mutual process of adaptation and influence, any of the actors can contribute to the evolution of one, and consequently the other, area of investigation of service innovation practice. These dynamics constitute a research imperative that requires a constant adaptation and evolution of theories and methods that can help to observe and investigate evolving areas of service innovation. This process requires the constant development of innovative research methods specifically developed for the areas of investigation under study or the strategic adaptation of existing methods to specific service innovation practices. The book and its chapters are proof of these two theoretical and methodological dynamics. Each chapter of the book deals with a specifically tailored method, created or adapted to the study of service innovation processes. Each chapter discusses the relevance of the method to the investigation of given aspects of service innovation in relation to the specific framework. The chapters also situate the presented methods in the epistemological and ontological landscape on which they are based. They provide suggestions for how the method can be applied (including more or less specific guidelines), discuss the potential and limitations of the method and its relevance and contribution to service innovation research and practice. To achieve this, each chapter will present research examples that serve to illustrate and discuss how the method has been specifically applied and with what benefits. Together they aim to fulfil the mission of this book: To be a first step in the creation of a systemic overview of innovative methods that the research community, students in the field and practitioners can explore and refer to.

The contributors to the book are members of the ISE (Innovation in Service and Experience) research group at Roskilde University, Denmark. The group's members have studied service innovation processes intensively during several decades and have been influential in service innovation literature and debates. The group has applied a variety of innovative methods in a large number of studies and research projects on innovation processes in public and private service organizations. It is a collection of these methodological experiences that is presented in the following chapters of the book.

While the chapters in general pursue a qualitative approach to service innovation research, Chapter 2, authored by Jon Sundbo discusses how a quantitative instrument can be developed to measure input to and output from specific innovation processes. However, the author also discusses how 'soft' variables other than economic ones may be relevant in order to measure the cost–benefits of service innovations at the firm level. These variables may include, for example, employee motivation and customer satisfaction. Such an instrument is relevant for practitioners to evaluate the benefits and costs of innovating, and for researchers, particularly in practice-oriented studies (such as those discussed in other chapters of the book), because it can provide a possibility for estimating the benefits of collaborative service innovation research projects. This is also relevant in many publicly funded collaborative research projects in which the impact of research on participating companies has become an important aspect for evaluations of such projects. The method developed in the chapter can make such evaluations more transparent. The chapter discusses what and how to measure, and why. It presents existing instruments for measuring the costs and benefits of innovation at the firm level (which are primarily focused on manufacturing sectors) and it discusses the particularities and challenges in measuring service innovations' inputs and outputs.

The next two chapters focus on two different interviewing techniques and their related methods. In Chapter 3, Lars Fuglsang argues that the critical incident technique (CIT) (Flanagan, 1954), combined with other more 'Heideggerian' approaches, provides a basis for analysing everyday experiences of innovation activity in services and can help people make sense of innovation. The author places CIT in three different research traditions with examples from services and innovations: a positivist-functional, a phenomenological and a process-oriented research tradition. The value of CIT as a special interview and research technique for service innovation research is discussed. The method may be particularly relevant in service sectors where, for example, innovation processes are often not strategically planned or intentional but occur as bricolage and are recognized in retrospect.

Niels Nolsøe Grünbaum places emphasis on the benefits of another type of particular interview technique and research method in Chapter 4: The Laddering Method in Service Innovation Research (Reynolds and Gutman, 1988). The author argues that the Laddering Method, which builds on means–end theory (Gutman, 1982), can beneficially be applied to service innovation research as it attempts to create an understanding of the value that users extract from service attributes and depicts mental or cognitive maps of consumers related to the consumption of specific services. In the chapter it is argued that knowledge derived from the Laddering Method is particularly relevant for guiding service innovations and, thus, to optimizing cost–benefits of service innovation and supporting user-based service innovation. While the Laddering Method has clear practical applications and implications for public and private service organizations it can also, for example, support service research by providing insights about different levels of service users' values.

In Chapter 5, Anne Vorre Hansen discusses the possible use of narrative methodology in service innovation research and, compared with the methods presented in the former chapters, she applies the method in a more collective set-up rather than in an interview setting. The potential use of narrative methods is illustrated by an empirical example of a service innovation process, which was planned and carried out as a collaborative research project involving researchers, a non-profit housing organization as well as its users. The author presents the design, the process and the outcome of an innovation workshop and shows how users can create stories of their service experiences and that employees and residents, by co-creating new service-stories, can find a fruitful and neutral place for development. The chapter suggests that narrative methodologies represent a beneficial 'mindset' in service innovation processes rather than a fixed method. The method facilitates user-based innovation and co-creation of value, thus it relates to important aspects currently emphasized in service innovation research.

Mapping innovation processes as visual techniques for opening up the black box of service innovation is the focus of Chapter 6, authored by Anne Rørbæk Olesen. The author argues how different mapping techniques, more or less simple and complex, can help structure, explore, analyse and present messy and complex innovation processes while not reducing their complexity too much. She argues that certain visual mapping techniques are particularly relevant for service innovation research processes, as such processes are exceedingly complex, fuzzy and difficult to make sense of because they often lack systematization and can involve a multitude of different actors. In particular, Olesen discusses the potential of service innovation research for the mapping techniques related to Situational Analysis

(Clarke, 2003, 2005) and a further development of these techniques, which the author calls Temporal Situational Analysis. The chapter illustrates the potential of mapping techniques by presenting findings from a case study of innovation processes in two museums, involving museum staff and digital designers.

While Chapter 6 suggests how the mapping of innovation processes that involve different actors can help sort out complex service innovation processes, Chapter 7 focuses more specifically on the importance of investigating the dynamic relations and networks among actors participating in service innovation processes. The chapter focuses on the potential of social network analysis (SNA) in service innovation research but advocates for applying a qualitative and interpretivist approach to SNA which is otherwise dominated by positivist and mathematical graph approaches. Because contemporary service innovation processes can involve many actors (e.g. individuals, companies and public organizations), they are often organized in complex and very dynamic networks. The authors argue that a qualitative approach to investigating a social network can provide complementary knowledge of such dynamic networks and how they influence, and are influenced by, innovation processes in which many different factors of relevance operate in concert. This is illustrated by a case of the development of an event in a local community. While the authors argue for the benefits of an interpretivist approach to SNA, they also acknowledge, however, the potentials of mixed methods approaches to SNA that combine positivist and interpretivist approaches simultaneously.

Chapter 8 by Ada Scupola focuses on the potential use of social media in service innovation research. Specifically, the author presents the use of blogs as a particular type of social media that can function as a means to collect ideas in open innovation processes for service innovation in engaged research. The potential for the use of blogs is illustrated by the case of a university library. The results of the case show that for service organizations, blogs can generate useful service innovation ideas from users and thus facilitate user-based innovation. From a research point of view the study indicates that the use of social media in service innovation research can provide knowledge about, for example, the value and types of different user inputs as well as about the potential role, use and set-up of different social media platforms.

In Chapter 9, Francesco Lapenta describes how methods, theories and inferences derived from future-oriented technology analysis can and should be developed and implemented in technology-dependent service businesses and activities. Advancements in technology and service innovation have always been intertwined. Information technologies, however, have profoundly reshaped the very nature, and many fundamental processes, associated with the service sector as a whole and with service innovation in general. This chapter specifically focuses on 'future scenario analyses' as a methodological tool that service companies in heavy technology-dependent business can utilize to maintain or build their business advantage. The chapter specifically looks at the banking sector and the fast changes that characterize the financial technologies services that depend as much on the comprehension of the banking practices of the past as the understanding, evaluation, development and adoption of the IT-based service practices of the future.

The relevance and potential of collaborative or engaged service innovation research, such as that illustrated in Chapters 5 and 8, are further discussed in the following chapters of the book. Chapter 10 illustrates how Future Workshops can be used in service innovation research that examines the relevance and ways of engaging users as well as employees in service innovation processes. The method presented is also an example of a collaborative research method that can benefit practitioners and researchers alike and can provide new knowledge and solutions to organizations. As such, the method can result in practically applicable knowledge in the shape of new innovation ideas. The future workshop method is exemplified by the case of Future Workshops conducted at a research library. The author discusses and illustrates the benefits of different types of set-ups of Future Workshops, for example, involving users, employees or both.

In Chapter 11, Flemming Sørensen argues that field experiments present an important potential for service innovation research. He argues that field experiments can sustain the development of new service innovation processes that can increase service organizations' innovativeness. Thus they comply with society's call for collaboration between academia and businesses and for the development of practically relevant knowledge. Furthermore, field experiments are argued to provide researchers with new knowledge about service innovation processes that could not be gained using other methods because they can test prototypes of service innovation procedures. The chapter illustrates the potential of field experiments in service innovation research, with the example of a simple experiment in a hotel where the joint development of new practices led to service innovations. The author also discusses certain limitations and risks of the experiment method.

The last chapter of the book follows in the footsteps of the former chapters dealing with collaborative and engaged research but changes perspective compared to those chapters. In this chapter Claire Esther Staddon Forder focuses on the set-ups of triple helix research projects that involve many different actors and the issues that follow from such set-ups. There is a growing interest in triple helix projects from society and from funding actors and this also includes applied service innovation research projects. However, knowledge on the process of developing service innovation triple helix projects and how they function in practice is still rather limited. By following the case of a large applied tourism service innovation research project that involved researchers, tourism companies, a labour union, sector organizations, educational institutions and other actors, the author discusses and exemplifies the inherent ontological and epistemological differences of various actors in service innovation-oriented triple helix projects, and the issues and controversies that these differences may cause during collaboration. The author discusses how bridging the ontological differences can facilitate service innovation in triple helix projects.

Thus, each chapter presents a specific method that is argued to be particularly relevant for service innovation research, taking into consideration the various characteristics of services, service innovation and service innovation processes, the relevant social conditions and the political and societal requirements of service innovation research. The result is the presentation of a varied collection of methods that can help focus on various aspects of service innovation processes. We hope that the book and its chapters can be inspiration for the application and further development of different methods and thus sustain the continuous development of new knowledge on service innovation and service innovation processes, thereby also sustaining the future innovativeness of the different service sectors.

REFERENCES

Ahuja, G., G. Soda, and A. Zaheer (2012), 'The genesis and dynamics of organizational networks', *Organization Science*, 23 (2), 434–448.

Alam, I. (2002), 'An exploratory investigation of user involvement in new service development', *Journal of the Academy of Marketing Science*, 30 (3), 250–261.

Amabile, T.M., R. Conti, H. Coon, J. Lazenby, and M. Herron (1996), 'Assessing the work environment for creativity', *Academy of Management Journal*, 39 (5), 1154–1184.

Anderson, L., A.L. Ostrom, C. Corus, R.P. Fisk, A.S. Gallan, M. Giraldo, J.D. Williams et al. (2013), 'Transformative service research: An agenda for the future', *Journal of Business Research*, 66 (8), 1203–1210.

Baines, T.S., H.W. Lightfoot, O. Benedettini, and J.M. Kay (2009), 'The servitization of manufacturing', *Journal of Manufacturing Technology Management*, 20 (5), 547–567.

Baines, T.S., H.W. Lightfoot, S. Evans, A. Neely, R. Greenough, J. Peppard, and J.R. Alcock (2007), 'State-of-the-art in product-service systems', *Proceedings of the Institution of Mechanical Engineers, Part B: Journal of Engineering Manufacture*, 221 (10), 1543–1552.

Beuren, F.H., M.G.G. Ferreira, and P.A.C. Miguel (2013), 'Product-service systems: A literature review on integrated products and services', *Journal of Cleaner Production*, 47, 222–231.

Bitner, M.J., B.H. Booms, and M.S. Tetreault (1990), 'The service encounter: Diagnosing favorable and unfavorable incidents', *The Journal of Marketing*, 1990, 71–84.

Bitner, M., A. Ostrom, and F. Morgan (2008), 'Service blueprinting: A practical technique for service innovation', *California Management Review*, 50 (3), 66–81.

Bornmann, L. (2013), 'What is societal impact of research and how can it be assessed? A literature survey', *Journal of the American Society for Information Science and Technology*, 64 (2), 217–233.

Boswijk, A., E. Peelen, S. Olthof, and C. Beddow (2012), *Economy of Experiences*. Amsterdam: European Centre for the Experience and Transformation Economy.

Boswijk, A., T. Thijssen, and E. Peelen (2007), *The Experience Economy: A New Perspective*. Upper Saddle River: Pearson Education.

Bryson, J.R. and P.W. Daniels (2015), 'Service business: Growth, innovation, competitiveness', in J. Bryson and P. Daniels (eds.), *Service Business*. Cheltenham, UK and Northampton, MA, USA: Edward Elgar Publishing, pp. 1–15.

Cabiddu, F., T.-W. Lui, and G. Piccoli (2013), 'Managing value co-creation in the tourism industry', *Annals of Tourism Research*, 42, 86–107.

Carayannis, E.G. and D.J.F. Campbell (2012), *Mode 3 Knowledge Production in Quadruple Helix Innovation Systems*. New York: Springer.

Carlborg, P., D. Kindström, and C. Kowalkowski (2013), 'The evolution of service innovation research: A critical review and synthesis', *The Service Industries Journal*, 34 (5), 373–398.

Carlzon, J. (1989). *Moments of Truth*. New York: HarperCollins.

Chesbrough, H. (2003). *Open Innovation: The New Imperative for Creating and Profiting from Technology*. Boston, MA: Harvard Business School Press.

Chesbrough, H. (2010), 'Business model innovation: Opportunities and barriers', *Long Range Planning*, 43 (2), 354–363.

Clarke, A.E. (2003), 'Situational analyses: Grounded theory mapping after the postmodern turn', *Symbolic Interaction*, 26 (4), 553–576.

Clarke, A.E. (2005), *Situational Analysis: Grounded Theory After the Postmodern Turn*. Thousand Oaks: Sage Publications.

Coombs, R. and I. Miles (2000), 'Innovation, measurement and services: The new problematique', *Economics of Science, Technology and Innovation*, 18, 85–103.

Cova, B. (1997), 'Community and consumption: Towards a definition of the "linking value" of product or services', *European Journal of Marketing*, 31 (3/4), 297–316.

Della Corte, V., A. Iavazzi, and C. Andrea (2015), 'Customer involvement through social media: The cases of some telecommunication firms', *Journal of Open Innovation: Technology, Market, and Complexity*, 1 (1), 1–10.

Drejer, I. (2004), 'Identifying innovation in surveys of services: A Schumpeterian perspective', *Research Policy*, 33 (3), 551–562.

Edvardsson, B., B. Gustafsson, M. Johnson, and B. Sandén (2000), *New Service Development and Innovation in the New Economy*. Lund: Studentlitteratur.

Eide, D. and L. Fuglsang (2013), 'Networking in the experience economy: Scaffolded networks between designed and emerging regional development', in J. Sundbo and F. Sørensen (eds.), *Handbook on the Experience Economy*. Cheltenham, UK, and Northampton, MA, USA: Edward Elgar Publishing, pp. 297–309.

Flanagan, J. (1954), 'The Critical Incident Technique', *Psychological Bulletin*, 51 (4), 327–358.

Fuglsang, L. (2010), 'Bricolage and invisible innovation in public service innovation', *Journal of Innovation Economics*, 5 (1), 67–87.

Fuglsang, L. and F. Sørensen (2011), 'The balance between bricolage and innovation: Management dilemmas in sustainable public innovation', *Service Industries Journal*, 31 (4), 581–595.

Gago, D. and L. Rubalcaba (2007), 'Innovation and ICT in service firms: Towards a multidimensional approach for impact assessment', *Journal of Evolutionary Economics*, 17 (1), 25–44.

Gallouj, F. and O. Weinstein (1997) 'Innovation in services', *Research Policy*, 27 (4–5), 537–556.

Gilsing, V.A. and G.M. Duysters (2008), 'Understanding novelty creation in exploration networks: Structural and relational embeddedness jointly considered', *Technovation*, 28 (10), 693–708.

Grissemann, U.S. and N.E. Stokburger-Sauer (2012), 'Customer co-creation of travel services: The role of company support and customer satisfaction with the co-creation performance', *Tourism Management*, 33 (6), 1483–1492.

Grönroos, C. and P. Voima (2013), 'Critical service logic: Making sense of value creation and co-creation', *Journal of the Academy of Marketing Science*, 41 (2), 133–150.

Gutman, J. (1982), 'A means–end chain model based on consumer categorization processes', *The Journal of Marketing*, 1982, 60–72.

Huizingh, E. (2011), 'Open innovation: State of the art and future perspectives', *Technovation*, 31 (1), 2–9.

Kallio, K. (2015), *Collaborative Learning with Users as an Enabler of Service Innovation*. Espoo: VTT Technical Research Centre of Finland.

Kanter, R.M. (1996), *The Change Masters. Corporate Entrepreneurs at Work*. Boston, MA: Thompson Business Press.

Koch, P., P. Cunningham, N. Schwabsky, and J. Hauknes (2005), *Innovation in the public sector. Summary and policy recommendations*. Public Report No. D24. Oslo: NIFU STEP.

Kristensson, P., J. Matthing, and N. Johansson (2008), 'Key strategies in co-creation of new services', *International Journal of Service Industry Management*, 19 (4), 574–591.

Leydesdorff, L. (2013), *Triple Helix of University–Industry–Government Relations*. New York: Springer.

Link, A.N. (2006), *Public/Private Partnerships: Innovation Strategies and Policy Alternatives*. Berlin: Springer Verlag.

Magnusson, P., J. Matthing, and P. Kristensson (2003), 'Managing user involvement in service innovation: Experiments with innovating end users', *Journal of Service Research*, 6 (2), 111–124.

Melton, H. and M.D. Hartline (2015), 'Customer and employee co-creation of radical service innovations', *Journal of Services Marketing*, 29 (2), 112–123.

Miles, I. (2005), 'Innovation in services', in Fagerberg, J. (ed.), *The Oxford Handbook of Innovation*. Oxford: Oxford University Press, pp. 435–458.

Mina, A., E. Bascavusoglu-Moreau, and A. Hughes (2014), 'Open service innovation and the firm's search for external knowledge', *Research Policy*, 43 (5), 853–866.

Mulgan, G. and D. Albury (2003), *Innovation in the Public Sector*. London: Strategy Unit, Cabinet Office.

Neely, A. (2009), 'Exploring the financial consequences of the servitization of manufacturing', *Operations Management Research*, 1 (2), 103–118.

Nickson, D., C. Warhurst, and E. Dutton (2005), 'The importance of attitude and appearance in the service encounter in retail and hospitality', *Managing Service Quality*, 15 (2), 195–208.

Nicolaisen, H.W., F. Sørensen, and A. Scupola (2016), 'The potential of workshops versus blogs for user involvement in service innovation', *International Journal of e-Services and Mobile Applications*, 8 (4), 1–19

Nijssen, E.J., B. Hillebrand, P.A. Vermeulen, and R.G. Kemp (2006), 'Exploring product and service innovation similarities and differences', *International Journal of Research in Marketing*, 23 (3), 241–251.

Novotny, H., P. Scott, and M. Gibbons (2001), *Re-thinking Science. Knowledge and the Public in an Age of Uncertainty*. Cambridge, UK: Polity.

OECD (2005), *The Measurement of Scientific and Technological Activities. Oslo Manual. Guidelines for Collecting and Interpreting Innovation Data* (33rd ed.). Paris: OECD.

Payne, A.F., K. Storbacka, and P. Frow (2008), 'Managing the co-creation of value', *Journal of the Academy of Marketing Science*, 36 (1), 83–96.

Pine, B.J. and J.H. Gilmore (2013), 'The experience economy: Past, present and future', in J. Sundbo and F. Sørensen (eds.), *Handbook on the Experience Economy*, Cheltenham, UK, and Northampton, MA, USA: Edward Elgar Publishing, pp. 21–44.

Prahalad, C.K. and V. Ramaswamy (2004), 'Co-creation experiences: The next practice in value creation', *Journal of Interactive Marketing*, 18 (3), 5–14.

Reynolds, T.J. and J. Gutman (1988), 'Laddering theory, method, analysis and interpretation', *Journal of Advertising Research*, 28, 11–31.

Rubalcaba, L., S. Michel, J. Sundbo, S.W. Brown, and J. Reynoso (2012), 'Shaping, organizing, and rethinking service innovation: A multidimensional framework', *Journal of Service Management*, 23 (5), 696–715.

Rusanen, H., A. Halinen, and E. Jaakkola (2014), 'Accessing resources for service innovation: The critical role of network relationships', *Journal of Service Management*, 25 (1), 2–29.

Salunke, S., J. Weerawardena, and J.R. McColl-Kennedy (2013), 'Competing through service innovation: The role of bricolage and entrepreneurship in project-oriented firms', *Journal of Business Research*, 66 (8), 1085–1097.

Sandström, S., B. Edvardsson, P. Kristensson, and P. Magnusson (2008), 'Value in use through service experience', *Managing Service Quality*, 18 (2), 112–126.

Schumpeter, J. (1969), *The Theory of Economic Development. An Inquiry into Profits, Capital, Credit, Interest and the Business Cycle*. Oxford: Oxford University Press.

Snyder, H., L. Witell, A. Gustafsson, P. Fombelle, and P. Kristensson (2016), 'Identifying categories of service innovation: A review and synthesis of the literature', *Journal of Business Research*, 69 (7), 2401–2408.

Sørensen, F. and L. Fuglsang (2014), 'Social network dynamics and innovation in small tourism companies', in M. McLeod and R. Vaughan (eds.), *Knowledge Networks and Tourism*. Abingdon: Routledge, pp. 28–45.

Sørensen, F. and J. Mattsson (2016), 'Speeding up innovation: Building network structures for parallel innovation', *International Journal of Innovation Management*, 20 (2).

Sørensen, F., J. Mattsson, and J. Sundbo (2010), 'Experimental methods in innovation research', *Research Policy*, 39 (3), 313–322.

Sørensen, F., J. Sundbo, and J. Mattsson (2013), 'Organisational conditions for service encounter-based innovation', *Research Policy*, 42 (8), 1446–1456.

Stringer, E.T. (2013), *Action Research*. Thousand Oaks, CA: Sage Publications.

Sundbo, J. (1997), 'Management of innovation in services', *Service Industries Journal*, 17 (3), 432–455.

Sundbo, J. (1998), *The Organisation of Innovation in Services*. Roskilde: Roskilde University Press.

Sundbo, J. (2010), *The Toilsome Path of Service Innovation*. Cheltenham, UK and Northampton, MA, USA: Edward Elgar Publishing.

Sundbo, J. and F. Sørensen (2013), 'Introduction to the experience economy', in J. Sundbo and F. Sørensen (eds.), *Handbook on the Experience Economy*. Cheltenham, UK and Northampton, MA, USA: Edward Elgar Publishing, pp. 1–20.

Sundbo, J. and F. Sørensen (2014), 'The lab is back: Towards a new model of innovation in services', in C. Bilton and S. Cummings (eds.), *Handbook of Management and Creativity*. Cheltenham, UK and Northampton, MA, USA: Edward Elgar Publishing, pp. 57–72.

Sundbo, J. and M. Toivonen (eds.) (2011), *User-Based Innovation in Services*. Cheltenham, UK and Northampton, MA, USA: Edward Elgar Publishing.

Sundbo, J., F. Sørensen, and L. Fuglsang (2013), 'Innovation in the experience sector', in J. Sundbo and F. Sørensen (eds.), *Handbook on the Experience Economy*. Cheltenham, UK and Northampton, MA, USA: Edward Elgar Publishing, pp. 228–247.

Sundbo, J., D. Sundbo, and A. Henten (2015), 'Service encounters as bases for innovation', *The Service Industries Journal*, 35 (5), 255–274.

Toivonen, M. and T. Tuominen (2009), 'Emergence of innovations in services', *The Service Industries Journal*, 29 (7), 887–902.

Toivonen, M., T. Tuominen, and S. Brax (2007), 'Innovation process interlinked with the process of service delivery: A management challenge in KIBS', *Economies et Sociétés*, 41 (3), 355–384.

Van de Ven, A.H. (2007), *Engaged Scholarship: Creating Knowledge for Science and Practice*. Oxford: Oxford University Press.

Vargo, S. and R. Lusch (2004), 'The four service marketing myths remnants of a goods-based, manufacturing model', *Journal of Service Research*, 6 (4), 325–335.

Witell, L., H. Snyder, A. Gustafsson, P. Fombelle, and P. Kristensson (2016), 'Defining service innovation: A review and synthesis', *Journal of Business Research*, 69 (8), 2863–2872.

2. Quantitative measurement instruments: a case of developing a method for measuring innovation in service firms

Jon Sundbo

2.1 INTRODUCTION

This chapter treats quantitative instruments to measure input to and output from innovation processes. Such cost–benefit considerations stem from economics, but in most innovation research more than economic variables are measured—for example, employee motivation and customer satisfaction (as dependent as well as independent variables).

The chapter will briefly present and discuss instruments developed to measure innovation input and outcome at the macro (societal) and micro (firm) levels. This will be the basis for the main message of the chapter, which is to present a development in a research project of a quantitative instrument to measure service innovation input and outcome at the firm level. This presentation has a twofold dimension: first, it presents and discusses the instrument that was developed. Second, it presents the research method, process and problems that appeared in the research project on how to measure service firms' innovation. The first is the presentation of measurement instruments that practitioners can use to observe their innovation capability, but data that the measurement provides can also be input to scientific analyses and these instruments are thus also research techniques. The second is a discussion of an attempt to innovate measurement instruments via a new and exploratory research method. This topic is emphasized since this book is about innovation research methods and this case illustrates one such method: development of quantitative measurement instruments in cooperation with firms. The methodological approach of this project was the co-creation of knowledge with practitioners (cf. Johannisson et al., 2008) or mode 2 research (as it has been defined by Nowotny et al., 2001).

The first section of the chapter will be a theoretical discussion of the measurement problem—what and how to measure, and why. Next, existing measurement instruments at the macro level will be presented and discussed, followed by the presentation and discussion of existing instruments for measuring innovation at the firm level in general (which by and large means the manufacturing sector). The particularity and challenges in measuring service innovations will then be discussed based on investigation of existing attempts at such measurement. Then the attempt in this piece of research to develop a new instrument to measure service innovation at the firm level will be presented and discussed. Finally, the conclusion will examine the general situation concerning innovation measurement instruments and what we can learn from this scientific attempt to develop a new instrument to measure service firms' innovation efforts.

2.2   THE MEASUREMENT PROBLEM: THEORETICAL DISCUSSION

Economic and management science has an interest in understanding the economics of innovation, that is, how innovation contributes to the economy and how that contribution can be measured. One line of thinking, often based on Schumpeter's (1934, 1939) theories, is that innovation creates economic growth. This idea has almost become a dogma within evolutionary economic theory (e.g. Freeman and Soete, 1997; Fagerberg et al., 2005; Andersen, 2008). Governments and supranational organizations such as the OECD and the EU have an interest in measuring innovation input and outcomes at a societal level to assess whether industrial policy, which is often based on innovation incentives, works and leads to economic growth (e.g. Rothwell and Zegveld, 1985; Borras, 2003).

It may be true that economic growth can be explained by innovation, but that does not mean that every attempt to innovate leads to economic growth. Indeed, this is far from the case as many—maybe most—attempts or projects lead to losses. The market may reject the innovation, development costs can be too high or organizational barriers and other obstacles may appear in the process (cf. Sundbo, 2013). We do not know how big the losses generally are; they might be as large as the growth effect of the successful innovations. One hypothesis might be that innovation can be both good and bad, and that the losses incurred in attempts to innovate may be of the same magnitude as the growth effect, at least for a period of time. These periods of loss could, theoretically, be assumed to be periods of depression. The problem with ascertaining the veracity of these claims is that we currently lack a way of measuring the losses and gains. Despite all the attempts to measure innovation input and output (i.e. Arundel et al., 2007; CIS, 2009; EU, 2013), we do not have a full picture of the value of innovation because the unsuccessful innovation projects that are ended halfway through the development process are not measured or included in the statistics. The losses are therefore underestimated. To get a more correct picture of the economic effect of innovation behavior for both society and individual firms, we need to count the input and outcome of *all* innovation attempts, not only the successful ones. This requires tools that can measure the total input and outcome of each innovation project that firms or individual entrepreneurs attempt to carry out (Daly, Sætre, and Brun, 2012). To specify and implement such instruments is difficult, both theoretically and practically, particularly within more complex innovation activities such as service innovation (cf. Gallouj and Djellal, 2010), experience innovation (Fuglsang et al., 2011) and open innovation (Chesbrough, 2006, 2011).

Thus, there is a need for an instrument that can measure the total input and output at both a macro (societal) level and a micro (firm) level. No perfect instrument to measure any of these levels exists—just imperfect ones that measure only some of the necessary variables, do not measure the real variables (such as economic input or outcome) but rather indicators for the real variables, or which do not reveal the pure effect of innovation investments but only some rough estimations of the outcome. By nature, the isolated effect of innovation input is difficult to measure because the effect appears some time after the input and other factors influence the result (for example, economic growth in a society or increased profit in a firm). Science therefore continuously looks for improved, though still imperfect, measurement instruments.

2.3 EXISTING MEASUREMENT INSTRUMENTS

2.3.1 Macro-level Instruments

The issue of measuring inputs to and outcomes of innovation processes has been emphasized for a long time, examples being the Frascati manual and Eurostat's CIS surveys. The Frascati manual was created in 1963 and defined innovation and which indicators should be used to measure inputs to and outputs of innovation processes (OECD, 2002). It was a quite narrow instrument that measured economic factors and was based on R&D as the leading innovation activity. In 1992, it was extended to include the Oslo manual with more organizational input indicators and more output indicators than just growth and profit (OECD and Eurostat, 2005).

The Oslo manual is the basis for the CIS surveys that Eurostat carries out regularly (Eurostat, 2004). The CIS survey is quite a wide survey that now includes many different variables, from economic ones such as investment in R&D to sociological and managerial ones such as which information sources firms use to get ideas for innovations (e.g. Aschhoff et al., 2013; see also Gault, 2013, for a critical discussion).

Later instruments that measure innovation inputs and outcomes more specifically from a societal benchmarking view have been developed. They are often called innovation scoreboards and are intended to provide instruments to benchmark nations or regions (e.g. Dutta, 2012). The EU has, for example, introduced such a scoreboard (EU, 2014) that measures and compares the member states' innovation performance using eight innovation dimensions and 25 indicators. The input indicators include, for example, the number of PhD graduates, venture capital investments and innovative SMEs collaborating with others. The output indicators include, for example, the number of SMEs with organizational and marketing innovations, employment in knowledge-intensive activities, and license and patent revenues from abroad.

2.3.2   Micro-level Instruments

Many other research-based models and instruments to guide innovation processes and innovation investment in firms have been offered (e.g. Cooper, 1988; Burgelman et al., 2004; Lundvall and Nielsen, 2007, based on a knowledge economy approach; or Foss, 2003, based on the resource-based view). These instruments are primarily grounded on the R&D approach and are generally oriented towards manufacturing (although some such as Cooper and Edget [1999] have been applied to services). However, micro-level instruments that quantitatively measure innovation input and output are rarer. Other instruments such as the European Service Innovation Scoreboard introduce a process measurement instrument with input, throughput and output factors particularly for measuring service innovation. Measurement instruments for innovative capability (Teece and Pisano, 1994) have been introduced (Forsknings og Innovationsstyrelsen, 2008; Damvad, 2011, 2013). Instruments to measure a firm's total dynamic innovation capability including intrapreneurship, strategic capacity, leadership and value chain positioning have been launched (e.g. Dewangan and Godse, 2014; Sicotte et al., 2014). However, these models do not measure concrete input and output at a project level (the single innovation), but only as a general firm innovation capability.

The first models developed to measure innovation performance at the micro level emphasized technological innovations and measured only R&D

investments as the input (e.g. Cordero, 1990). Later, more variables were included, but still connected to technological innovations. For example, besides R&D investments, Hagedoorn and Cloodt (2003) included a number of patents and even marketing of new products (announcement of new products). Later research has attempted to provide more holistic measurement instruments that include managerial, organizational and market-oriented variables such as knowledge absorption, organizational culture and commercialization (e.g. Adams et al., 2006). However, many of these model suggestions are not operationalized into quantitatively measurable instruments, and they still emphasize the input and not the output.

2.4 STATE OF THE ART OF INNOVATION MEASUREMENT IN SERVICES

Measurement is more difficult in services than in traditional manufacturing innovation because a service is an immaterial product in which employee and customer behavior and state of mind play a larger role. Thus, the market acceptance of the innovation may be more difficult to predict because of these subjective factors, in addition to the ever-present insecurity about market reactions.

Further, the innovation process is more complex in services because many employees are involved for only part of the time, users are often involved and the innovation activities are spread throughout the organization (Sundbo, 1998; den Hertog et al., 2006). Such inputs are therefore more difficult to calculate. Further, the measures generally emphasize the macro level. Thus, a research aim would be to develop measurements at a micro or firm level that can measure, or at least provide indications of, the input and outcome of service innovation processes. This is not easy because many factors are involved, of which several cannot be measured with any precision, and definitely not in monetary terms.

The theoretical problems of the measurement of service innovation have been discussed (Drejer, 2004), as have the methodological aspects of measurement itself (Djellal and Gallouj, 2001). Some attempts have been made to measure input and innovation capabilities in service companies (SIC, 1999; Djellal and Gallouj, 1999, 2001; INNO-Studies, 2004). New contributions have identified and measured some dimensions of dynamic capabilities in service innovation (den Hertog, 2010; Damvad, 2011; Janssen et al., 2012). Other contributions have developed insights into employee innovation (Sundbo, 1998; ICE, 2010, 2012) and the soft (social, organizational) side of service innovation (den Hertog et al., 2006), as well as involvement of users and other external actors in innovation networks

(Kristensson et al., 2008; Fuglsang, 2010; Sundbo and Toivonen, 2011), however, these are rarely based on quantitative measures. Suggestions for indexes that include employees' corporate entrepreneurship and management capability exist (e.g. Sundbo et al., 2001; Bryson et al., 2012), but these are few and not very well developed. This has led to the inclusion of new indicators in CIS to capture specific characteristics of service innovation. Gotsch and Hipp (2012) have, for example, developed a specific market indicator (trade mark) while Krizaj et al. (2012) have developed an instrument that measures tourism innovation output (but not input).

There has been a focus on customer involvement in service innovation processes, called co-creation (e.g. Prahalad and Ramaswamy, 2004; Kristensson et al., 2004; Kristensson et al., 2008) or co-innovation (Sundbo et al., 2015). This aspect is valuable for creating successful innovations, but also costly because it requires time for employees or managers to interact with customers or analyse customer data. Much literature has praised the outcome of co-creation activities and some literature also refers to its measurement (Li et al., 2009; Edvardsson et al., 2012; Gustafsson et al., 2012; Perks et al., 2012). However, such measures are of customer satisfaction with the delivery of existing services. Very little literature has attempted to measure the outcome in terms of innovations; in particular, there have been few attempts to establish quantitative measures (some of the rare examples are Li et al., 2009, and Perks et al., 2012). This is also true of required input in relation to customer co-innovation (Sundbo et al., 2015).

2.5   MEASUREMENT OF SERVICE INNOVATION AT THE FIRM LEVEL

2.5.1   Research on Service Innovation Measurement

In this chapter, a first attempt to develop service innovation measures is presented. Since the aim is to develop tools that can be used by service firms, it is not sufficient to develop a theoretical instrument. If service firms will not use the measure because it is difficult, or impossible, to use in practice or because the service firms do not find it appropriate—despite its theoretical eminence—we will not get a valid measure nor will service firms get a usable decision tool. The research referred to in this chapter is therefore an attempt to theoretically develop an appropriate measurement instrument and a test of whether service firms would be likely to use it. If we cannot perform laboratory experiments, which we cannot in economics, we are dependent on economic actors' willingness to provide the necessary empirical data. This may not, sometimes, lead to the most perfect measures, but to optimal ones (a compromise between the theoretically desirable and the practically possible). However, we do not even know what the practically possible is. Therefore, the investigation into which factors service firms are willing and motivated to measure is crucial for establishing a scientific measure and for developing measurement tools that firms can use.

Such an investigation has not been done before. Theoretical models of service innovation (e.g. Sundbo and Gallouj, 2000; Gallouj, 2002) and prescriptions for organization of service innovation activities exist (e.g. Cooper and Edget, 1999), but no concrete measurement tools that can inform about the outcome related to the input have been developed. The research referred to in this chapter will fill a gap in the scientific knowledge concerning which input and outcome factors are really important to service firms and which factors are crucial for success in service innovation processes. In the following sections, the theoretical foundation for a service innovation project measurement tool and, based on this, a suggestion for a practical tool is put forward. The tool has been tested with a group of service innovation managers (a kind of longitudinal focus group; see Puchta and Potter, 2006) and thereafter in two service firms in an exploratory study. The results are discussed in the conclusion.

2.5.2 What to Measure?

Since no appropriate measure exists that firms can use to assess different innovation projects, one may turn to what the service innovation research says about the drivers of innovation processes and the useful outcomes of such processes for service firms. This can be the basis for an ideal model of a measure of service innovation efficiency. A review of the service innovation research (e.g. Evangelista and Sirilli, 1998; Sundbo, 1998; Sundbo and Gallouj, 2000; Gallouj, 2002; van den Aa and Elfring, 2002; Drejer, 2004; Kristensson et al., 2004; Hipp and Grupp, 2005; Tidd and Hull, 2005; Edvardsson et al., 2006; Cainelli et al. 2006; Gallouj and Savona, 2009; Gallouj and Djellal, 2010; particularly Howells, 2010; Sundbo and Toivonen, 2011; Perks et al., 2012; Rubalcaba et al., 2012) suggests that a broad measure is desirable, including both quantitative indicators and qualitative factors that are difficult to quantify. This also suggests that it will be extremely difficult to create one index that contains all input or all output factors. How to characterize the result of the innovation process has been discussed (Damvad, 2011)—whether it should be in terms of output or outcome. The former is considered a more quantitative, narrow income or profit measure, which may usually be expressed in money terms.

The latter is a wider measure that includes more than the narrow economic income. Outcome will therefore be chosen here.

A review of the above-mentioned service innovation research literature that has been carried out by the author suggests that the following are relevant input and outcome factors:

Input factors
These are investments in either money or time (the latter can in principle be converted into money terms).

- *Working hours within the firm* (at all levels and including all activities, such as interacting with customers in co-creation activities (Prahalad and Ramaswamy, 2004; Payne et al., 2009; Witell et al., 2011), converted into money terms)
- *External advice and knowledge procurement* (both of which can be expenses, for example, consultancy or paid research)
- *Expenses for technology and other materials*
- *Public support* (an income, for example, public grants or researchers giving free advice)
- *Network benefits* (for example, competitors who are also collaborators, representatives from the value chain and others from networks; the input from network activities is normally free, however, the firm's time use in network activities should be deducted from that; cf. Hakonsson and Snehota, 1989; Pyka and Küppers, 2002).

Outcome factors
Four types of outcome factors are seen as important in the literature: income and growth (including productivity), employee (such as motivation and competence), customer/market (such as branding and experienced customer quality) and strategic/business model factors (cf. Osterwalder and Pigneur, 2010).

Income and growth

- *Turnover* (more sales—increased turnover)
- *Profit* (either positive or negative).

Employee factors

- *More employees* (an indicator of growth—may be a power factor for departmental managers)
- *Productivity*

- *Employee motivation and competence* (more satisfied and efficient employees)
- *Employee entrepreneurship* (employees more engaged in innovation activities).

Customer/market factors

- *Increased service quality and customer satisfaction* (which in theory are supposed to be connected; cf. Edvardsson et al., 1994; Grönroos, 2000)
- *Branding and PR* (the firm becomes better known by the market because of the innovation)
- *Penetration into new markets* (a new product launched in a new market can result in firms being able to sell other services in that market).

Strategic/business model factors

- *Organizational learning* (the firm learns how to innovate better and more efficiently next time)
- *Changed strategy* (the firm may change to a more appropriate strategy because of the innovation)
- *New networks* (if the innovation required a relation to new external actors, these can be an innovation resource in the future).

2.5.3 Practical Usability

This theoretical model was tested for its practical usability in a group of 11 innovation managers (of which some were the managing directors) from different service industries and different sizes of service firms.[1] Three researchers held discussions with this group for a period of one year. The aim of the discussion was to find which input and outcome factors were meaningful to the innovation managers in their business activities and which measures were appropriate—that is, those they would carry out in their firm as tools to assess and choose between different innovation ideas. Thus, these measures are also tools in organizational learning (cf. Senge, 1990; Argyris, 1992).

The researchers made notes during the meetings to collect information. These notes were analysed and systematized by the researchers, and the results of this analysis were discussed with the group.

One general result was that none of the firms made an exact economic calculation of the total cost–benefit of the innovation processes. Some of the larger ones, and the consultancy firms, registered the number of man-hours used; they could easily find these data and some of them used them. However, they rarely learned from them; that is, they rarely compared them with the outcome and did not compare different innovation projects. In general, they all expressed that more comprehensive and exact measurements, possibly converted into money terms, were not very interesting to them—they considered this theoretical, desktop research. They would prefer to use their sparse resources on developing and improving the organizational processes, customer interaction and market knowledge instead of using them on measurement exercises. This may be an effect of a particular national corporate culture. Danish corporate culture is characterized by little formality and an emphasis on practice-based entrepreneurial behavior, not a big planning approach (cf. Hofstede, 1991; see also Sundbo, 1998, on Danish service firms). The results may be different, for example, in the US, France or Germany, which are more dominated by a systematic planning approach (cf. Hofstede, 1991).

Having said that, the managers found all the above factors interesting; however, the outcome factors remained more interesting than the input ones. The managers agreed with what the literature says (e.g. Djellal and Gallouj, 2008), namely, that the exact economic effect of innovation attempts is difficult to measure. This is because the effect on profit in particular, but also turnover, can be difficult to isolate from other factors' effects—business cycles, for example. Measurement is also difficult and resource-demanding in an individual firm; thus, the advantages of such a measure often do not match the costs of measuring. Those were two arguments given by the managers for not being *very* interested in all the factors included in the list above. The managers were interested in all the factors, but to different degrees in different firms.

2.6   EXPLORATORY EXPERIMENTS IN TWO SERVICE FIRMS

The next step was to conduct experiments (cf. Chapter 11 in this book) in two selected knowledge service organizations (so-called KIBS). One was a large public organization (here called 'Tax'—a Danish tax authority), the other a small consultancy firm (here called 'Consult'). The public organization considers itself a service organization and wants to be innovative; hence its relevance for the current purpose. The experiments were exploratory as they were to investigate the research questions in practice, that is, which measures are meaningful to the firms and which measures are practicable. The experiments greatly depended on what the firms, in their actual situation, wanted to do. The answer to that was established and it was that the firms did not necessarily want to do very much. This was, from a scientific point of view, not very satisfactory because it did not lend itself to a perfect test of the hypotheses. On the other hand, it was an empirical-inductive test of service firms' interest in investing resources in measuring innovation input–output, which is also an aim of this research.

2.6.1   Method

In each firm, we started with a meeting with the innovation managers (who in Consult's case was the owner). We suggested our plan for an ideal measurement and they responded by saying what they thought was practicable and what they wanted to measure, which was not the whole range of factors in the above list. They then collected data concerning existing innovation activities or developed new measurement activities for a period of six months. The data was connected to a few concrete innovations that were under development at the time. The researchers met the innovation managers and other employees regularly during the data collection period. At the end of the period, the researchers and the innovation managers met for a final evaluation of the experiment. This evaluation was based on a diary method, which means that the researchers interviewed the innovation managers about their impression of the measurement experience combined with some statistical data. The research questions investigated at these meetings were the following: (1) How did the measurement experiment go—was it carried out as planned, and if not, why not? (2) What was the result? That is, which values of the input and output were measured? (3) Is it possible to make a quantitative or mixed quantitative–qualitative calculation of the innovation result, that is, output minus input (ideally an index)? (4) How do the innovation managers assess the experiment and the results? Namely, are the results useful to the firm and will the firm use them in the future? The next two sections briefly explain the innovations and the measurement activities in each firm and discuss the answers to the four research questions.

2.6.2   Tax

One innovation was selected, namely, the development of a service letter to entrepreneurs who had abandoned their business and who should be reminded of declaring their income over the last year of the firm's existence. This was a new service. The letter was developed and a test distribution was made before it was finally sent.

At the first meeting, an agreement was made about measures of innovation input and output variables. The outcome variables were to measure how much this particular innovation contributed to outcomes that were considered important by Tax. The variables were:

Input

- Working hours (salary costs) for development of the activities
- external consultant
- letter prototypes—expenses for printing, working hours
- telephone calls (reminders).

Outcome

- Direct effect ('income' defined as the number of self-declarations)
- saved costs (fewer cases where Tax should calculate the debt-hours with saved salaries)
- branding (the clients found the innovation a good idea—measured in a survey)
- clients' satisfaction with the innovation (the reminder letter; measured in a survey)
- clients' general satisfaction with Tax (measured in a survey)
- employee satisfaction (interviews, survey).

The results of the evaluation interviews can be summarized as follows.

1. How did the measurement experiment go?   All the agreed-upon measurements were carried out except the interviews and survey output measure of employee satisfaction. In the final evaluation meeting, the innovation manager still found this a very important factor, but Tax had not made the interviews (except a couple of test interviews) or the survey. This was because answering a survey would require some work by several employees and the time needed would be taken from their normal work. This was not so popular, whether among the employees or the managers in different departments, particularly since Tax was undergoing budget cuts and employees were being laid off.

We might conclude from this interview that employee satisfaction is considered an important output variable, but measurement can be very sensitive. The service firm may, as in this case, prioritize productivity and internal peace over innovation aims.

2. What was the result?   Tax could measure all the input variables in money terms (for example, by measuring hours used on the specified activities). A total measure in money terms of the investment in the innovation could be established (which in this case was €12 000). Of the output variables, only the direct effect and saved costs could be measured in money terms (which was €13 700).

3. Can we make a quantitative or mixed quantitative–qualitative calculation of the innovation result? Already, based on the above two variables, we can establish that the innovation resulted in a surplus. The branding and clients' satisfaction was measured in a survey. There were no significant effects of this innovation. The total result—excluding the effect on employee satisfaction, which was not measured—was the surplus of €1700, though of course there was much uncertainty about the result. The innovation manager emphasized that the costs of measuring the variables were not calculated. If they were, it would probably lead to a deficit, according to the interview, particularly if the employee satisfaction measurement had been effectuated.

4. How did the innovation manager assess the experiment and the results? This was a general question in the interview. The manager thought that it was an interesting exercise that could be used in her actual and future jobs. From a follow-up interview some months later, we know that she wrote an article and made speeches about this experiment and the model. However, she was soon let go and the innovation department closed down in a rationalization round.

From the latter information, one might conclude that to Tax the experiment and the results were not that important, or at least they did not want to invest in a specific innovation department.

2.6.3 Consult

Three innovations were selected. One was 'Competencies on IPad', a service system which provides information about labor-force competencies, which can be used by firms, unions and public employers. Another was 'Employment Indicators', which is an information system about the degree of employment and unemployment in different industries and geographical areas; customers are the municipalities, unions, employers' associations and analysis bureaus. The third innovation was 'My Doctor Friend', a system to find disease diagnoses on the Internet; customers would be all citizens.

The innovations were already in progress when we, the researchers, became involved. At the first meeting, we agreed on the following measurement variables, which the firm should attempt to collect:

- *Input*: Investment in the innovations (man-hours where a total price could be estimated)
- *Outcome*: Income and surplus (in money terms)
- *PR*: Improved network relations to customers; increased service quality; increased personnel motivation; increased personnel competencies.

The results of the evaluation interviews can be summarized as follows.

1. How did the measurement experiment go? The counting of investment in working hours in money terms was found quite easy by the owner because of a system in which all employees register their hours. The outcome was difficult to measure in his opinion. The firm did not have any quantitative measures and had no interest in developing and using them. The owner explained that it would be expensive and saw no need for doing this. It is a small firm and he claimed to know the employees and the customers. Thus, the measurement of the outcome by the owner was achieved by calculating the income in money terms from these innovations and in qualitative terms by his personal evaluation combined with interviewing two of the employees.

2. What was the result? The financial investment was calculated by the owner. The economic outcome was partly calculated, and partly assessed qualitatively by the owner. The owner's interviews with the two employees were the basis for a qualitative assessment of customer and employee effects of the innovations; the results of the interviews were imparted to the researchers by the owner in their interview.

3. Can we make a kind of quantitative or mixed quantitative–qualitative calculation of the innovation result? The owner provided some statistical data. Investments were €13 400 in 'Competencies on IPad', €47 000 in 'Employment Indicators' and €8700 in 'My Doctor Friend' (all during working hours). The economic benefit of 'Competencies on IPad' was estimated to be small as the turnover of this product was small; no exact figures could be found. The outcome of 'Employment Indicators' was quite high; the innovation led to an increased turnover of about €1.2 million and it was the basis for a public development grant of €2 million. Although the exact profit could not be measured, the owner saw it as a clear surplus. 'My Doctor Friend' was not sold at all, so all investments resulted in a deficit.

The owner and his employee-interviewees expressed that the firm had benefited from the innovations in the following ways: they strengthened their network with customers, increased employee competencies and had a clearer customer interface in IT-based service deliveries. These were positively assessed by the owner and the employees, but no monetary value could be placed on them.

4. How did the innovation manager assess the experiment and the results?
This was a general question in the interview. The owner thought the experiment was interesting, but he was not sure how useful it really was. As an entrepreneur, he expressed that he was more occupied by creating jobs and customer satisfaction than in performing comprehensive calculation systems.

2.6.4 Summary and Discussion

From this research we can conclude:

- It is possible to construct reasonable measurement instruments based on theoretical and empirical scientific knowledge. However, they become compound and cannot reasonably be combined into an index.
- Service firms can measure the relevant factors although a few of the factors would be difficult and expensive to measure and they have not been part of these measurement attempts (e.g. network benefits, productivity, branding and PR, and organizational learning).
- The service firms were not overly interested in developing and using the—seen from a theoretical perspective—'perfect measure'. They assessed that the utility of many measures does not always justify the use of the resources necessary to measure them. The most important factors for the firms (which interested them and which demanded limited resources to measure) were:
  - input factors:
    - working hours within the firm
    - expenses to technology and other materials
    - public support.
  - outcome factors:
    - *income and growth*: turnover
    - *employee factors*: employee motivation and competence; employee entrepreneurship
    - *customer/market factors*: increased service quality and customer satisfaction
    - *strategic/business model factors*: changed strategy; new networks.

It was quite surprising that the service firms were not more interested in using quantitative measurement instruments (and not more intensively focused on profit measurement). Some of them, especially those in the financial services sector, used measures (particularly of man-hour input), but not very detailed ones. They were more interested in directly creating customer satisfaction and employee engagement than in technicalities in quantitative measurement. This preliminary piece of research shows that at least some service firms are more dominated by entrepreneurial trial-and-error than by a systematic quantitative scientific approach. This may be suggested as a general hypothesis for the service sector.

The issue of quantitative service innovation measurement requires more research in order to form conclusions about service firms' attitudes and which factors should be included in a measurement. The firms may also accept measurement instruments if researchers present one that is fully developed and based on what is fairly easy for service firms to use (i.e. demands few resources) and which they find relevant for their way of handling their businesses.

2.7   CONCLUSION

Despite a growing interest in developing research-based instruments to measure innovation input and output, still few instruments exist and they are imperfect: either they only measure input or innovation capability or (rarely) only outcome, or they do not include all relevant variables. The most complete instruments that exist measure innovation performance at a macro (societal) level. The most complete of the imperfect instruments at the micro level measure innovation performance or capability at the firm level. Generally, they measure input; few of them measure output. Many of them do not quantify all variables. Instruments that quantitatively measure innovation input and outcome at the single innovation, or project, level (a cost–benefit analysis of the attempt to develop a single innovation) are almost non-existent. This situation also characterizes attempts to develop quantitative measurement instruments to measure input to and outcome of innovation in service firms. The particularities of service innovation have been emphasized; thus, particular instruments should be developed to measure service innovations.

This chapter has reviewed research that has attempted to develop a quantitative measurement instrument based on a co-development method in which the instrument has been developed in cooperation with service firms to ensure the usability of the instrument. This research has provided both input and outcome variables that have a research background and are assessed as usable by service firms. It has also demonstrated a specific research method to develop such instruments. This method still is assessed to be adequate;

however, the instrument that was created still needs further development to perfect it. For firms, this research can provide a suggestion for a rather simple measurement instrument that is both research-based and practically usable. This should be further investigated in practical experiments in firms.

LEARNING POINTS

- Quantitative measurement at the micro level of innovations in services is rare but possible—although difficult.
- A suggestion for a measurement instrument has been presented in this chapter.
- Practitioners do not always want to measure the innovation factors that theory has deemed the most important.
- Measurement can be costly to firms and might induce unrest in the firm organization.

DISCUSSION TOPICS

- How useful is quantitative measurement of input and output factors in service innovation?
- Which factors could, or should, be measured in different service firms?
- How can firms create employee involvement and avoid unrest in the organization when inducing and measuring innovation activities?

NOTE

1. Members of the group were innovation managers from a building society; a film producer; a post company; a tax authority organization; a bank; two small consultancy firms; a film distributor; a large manual service firm providing cleaning, catering, building facilities management, etc.; a hotel; and a financial IT-advising organization.

REFERENCES

Adams, R., J. Bessant, and R. Phelps (2006), 'Innovation management measurement: A review', *International Journal of Management Review*, 8 (1), 21–47.
Andersen, E.S. (2008), *Schumpeter's Evolutionary Economics: A Theoretical, Historical and Statistical Analysis of the Engine of Capitalism*. Aalborg: Aalborg University.

Argyris, C. (1992), *On Organizational Learning*. Cambridge, MA: Blackwell.
Arundel, A., M. Kanerva, A. van Cruysen, and H. Hollanders (2007), 'Innovation Statistics for the European Service Sector', INNO Metrics 2007 Report, Brussels: European Commission, DG Enterprise.
Aschhoff, B., E. Baier, D. Dirk Crass, M. Hud, P. Hünermund, C. Köhler, B. Peters, C. Rammer, E. Schricke, T. Schubert, and F. Schwiebacher (2013), *Innovation in Germany—Results of the German CIS 2006–10*. Manheim: Zentrum für Europäische Wirtschaftsforschung, Mannheim.
Borras, S. (2003), *The Innovation Policy of the European Union*. Cheltenham, UK and Northampton, MA, USA: Edward Elgar Publishing.
Bryson, J., L. Rubalcaba, and P. Strom (2012), 'Services, innovation, employment and organisation: Research gaps and challenges for the next decade', *Service Industries Journal*, 32 (4), 641–55.
Burgelman, R., C. Christensen, and S. Wheelwright (2004), *Strategic Management of Innovation*. Boston, MA: McGraw-Hill.
Cainelli, G., R. Evangelista, and M. Savona (2006), 'Innovation and economic performance in services: A firm-level analysis', *Cambridge Journal of Economics*, 30 (3), 435–58.
Chesbrough, H. (2006), *Open Innovation*. Boston, MA: Harvard Business School Press.
Chesbrough, H. (2011), *Open Services Innovation: Rethinking Your Business to Grow and Compete in a New Era*. Chichester: Wiley.
CIS (2009), *Community Innovation Survey*, http://www.dst.dk/fui (accessed January 10, 2014).
Cooper, R.G. (1988), *Winning at New Products*. Ontario: Addison-Wesley.
Cooper, R.G. and S.J. Edget (1999), *Product Development for the Service Sector*. Massachusetts: Perseus Books.
Cordero, R. (1990), 'The measurement of innovation performance in the firm: An overview', *Research Policy*, 19, 185–92.
Daly, J., A. Sætre, and E. Brun (2012), 'Killing mushrooms: The realpolitik of terminating innovation projects', *International Journal of Innovation Management*, 16 (5), 1–30.
Damvad (2011), *Service Innovation: Impact Analysis and Assessment Indicators*. Prepared by DAMVAD for Task Force 2 of EPISIS. Copenhagen: Damvad.
Damvad (2013), *Service Innovation in the Nordics*. Copenhagen: Damvad.
den Hertog, P. (2010), 'Managing service innovation—Firm-level dynamic capabilities and policy options', PhD thesis, Dialogic Innovatie & Interactie, Utrecht.
den Hertog, P., G. Poot, and G. Meinen (2006), 'Towards a better measurement of the soft side of innovation', in J. Sundbo, A. Gallina, G. Serin, and J. Davis (eds.), *Contemporary Management of Innovation*. London: Palgrave, pp. 181–202.
Dewangan, V. and M. Godse (2014), 'Towards a holistic enterprise innovation performance measurement system', *Technovation*, 34, 535–46.
Djellal, F. and F. Gallouj (1999), 'Services and the search for relevant innovation indicators: A review of national and international surveys', *Science and Public Policy*, 26 (4), 218–32.
Djellal, F. and F. Gallouj (2001), 'Innovation in services, patterns of innovation organisation in service firms: Postal survey results and theoretical models', *Science and Public Policy*, 28 (1), 57–67.
Djellal, F. and F. Gallouj (2008), *Measuring and Improving Productivity in Services*. Cheltenham, UK and Northampton, MA, USA: Edward Elgar Publishing.

Drejer, I. (2004), 'Identifying innovation in survey of services: A Schumpeterian perspective', *Research Policy*, 33 (3), 551–62.

Dutta, S. (ed.) (2012), *Global Innovation Index*, INSEAD, http://www.globalinnovationindex.org/gii/main/fullreport/index.html (accessed January 10, 2014).

Edvardsson, B., A. Gustafsson, P. Kristensson, P. Magnusson, and J. Matthing (eds.) (2006), *Involving Customers in New Service Development*. London: Imperial College Press.

Edvardsson, B., P. Kristensson, P. Magnusson, and E. Sundström (2012), 'Customer integration within service development: A review of methods and an analysis of insitu and exsitu contributions', *Technovation*, 32 (7–8), 419–29.

Edvardsson, B., B. Thomasson, and J. Øvretveit (1994), *Quality of Service*. Maidenhead: McGraw-Hill.

EU (2013), *InnoBarometer—Investment in Intangibles: Economic Assets and Innovation Drivers for Growth*. Brussels: EU.

EU (2014), *Innovation Union Scoreboard 2014*. Directorate-General for Enterprise and Industry, Brussels: EU.

European Commission (2004), *Innovation in Europe, Luxembourg* (European Communities).

Evangelista, R. and G. Sirilli (1998), 'Innovation in the service sector: Results from the Italian statistical survey', *Technological Forecasting and Social Change*, 58 (3), 251–69.

Fagerberg, J., D. Mowery, and R.N. Nelson (2005), *The Oxford Handbook of Innovation*. Oxford: Oxford University Press.

Forsknings og Innovationsstyrelsen (2008), *Inside Service Innovation—Challenging Policy*, prepared by Damvad, Copenhagen: Forsknings og Innovationsstyrelsen.

Foss, N. (2003), 'Bounded rationality and tacit knowledge in the organizational capabilities approach: An assessment and a re-evaluation', *Industrial and Corporate Change*, 12 (2), 185–201.

Freeman, C. and Soete, L. (1997), *The Economics of Industrial Innovation*. London: Pinter.

Fuglsang L. (2010), 'Bricolage and invisible innovation in public service innovation', *Journal of Innovation Economics*, 1 (5), 67–87.

Fuglsang, L., J. Sundbo, and F. Sørensen (2011), 'Dynamics of experience service innovation: Innovation as a guided activity—results from a Danish survey', *Service Industries Journal*, 31 (5), 661–77.

Gallouj, F. (2002), *Innovation in the Service Economy*. Cheltenham, UK and Northampton, MA, USA: Edward Elgar Publishing.

Gallouj, F. and F. Djellal (eds.) (2010), *Handbook of Innovation and Services*. Cheltenham, UK and Northampton, MA, USA: Edward Elgar Publishing.

Gallouj, F. and M. Savona (2009), 'Innovation in services: A review of the debate and a research agenda', *Journal of Evolutionary Economics*, 19 (2), 149–72.

Gault, F. (2013), *Handbook of Innovation Indicators and Measurement*. Cheltenham, UK and Northampton, MA, USA: Edward Elgar Publishing.

Gotsch, M. and C. Hipp (2012), 'Measurement of innovation activities in the knowledge-intensive services industry: A trademark approach', *Service Industries Journal*, 32 (13), 2167–87.

Grönroos, C. (2000), *Service Management and Marketing*. New York: Wiley.

Gustafsson, A., P. Kristensson, and L. Witell (2012), 'Customer co-creation in service innovation: A matter of communication?', *Journal of Service Management*, 23 (3), 311–27.

Hagedoorn, J. and M. Cloodt (2003), 'Measuring innovative performance: Is there an advantage in using multiple indicators?', *Research Policy*, 32, 1365–79.

Hakonsson, H. and I. Snehota (1989), 'No business is an island: The network concept of business strategy', *Scandinavian Journal of Management*, 5 (5), 187–200.

Hipp, C. and H. Grupp (2005), 'Innovation in the service sector: The demand for service specific innovation measurement concepts and typologies', *Research Policy*, 34 (4), 517–35.

Hofstede, G. (1991), *Cultures and Organizations*. London: McGraw-Hill.

Howells, J. (2010), 'Service and innovation and service innovation: New theoretical directions', in F. Gallouj and F. Djellal (eds.), *The Handbook of Innovation and Services*. Cheltenham, UK and Northampton, MA, USA: Edward Elgar Publishing, pp. 68–83.

ICE (Innovation, Customers, Employees) (2010), *Servicevirksomhedernes organisering af innovationsarbejdet* [Service firms' organization of innovation work], ICE project. Roskilde: Roskilde University.

ICE (2012), *Metoder til inddragelse af brugere i service innovation* [Methods for involvement of users in service innovation], ICE project. Roskilde, http://ice-project.dk/Download.html (accessed January 10, 2014).

INNO-Studies (2004), *Innovation in Services: Issues at Stake and Trends*, INNO-Studies 2001: Lot 3 (ENTR-C/2001). Brussels: EU Commission.

Janssen, M.A., A.S. Alexiev, P. den Hertog, C. Castaldi, and C. de Blok (2012), 'Towards a new scale for measuring dynamic capabilities in service innovation management', Paper presented at the European Academy of Management Conference, Rotterdam, 6–8 June 2012.

Johannisson, B., E. Gunnarsson, and T. Stjernberg (eds.) (2008), *Gemensamt kunspapande* [Cooperative knowledge creation]. Växjö: Växjö University Press.

Kristensson, P., A. Gustafsson, and T. Archer (2004), 'Harnessing the creative potential among customers', *Journal of Product Innovation Management*, 21 (1), 4–14.

Kristensson, P., J. Matthing, and N. Johansson (2008), 'Key strategies for the successful involvement of customers in the co-creation of new technology-based services', *International Journal of Service Industry Management*, 19 (3–4), 474–91.

Krizaj, D., A. Brodnik, and B. Bukovec (2012), 'A tool for measurement of innovation newness and adoption in tourism firms', *International Journal of Tourism Research*, 16, 113–25.

Li, J.-H., L. Xu, and X.-L. Wu (2009), 'New service development using GAP-based QFD: A mobile telecommunication case', *International Journal of Services Technology and Management*, 12 (2), 146–74.

Lundvall, B.-A. and P. Nielsen (2007), 'Knowledge management and innovation performance', *International Journal of Manpower*, 28 (3–4), 207–23.

Nowotny, H., P. Scott, and M. Gibbons (2001), *Re-Thinking Science: Knowledge and the Public in an Age of Uncertainty*. Oxford: Polity Press.

OECD (2002), *The Frascati Manual. Proposed Standards Practice for Surveys on Research and Experimental Development*. Paris: OECD.

OECD and Eurostat (2005), *Oslo Manual: Guidelines for Collecting and Interpreting Innovation Data*. Paris: OECD.

Osterwalder, A. and Y. Pigneur (2010), *Business Model Generation*. New York: Wiley.

Payne, A., K. Storbacka, P. Frow, and S. Knox (2009), 'Co-creating brands: Diagnosing and designing the relationship experience', *Journal of Business Research*, 62 (3), 379–89.

Perks, H., T. Gruber, and B. Edvardsson (2012), 'Co-creation in radical service innovation: A systematic analysis of microlevel processes', *Journal of Product Innovation Management*, 29 (6), 1–17.

Prahalad, C.K. and V. Ramaswamy (2004), *The Future of Competition: Co-Creating Unique Value with Customers*. Boston, MA: Harvard Business School Press.

Puchta, C. and P. Potter (2006), *Focus Group Practice*. London: Sage.

Pyka, A. and G. Küppers (eds.) (2002), *Innovation Networks—Theory and Practice*. Cheltenham, UK and Northampton, MA, USA: Edward Elgar Publishing.

Rothwell, R. and W. Zegveld (1985), *Reindustrialization and Technology*. Harlow: Longman.

Rubalcaba, L., S. Michel, J. Sundbo, S. Brown, and J. Reynoso (2012), 'Shaping, organizing, and rethinking service innovation: A multidimensional framework', *Journal of Service Management*, 23 (5), 696–715.

Schumpeter, J. (1934), *The Theory of Economic Development*. Cambridge, MA: Harvard University.

Schumpeter, J. (1939), *Business Cycles*. New York: McGraw-Hill.

Senge, P. (1990), *The Fifth Discipline*. London: Century Business.

SIC (Service development, Internationalisation and Competence development) (1999), 'Danish service firms' innovation activities and use of ICT, based on a survey', Report no. 2, Centre of Service Studies, Roskilde University, Roskilde.

Sicotte, H., N. Drouin, and H. Delerue (2014), 'Innovation portfolio management as a subset of dynamic capabilities: Measurement and impact on innovative performance', *Project Management Journal*, 45 (6), 58–72.

Sundbo, J. (1998), *The Organization of Innovation in Services*. Copenhagen: Roskilde University Press.

Sundbo, J. (2013), 'Blocking mechanisms in user and employee based service innovation', *Economies et Sociétés, Serie Économie et gestion des services*, 14 (3–4), 479–506.

Sundbo, J. and F. Gallouj (2000), 'Innovation as a loosely coupled system in services', *International Journal of Services Technology and Marketing*, 1 (1), 15–36.

Sundbo, J. and M. Toivonen (eds.) (2011), *User-Based Innovation in Services*. Cheltenham, UK and Northampton, MA, USA: Edward Elgar Publishing.

Sundbo. J., L. Fuglsang, and J.N. Larsen (2001), *Innovation med omtanke* [Innovation with care]. Copenhagen: Academia.

Sundbo, J., D. Sundbo, and A. Henten (2015), 'Service encounters as basis for innovation', *Service Industries Journal*, 35 (5), 255–74.

Teece, D.J. and G. Pisano (1994), 'The dynamic capability of firms: An introduction', *Industrial and Corporate Change*, 3 (3), 537–56.

Tidd, J. and F. Hull (2005), *Service Innovation*. London: World Scientific Publishing.

van den Aa, W. and T. Elfring (2002), 'Realizing innovation in services', *Scandinavian Journal of Management*, 18 (2), 155–71.

Witell, L., P. Kristensson, A. Gustafsson, and M. Löfgren (2011), 'Idea generation: Customer co-creation versus traditional market research techniques', *Journal of Service Management*, 22 (2), 140–59.

3. The critical incident technique and everyday innovation

Lars Fuglsang

3.1 INTRODUCTION

This chapter discusses how the critical incident technique (CIT) can be a relevant, practically oriented research technique in service innovation research. Research has pointed to several characteristics of innovation processes in services. Innovation in services is often incremental, and it can emerge from the provision and delivery of services or from the service encounter between the provider and the receiver of the service (Sørensen, Sundbo, and Mattsson, 2013). Innovation is sometimes not even a deliberate action but is recognized as innovation only in retrospect, and may have blurred outcomes (Toivonen and Tuominen, 2009). Innovation theory has argued that, to count as innovation, an invention must have a clear economic impact (Drejer, 2004). This criterion is applicable to some technological innovations, but is more difficult to apply to services. Service theories instead call for more practice-based theorizing – investigating services in their context of use and exploring the organizational conditions for innovations (Sørensen et al., 2013). In this chapter it will be argued that the CIT is useful in practice for uncovering and recognizing innovations in services and can also contribute to theoretical understandings of service innovation as an everyday phenomenon. The method needs to be extended with phenomenological and reflexive approaches if it is to capture not just single incidents but also the broader context of innovation. In this way, the CIT method can be situated within a research tradition that sees innovation as being related to everyday practices and experiences (Fuglsang and Sørensen, 2011). The chapter builds on, extends and develops an article that has previously been published in Danish (Fuglsang, 2007).

The CIT was introduced to research by Flanagan in a seminal article in Psychological Bulletin (Flanagan, 1954). Flanagan suggested a flexible use of the method, and hence it was not bound to a specific research tradition. Instead, it was a practical method to uncover people's situated experiences. Essentially, what Flanagan presented, based on experiences from an aviation psychology programme in the Second World War, was an interview technique that allowed the researcher to collect subjective information about incidents that often had not previously been verbalized. The strength of the method is that it allows the researcher to collect subjective information about a phenomenon in a structured way. During the Second World War, CIT based on real life experiences had been used to select flight crews and make innovations to the aircraft cockpit, in order to, among other things, avoid severe vertigo during combat.

While the method is mostly used in a straightforward positivist/ naturalistic or functional way to find out how something functions in practice, we shall discuss how it can also be used to collect subjective experiences in a more phenomenological sense, and how a more reflexive process-oriented approach to CIT can be introduced. The technique can be used to ask questions about how actors experience and learn from incidents, and this can be contrasted with extant theories. The flexibility of the method has been seen as a strong point that allows it to be used for various purposes, but the downside is that this makes it more difficult to develop the method systematically (Butterfield et al., 2005).

The following discussion seeks to place the CIT in three different research traditions: a positivist–functional, a phenomenological–interpretivist and a reflexive process-oriented tradition. The kind of research issues that follow from these three traditions will be explored. Further, the value of the CIT as a special interview technique for service innovation research is discussed.

The three traditions are rooted in different philosophies of science, methods and interviewer strategies, but the chapter attempts to show how these traditions can be pragmatically applied to different research contexts. CIT can be used to analyse innovative solutions to problems, to uncover the experiences and challenges of innovation and to investigate the process dynamics of innovation, depending on the researchable context.

The chapter is structured as follows. First, Flanagan's (1954) original presentation of the method is described, together with some weaknesses of this method. The three different research traditions are then discussed in service research: positivist–functional research, the newer phenomenological–interpretivist tradition and a possible more process-oriented reflexive approach. Innovation cases are given as examples of each of these traditions. Finally, the use of CIT in innovation research, and its limitations, is discussed.

3.2 THE METHOD AND ITS POSSIBLE APPLICATION IN INNOVATION RESEARCH

In this section, the method, as Flanagan initially developed it, is presented. Some potential applications to service innovation research, and their limitations, are briefly discussed.

3.2.1 The Method in its Initial Form

In his initial presentation of the method (Flanagan, 1954), Flanagan was interested in the functional use of the method to solve practical problems, and the method was presented in a straightforward positivistic way. Flanagan describes the overall approach as follows:

> The CIT consists of a set of procedures for collecting direct observations of human behaviour in such a way as to facilitate their potential usefulness in solving practical problems and developing broad psychological principles. The CIT outlines procedures for collecting observed incidents having special significance and meeting systematically defined criteria. (Flanagan, 1954, p. 327)

Flanagan emphasizes that the method should be used to clarify how certain actions are useful for solving certain practical, observed problems, and also to develop broad psychological principles for such actions. Flanagan understands 'an incident' as:

> observable human activity that is sufficiently complete in itself to permit inferences and predictions to be made about the person performing the act. To be critical, an incident must occur in a situation where the purpose or intent of the act seems fairly clear to the observer and where its consequences are sufficiently definite to leave little doubt concerning its effects. (1954, p. 327)

Note that Flanagan refers to an incident as an 'observable activity' that is complete in itself; he therefore assumes that actions can be distinguished in a clear way. His approach also implies a clear cause–effect relationship between an incident and the (positive/negative) effect. Flanagan implicitly also seems to think that there are effective new actions (cf. innovations) in a situation that can remedy incidents that cause negative outcomes, and that a key issue is to make such actions occur in the right way. By gathering experiences from many actors who think back on a situation that they have experienced, and who are encouraged to verbalize about it, one can identify the problems and the innovative solutions.

As an illustration of the method, Flanagan refers to the initial application of the method in The Aviation Psychology Program in the US Air Force in the early 1940s. This programme was made to develop methods 'for selection and classification of aircrews' based on subjective experiences of flight crews during bombing missions and battle management. Researchers asked the aircrew to report their experiences, using questions like, 'Describe the officer's action. What did he do?' In another study, researchers studied the circumstances during a flight that caused vertigo. The pilots were asked to think about events that led to severe vertigo. Based on this study, recommendations for the training of pilots and the design of the cockpit were made. In his description of the method, Flanagan quotes from a report he wrote in 1946:

> The principal method of job analysis procedures should be the determination of critical requirements. These requirements include those which have been demonstrated to have made the difference between success and failure in carrying out an important part of the job assigned in a significant number of instances. (Flanagan, 1954, p. 329)

The method was eventually used in contexts other than military ones, but often in a similar functional way to identify the requirements for solving specific problems. Flanagan mentions, for example, a number of studies from the Department of Psychology of the University of Pittsburgh that were conducted in the late 1940s and early 1950s. One example, which comes close to later service encounter studies, is a dissertation on the critical requirements for dentists' work, where critical events related to a dentist's work were collected from patients, dentists and instructors at dental schools. The collected events were then grouped into four broad themes: 1) technical skills, 2) the handling of the patient relationship, 3) the ability to take professional responsibility, and 4) the ability to take personal responsibility.

Another 'service' study focused on the requirements for teaching psychology courses. It collected incidents from teachers and students, and showed how teachers and students emphasized different requirements for teaching the course. The teachers emphasized performing demonstrations and experiments, using discussion group techniques and encouraging and ascertaining students' ideas and opinions. The students paid more attention to exams, grades, lecture techniques and project work, and emphasized the problems the teachers had with presenting the course requirements, expressing themselves effectively, answering students' questions and summarizing facts and principles (Flanagan, 1954, p. 333). The different perspectives of the students and the teachers explained the difference between their focal requirements for successfully teaching a course:

students focused on short-term needs, while teachers had a longer-term perspective on teaching.

A third study was more oriented towards research. Its aim was to develop a functional description of emotional immaturity. Various professionals in psychiatry and psychology were asked to give examples of emotional immaturity: 'Have you recently thought of someone as being emotionally immature (regardless of diagnosis)?' The descriptions of immaturity were then divided into a number of themes that were reviewed and evaluated by some experienced psychiatrists. In this way the method was used inductively to create a theory on immaturity in a way that could be used functionally in psychiatry to uncover personalities.

Based on these and other studies, Flanagan divides the method into five stages, which he calls: 1) the general aims, 2) plans and specifications, 3) collecting data, 4) analysing the data, and 5) interpreting and reporting.

1. The first task of the researcher is to specify the aims of the behaviour that constitutes the starting point for the investigation. The researcher must give a functional description of an activity such as going to the dentist.
2. The next step is to identify a situation to be observed, its relation to the overall aim, and the people who observe the situation, who need to be familiar with the activity.
3. Data are collected through interviews. The interviewer should try to make the respondent tell a story based on the lived situation. The question could be asked in the following way: 'Think about the last time you saw one of your subordinates do something that was very helpful to your group in meeting their production schedule', 'Tell me exactly what this person did', etc. The interviewer can ask further about the behaviour, what effect it had, what led up to the action, why it was so important, when it happened, who performed the action, what her experience was, how old she was, and so on. The size of sample can, according to Flanagan, vary from situation to situation. In simple job situations 50 events may be sufficient, while in more complex situations the interviewer may need to collect up to 4,000 events. Flanagan's understanding of the problem is that it is necessary to collect descriptions of almost all the critical events in the situation, and to get many examples for the same incident, in order to be able to state meaningful results.
4. Flanagan sees the above three stages of the analysis as inductive and objective, while the two subsequent steps are more subjective (or reflexive), since they are based on the analyst's interpretations. However, it is through the analysis and the interpretation of the results

that the method becomes useful. The purpose of the analysis is to categorize the incidents and behaviour within overall themes or frames of reference.

5. The interpretation of the analysis aims to assess the incidents that are critical in a situation, and to discover how concrete action (cf. innovations) can remedy the problems. The interpretation of the results is associated with a certain responsibility, and there may be a tendency for analysts to try to avoid interpretation to avoid responsibility, says Flanagan. The analyst must, however, assess the value of the results and try to assess how they can be used.

3.2.2 Possible Application in Innovation Research, and Limitations

The method can be used for collecting subjective experiences of a service problem and of how the problem can be handled, to the extent that it is possible to clarify the aims, the situations to be observed and clear incidents. For example, the method could be used to collect experiences from service users about problems during service delivery such as long waiting times (Ramseook-Munhurrun, 2016). It may be used to identify customer satisfaction and dissatisfaction (Edvardsson, 1992, 1998). In this way, collecting and assessing critical incidents may help an organization to change existing practices and remedy problems. In other words, the method can give valuable input about valuable action for an innovation process.

However, there are some limitations to and problems with the method. First, the method relies on definitions of general aims and situations. The respondents' role is to provide experiences of incidents of such situations that relate to the general aims. Incidents and behaviours are collected and interpreted by the researcher, leading to overall suggestions for changing practice. However, one may question whether it is always relevant and even possible to define a relationship between aims, situations, incidents and behaviours in a completely objective way, and whether clear incidents can always be identified. It may be possible and valuable to do this in certain situations that require functional intervention, but this limits the application of the method to such situations. This also limits the value of the method, because a broader range of incidents as they appear to the respondent (for example, incidents related to a wider context, such as family or life situation) may not be captured. The researcher can find it fruitful to define a situation in a more tentative way, and let respondents tell broader stories of what happened, thereby allowing for more insight into the contextual aspects.

Second, the method is meant to bring out knowledge of incidents that have a clear impact. By collecting a large number of incidents, the researcher is supposed to get a clear picture of negative and positive incidents with respect to a given outcome. However, respondents may perceive a situation differently, and incidents can have different meanings depending on respondents' different perspectives. The method tends to ignore the fact that there can be different groups and interests at play, and that good and bad incidents are valued in different subjective ways and can emerge from the interaction of various interests, preferences and plans.

Third, a more practical problem with the method is that it is based on semi-structured interviews in which the interviewer must ask the respondent about a particular event that the respondent can 'remember'. The interviewer asks the respondent to 'think of an event' that, in his or her view, was important in the given situation with respect to the general aim. One potential problem is that this puts great demands on the respondent's ability to remember and clearly describe or write about the important events. It may perhaps also lead the respondent to overstate or exaggerate what actually happened.

According to Flanagan the various applications of CIT show that CIT consists of a set of flexible principles that must be adapted to the situation to be studied. The use of the method depends, according to Flanagan, on whether the situation to be observed and its characteristics are defined with enough precision and whether the respondents are able to interpret the situation. While the method may be criticized for being too flexible (and hence difficult to systematize), leading to a proliferation of approaches and terminology (Butterfield et al., 2005), it may also be criticized for being too rigid. It assumes that aims, situations, incidents and behaviours with clear borderlines can be detected in an objective way. Making this a starting point for the use of the method may prevent a researcher from grasping the flow of everyday experience and studying the wider context of service experiences and value creation.

3.3 APPLICATIONS TO SERVICES AND INNOVATION RESEARCH

In this section, three more recent approaches to the CIT in service and innovation research are discussed: a positivist–functional approach in the service literature, a phenomenological–interpretivist approach and a process-oriented reflexive approach. Each sub-section in the following contains a presentation of the method and a brief discussion of its limitations.

3.3.1   Positivist–Functional Approach in Service Research

3.3.1.1   Presentation

One of the first uses of the CIT in service research was reported by Bitner, Booms and Tetreault (1990; see also Gremler, 2004). This was followed by several other studies in service marketing and management, many with a focus on service quality and customer dissatisfaction (Edvardsson, 1992, 1998; Johnston, 1995). Bitner et al. (1990) examined customer experiences in service encounters by collecting 700 incidents from airlines, hotels and restaurants. They used the method to collect data on employee behaviour by asking customers the following question: 'Think of a time when, as a customer, you had a particularly satisfying (dissatisfying) interaction with an employee of an airline, hotel, or restaurant . . . Exactly what did the employee say or do?' (p. 74). They then sorted the incidents into three groups according to the main employee response: 1) responses to service delivery system failure; 2) responses to customer needs and requests; and 3) unprompted and unsolicited employee action. These were then further divided into 12 categories, such as: 'They lost my room reservation but the manager gave me the V.P. suite for the same price'. Or: 'We had made advance reservation at the hotel. When we arrived we found that we had no room—no explanations, no apologies, and no assistance in finding another hotel' (Bitner et al., 1990, p. 77). The authors also used this procedure to speculate about underlying and generic events and behaviours.

From this study it can be seen how important the analysis (thematic grouping and categorization of behaviour) really is for the results, and how this analysis in turn can directly inspire practical measures that can be taken for a given service. A service company may use the method to understand its customers' different experiences and how to respond to them in an innovative way. In addition, the classification scheme may be useful for a service company as a kind of checklist for analysing possible problems. Further, the method can be used for speculating and proposing theories about the service encounter between frontline employees and customers with respect to the generic features of the service. For example, the study contributes to research on service encounters by creating a generalizable classification scheme for understanding the sources of satisfaction and dissatisfaction in the service encounter.

3.3.1.2   Criticisms and limitations

Inger Roos (2002) argues that service encounter research has developed the CIT in new directions, moving from focusing on the individual service encounter towards paying more attention to the 'criticality' of the customer's relationship and the customer context. A piece of research may, for example, explore how people associated with a customer (family, friends, etc.) have an impact on the service experience. This would lead to a new research focus on the dynamics and shifts between different types of services. What are the contextual circumstances that lead a customer to emphasize one service relationship in favour of another? Answers to the question may include changes in the client's own situation, the influence of other service providers, or reactions to bad service. This perspective corresponds to the suggestion by Helkkula and Pihlström (2010) that CIT should be combined with a narrative approach that includes the narratives of other lived events. They argue that such an approach can be useful for yielding new service ideas and evaluating current services. The narrative approach focuses on events over a longer period of time across situations, rather than on specific incidents in a micro-situation.

The method has also found its uses in healthcare services – for example, in examining the information search behaviour of employees (Urquhart et al., 2003). The aim in this case was mostly practical, to improve the opportunities for health staff to carry out a relevant information search. However, Urquhart et al. (2003) criticize the method for not going deeply enough into the cognitive processes of information searching and for having a predominantly individualistic methodological basis. Urquhart et al. therefore suggest that the 'explicitation' method is used as a supplement or alternative to the CIT. This approach would emphasize the need for a full description or explicitation of an event or sequence of events, rather than exclusively focusing on critical events. This may increase the knowledge and awareness of how cognitive processes, including the cognitive problems that arise in the course of events when a healthcare service is delivered, proceed.

In his review of 141 critical incident studies in service research, Gremler (2004) summarizes some criticisms and recommendations. The method is a retrospective method and can therefore suffer from the possibility that respondents cannot remember what happened in the situation. The method also requires a very active involvement of respondents, who must tell or write a story. This can lead to a poor response rate or a poor quality of answers. In addition, analysts subsequently easily misunderstand or misinterpret the interviewees' answers. There may also be problems with the events recounted. Are they sufficiently complete and representative? Respondents provide examples of 'critical' events, but what about the more normal or typical events? Should they not also be included? Lastly, Gremler finds that the method is used exploratively for generating new theory by grounded theory principles (cf. Glaser and Strauss, 1967). In this connection it may be necessary to supplement the method with other methods, which does not often happen. The method therefore appears more objective and isolated than it is meant to be.

Gremler recommends, among other things, that instead of solely focusing on the customer or user side, which most CIT-inspired service studies do, it might be valuable to bring a 'dyadic' perspective on the relationship between the customer and the provider. Gremler cites, as an example, a study that focused on how friendships are formed between staff and users (Price and Arnould, 1999), which could provide a framework for how the CIT can be used. In addition, Gremler mentions that the physical environment is rarely investigated in connection with the CIT. Some studies on the physical environment are mentioned, including studies of 'servicescapes' (Hoffman, Kelley, and Chung, 2003) and studies of the self-service environment and the impact of this on the user experience (Meute et al., 2000).

Finally, Gremler recommends that the method be used to a greater extent in an exploratory and interpretative way, rather than solely to provide descriptions of the respondents' answers. He recommends ethnographic and narrative approaches to the analysis, which, among other things, can focus on the relationship between emotions and practice in a context in which the respondents create critical events.

3.3.2 The Phenomenological–Interpretivist Approach

3.3.2.1 Presentation
In continuation of the above, a phenomenological–interpretivist tradition has been developed by Elizabeth Chell, in particular, in various articles (Chell, 1998; Chell and Pittaway, 1998; Chell, 2014; Chell and Allman, 2003; Chell, 2004; see also Cope, 2005). Phenomenology originally focused on subjective experiences in a naturalistic–realistic setting, but Chell combines phenomenology with an interpretivist and hermeneutic approach in a Heideggerian tradition, in which the researcher's pre-understanding is important to the research.

In Chell's development of the method, a critical incident no longer consists of hard facts, but is something that emerges from a respondent's situated experiences within a societal and historical context. The focus is on the cognitive, affective and behavioural aspects of these experiences (Chell, 1998) and their meaning in context (Chell, 2014). Chell thus changes the analytical perspective from an approach that aims to make scientific discoveries of negative and positive incidents 'out there' to an approach that inquires into observations and experiences of incidents that are inherent to the respondent's subjective life context or lifeworld. Referring also to a constructivist tradition, Chell and Pittaway argue:

> The main principles of social constructivism suggest that behaviour arises out of a combination of the individual and their environment and that an

individual's personality is constructed from perceptions of all actors in any given situation. Personality *is not* considered to be internal and consistent as in trait theory but personality is considered to derive from an actors [sic] interpretation of their own behaviour as well as the interpretation of others involved in the social context. (Chell and Pittaway, 1998, p. 25)

The researcher must carefully examine her own pre-understandings in order to be able to understand the respondent and her context, and the technique must be adapted to the context of the persons investigated. The researcher 'thinks through *how* the technique may most appropriately be applied in the particular researchable case' (Chell, 1998, p. 51). The method is thus used to explore and interpret how subjects, for example, business owners or employees, experience certain occurrences, such as innovations, and what strategies they use to deal with them:

> The CIT is a qualitative interview procedure, which facilitates the investigation of significant occurrences (events, incidents, processes or issues), identified by the respondent, the way they are managed, and the outcomes in terms of perceived effects. The objective is to gain an understanding of the incident from the perspective of the individual taking into account cognitive, affective and behavioural elements. (Chell, 2014, p. 108; see also Chell, 1998)

The advantage of this version of CIT, in comparison to other qualitative and narrative methods, according to Chell, is that the relationship between context, strategy and outcome has a much better focus: the CIT interviewer inquires into an event that is explained in relation to what happened, how the event was handled and what the consequences were. For example, in the case of innovation in services, the method can be used to collect individual experiences about how innovations occur, how they are then handled and what the consequences are. Because the respondents can speak freely about incidents, many topics can be taken into consideration.

In this approach, incidents are thus seen as embedded in the respondent's perspective, her life story and her self-understanding. Examples are studies of innovative entrepreneurs, the incidents to which they pay attention (such as family incidents), and how they manage and cope with such incidents. Further, these incidents can be compared across contexts through multiple cases. Multiple cases can lead the researcher to examine and compare different situated perspectives: certain actors may tend to stress certain incidents and experiences, while others may stress other types. While the pure phenomenological analysis places the emphasis on the individual's unique experiences in an essentialist way, the phenomenological–interpretivist analysis offers a broader view. Chell argues:

Whilst phenomenology assumes the uniqueness of individual consciousness, the CIT enables the researcher to gain insights both into particular cases and across a sample of cases. For example, if the subset of cases is self-employed women with children, single parents, business owners at start-up, etc. then what are the typical issues which are raised by the particular subset? Is there a common set of problems? What do they need to know in order to be able to handle those problems (Chell, 1998, p. 68)

While incidents are subjective and unique to individuals, they are also contextually embedded and articulated through language, and behavioural consequences are observable. Therefore subjective incidents can be objectified and generalized to theory (Chell, 2014, p. 112). The method is, however, not a scientific tool used to solve problems by making incidents occur, but an 'investigative tool' that can be used in a phenomenological or interpretative approach (Butterfield et al., 2005) to explore different life situations and coping strategies in context.

Chell and Pittaway (1998) have used the method to analyse behaviours associated with entrepreneurship in the restaurant and café industry. The method was used, following a grounded theory approach, to codify certain incidents that were stressed by the business owners. These were grouped into: pro-active and re-active; tangible and intangible; and positive and negative incidents. They were then correlated with the different growth types of the businesses being investigated. Chell and Pittaway conclude that the CIT was useful for revealing the heterogeneity of small business owners. They relate information about this to business performance (p. 31). They found differences in what was done by different types of business owners, in how it was done (whether the behaviour was pro-active or re-active, for example) and in why it was done (for example, as an extension of personality).

Another example is a study by Cope (2011) on lived experiences of venture failure. The study is inspired by the CIT but also uses what he calls 'interpretative phenomenological inquiry' – stressing the researcher's interpretation of subjective experiences in a broader sense. The study uses a purposeful sampling technique to identify entrepreneurs who volunteer to report on their business failures. The interview technique that is used is called 'phenomenological interviewing'. The study demonstrates that entrepreneurs learn from failure and develop a capacity to do things in a radically different way (Cope, 2011, p. 618). This problematizes previous understandings of 'intelligent failure', which argued that failures need to be small in order not to create a negative response.

Chell (2014) makes a distinction between an interpretivist–hermeneutical approach and an interpretivist–social-constructivist approach. The difference between these, as described by Chell, is marginal. Both start from the assumption that knowledge about critical incidents is contextually grounded and relative. The interpretivist–hermeneutical approach develops subjective, particular, local and explorative knowledge of critical incidents, yet it may, as mentioned, seek to generalize to theory 'given sufficient cases and detailed content analysis'. The interpretivist–social-constructivist approach stresses a critical reflection on what the 'subject views as is or is not part of their world' (Chell, 2014, pp. 113–14). The studies of Cope (2011), mentioned above, and Chell tend to be positioned within an interpretivist–hermeneutical approach, and yet they overlap with the interpretivist–social-constructivist approach. For example, Cope uses the technique of purposeful sampling to identify actors' unique experiences of incidents of entrepreneurial failure. This leads him to indicate generalizable learning outcomes that transcend the participants' purely subjective experiences (p. 616). However, Cope's ambition in his study is also to critically reflect on what is part of the subject's world and question extant views and theories of venture failure.

In a similar way, in a study of change and innovation in a service organization, based on subjective accounts, it was questioned whether service innovation appeared as ready-made, planned entities. Instead it was concluded that they emerged from bricolage activity, using the resources at hand and solving problems on the spot (Fuglsang, 2010). Further, it was possible to explore the challenges and experiences that were involved in transforming bricolage into more reproducible innovations (Fuglsang and Sørensen, 2011).

3.3.2.2 Limitations

From a scientific point of view, it may be a problem that the interpretative research of this kind cannot be empirically generalized beyond the cases under investigation. The method instead offers unique insight into particular cases, which provides input for learning and theorizing. The detailed insight into single cases that the method can offer has explanatory power at the theoretical level (Chell, 2004). The phenomenological–interpretivist application of the method explains the heterogeneity of behaviours and how there are different strategies for coping with incidents. The method can also be useful in a practical way. It may help respondents to cope reflexively with what they can do, and how, why, and under what circumstances they can do it. In the context of service innovation, the practical use of the method can be to inquire more deeply into lessons that can be learned from innovations. For example, it may be used by service providers, such as business owners or employees, to investigate how subjects (employees, customers) experience incidents as part of their work or consumer practice, which may lead to learning and innovation.

It is difficult to formalize the method. The method relies on the successful interaction and fusion of the interviewers' and respondents' 'horizons'. Conducting the interviews requires particular skills. The investigator must examine her own assumptions (Chell, 1998, p. 51), and must be able to manage respondents' expressions of emotions and distress carefully (Chell, 2014). To increase the feasibility, two interviewers may be used. Two interviewers may provide a more complete picture by looking from different angles, and it also gives the interviewers time to reflect during the interviews and to check understandings and interpretations with the respondents (Chell, 2014, p. 126). However, the method cannot be isolated from the context of investigation, the pre-understandings of the researcher and the learned skills of a skilled interviewer.

A further problem of the method may be its origin in the phenomenological tradition. The interviewer is supposed to get access to the respondents' unique subjective experiences. As presented by Chell in most of her work, the phenomenological perspective is coupled with an interpretivist reflexive approach. Chell's approach clearly belongs to a Heideggerian version of hermeneutic phenomenology that stresses the researcher's explication of her pre-understandings rather than 'bracketing' her prejudices as in phenomenology. However, basically, Chell's method relies on a phenomenological strategy where the primary concern is to get access to contextual experiences and subjective interpretations of incidents. Chell makes this clear: 'The choice of what incidents to recount is entirely under the control of the subject; all that the researcher is doing is attempting to ensure that there is thorough coverage of the issues' (2014, p. 124). What is lacking in her work is, perhaps, a clearer positioning of the researchers' theoretical pre-assumptions. By comparison, the paper by Cope about venture failures (described above) indicates a slightly more theoretical way of using phenomenological–interpretivist analysis because it questions the extant theory about how entrepreneurs learn from failure. The empirical insights are compared to previous theoretical assumptions thereby leading to a revision of theory.

3.3.3   Reflexive Process Views of the CIT

3.3.3.1   Presentation
Process studies stress the temporal embeddedness of organizing and innovation. Process studies have for some years been extensively discussed in organizational studies and innovation research. Recent process studies are rooted in a 'process philosophy' that conceptualizes the world as process rather than substance. Process perspectives 'address questions about how and why things emerge, develop, grow, or terminate over time' (Langley,

Smallman, Tsoukas, and Van de Ven, 2013, p. 1). They 'provide the temporally embedded accounts that enable us to understand how . . . patterns come to be' (Langley, 2007, p. 273).

The process literature suggests that we may distinguish different types of process studies – such as weak, stronger and strongest. Weak process views focus on stages of development (like stages of innovation). Stronger process views explore the generative mechanisms that produce change. And the strongest process views conceive the world as process rather than substance, and hence are based in process philosophy (Welch and Paavilainen-Mantymaki, 2014).

Studies of service innovation are indeed process studies in their own right, since innovation can be understood both as process and as outcome. Process studies of innovation typically explore steps or stages in the innovation process. Yet the relationship between innovation studies and stronger process studies remains unclear. A stronger process approach to innovation would pay attention to innovation as an emerging pattern in ecologies of interrelated changes. It would also question previous understandings of innovation as a simple, planned, 'thing'-like or step-wise process.

The CIT can be used to conceptualize stages in the innovation process. This would be a 'weak' process perspective (Alam and Perry, 2002; Cooper, 2004). The CIT would then uncover the different periods/incidents that occur during the total innovation process. Further, the CIT can also provide a more detailed analysis of how actors experience and respond to these stages, how they cope with them, and with what consequences. The relevance of this to service theory and practice would be to make innovation and development more manageable (Alam and Perry, 2002) and to learn from experience. Alternatively, the critical incidents in the innovation process can be analysed as antagonistic episodes. For example, Van de Ven has interpreted innovation as a 'journey' (rather than being divided into neatly organized stages), where actors go through different periods of change that are mutually related in an antagonistic or dialectic/conflicted way (Van de Ven, 1999).

The CIT may perhaps also be used to pursue strong process studies. Innovation would within such a perspective be interpreted as an open-ended pattern that emerges over time from an ecology of many interacting actors with different intentions by processes of mutual connecting actions, into single acts that are retrospectively and reflexively recognized as innovations (Hernes, 2014, pp. 57–58). Thus the strong process perspective turns things around: incidents in this perspective are thought of as accomplished acts that are recognized retrospectively and reflexively, rather than as occurrences that trigger action or cause something to happen. The CIT could thus be used as a method to uncover innovative behaviours in a company and to recognize innovations in the past that point to the future.

3.3.3.2 Limitations

In the context of a strong process view, the CIT can be used to 'think back' and retrospectively recognize innovative behaviours/incidents in the past that can then be further developed in the future. One limitation of this use of the technique is that the technique uncovers 'old' practices rather than it develops new practices from experiences and new solutions to problems. A strong process view would stress cumulative change rather than radical change.

In a practical context of problem-solving, focusing cumulative processes of change may prevent a company from replacing existing routines and practices with new relevant routines and practices that create new value for the company and its customers. This is different from the original use of the technique, where rather the idea was to identify inadequate behaviours in order to replace them with new behaviours to solve problems.

However, such critique does not do full justice to a strong process view, because retrospectively recognizing adequate behaviours in the past is always an enactment in the present of some past experiences that point to the future.

3.4 DISCUSSION

The chapter has explained how the CIT can be used to study services and services innovation in a positivist–functional, a phenomenological–interpretivist or a process-oriented reflexive perspective.

CIT has been used in service research to analyse successes and failures in service encounters. The language is often positivistic and functional. The aim is to point to particular incidents and behaviours 'out there' in order to remedy these. For example, the method can be used to explore instances of customer dissatisfaction, and suggest innovative solutions to these. Yet, in services, the method may also be used to explore how respondents within their lifeworld experience innovations. Using the CIT in a phenomenological–interpretivist way may generate a sense-making process between the interviewer and the respondent in which the respondent can report important lessons learned during an innovation process which can be useful for future developments. Furthermore, CIT may also be used to reflect about temporal dynamics of innovation and to enact the past in the present pointing to the future.

While there are great differences between these approaches in terms of theory of science, method and interviewer strategy, we suggest that they can be used in different types of research contexts as explained in Table 3.1 below.

Table 3.1   Different approaches to CIT and the situations in which they may be applied

Approach to CIT	Research context	Interview questions	Incidents	Results
Positivist–functional	If aim and situation can be clearly stated and delimited, then the positivist–functional perspective can be applied.	Objective. What did someone do? With what effect with respect to what general aim?	Observable in terms of specific incidents with clear causal effects.	Solutions to problems, making things work better.
Phenomeno-logical–interpretivist	If aim and situation are understood as broad headings (such as entrepreneurship or service encounter), then the phenomenological–interpretivist perspective can be used.	Subjective, value-bound, contextual. What incidents were experienced? How were they handled and with what consequences?	Freely emphasized by the interviewee as experienced and coped with by the interviewee.	Learning about experiences with innovation and the challenges they pose in a life context.
Process-oriented reflexive	If aim and situation are understood as emerging patterns of innovation, which are rooted in the past and experienced in the present, then the process-oriented reflexive perspective can be applied.	Retrospective, key moments. What key moments in the history of the organization are currently pointing towards the future?	Something that presently seems an important act in the past.	Retrospectively recognizing innovations in the past that point to the future.

In the different research contexts, the notion of incident takes quite different meanings. In a positivist–functional research context, incidents are hard facts 'out there'. The researcher must specify general aims and identify situations that relate to those aims. The research question concerns what happened that produced certain outcomes in a causal way. This may be possible and relevant in some areas of service development. An example is the service encounter between an employee and a customer. However, this use of the method does not capture the wider context of the actors and how they understand and are able to cope with a situation. In a phenomenological–interpretivist approach, the aims and situations, such as the service encounter, are broad headings the interviewee can freely talk about. The researcher and the respondent seek to understand the situation through their interactive conversations. The focus is on the experiences of the respondent and on how the respondent deals with the reported incidents, as well as lessons learned. In a possible process-oriented reflexive approach, the focus is on events in the past that point to the future and thus retrospectively recognizing innovations.

The method can thus be used to analyse the role of specific incidents for innovation, lessons learned and temporal dynamics of innovation. As such, the approach falls within the broader quest of innovation theory to study 'how innovation takes place and what the important explanatory factors and economic and social consequences are' (Fagerberg, Fosaas, and Sapprasert, 2012). Yet the method mainly focuses on the individual and organizational level, seldom the macro- or system-levels. The method may be particularly relevant in services, where innovative solutions can be hidden in the service encounter, where the experience of innovation can be more blurred, and where the key moments and impacts of innovation are fuzzier than in technological innovation.

LEARNING POINTS

- The CIT can be used in a positivist–functional way to uncover concrete innovative solutions, in a phenomenological–interpretivist way to uncover the experiences and challenges of innovation in practice, and in a process-oriented reflexive way to uncover the temporal dynamics of innovation.
- The CIT relies on quite different philosophies of science and interviewer strategies, but the different approaches may also be used more pragmatically for different types of research problems or practical problems concerning innovation.

DISCUSSION TOPICS

- How can the CIT help spur innovation? An example could be the development of tourist services in a tourist destination.
- Give examples of researchable contexts in which each of the three approaches to CIT (positivist–functional, phenomenological–interpretivist and process-oriented) can be applied.
- How can the CIT be applied in a quantitative way?

REFERENCES

Alam, I., and C. Perry (2002), 'A customer-oriented new service development process', *Journal of Services Marketing*, 16(6), 515–534.

Bitner, M.J., B.H. Booms, and M.S. Tetreault (1990), 'The service encounter: Diagnosing favorable and unfavorable incidents', *Journal of Marketing*, 54(1), 71–84.

Butterfield, L.D., W.A. Borgen, N.E. Amundson, and A.S. Maglio (2005), 'Fifty years of the critical incident technique: 1954–2004 and beyond', *Qualitative Research*, 5(4), 475–497.

Chell, E. (1998), 'Critical incident technique', in G. Symon and C. Cassell (eds.), *Qualitative Methods and Analysis in Organizational Research: A Practical Guide.* London: Sage Publications, pp. 51–72.

Chell, E. (2004), 'Critical incident technique', in C. Cassell and G. Symon (eds.), *Essential Guide to Qualitative Methods in Organizational Research.* London: Sage, pp. 45–60.

Chell, E. (2014), 'The critical incident technique: Philosophical underpinnings, method and application to a case of small business failure', in E. Chell and M. Karatas-Özkan (eds.), *Handbook of Research on Small Business and Entrepreneurship.* Cheltenham, UK and Northampton, MA, USA: Edward Elgar Publishing, pp. 106–129.

Chell, E., and K. Allman (2003), 'Mapping the motivations and intentions of technology-orientated entrepreneurs', *R&D Management*, 33(2), 117–134.

Chell, E., and L. Pittaway (1998), 'A study of entrepreneurship in the restaurant and café industry: Exploratory work using the critical incident technique as a methodology', *Hospitality Management*, 17, 23–32.

Cooper, R.C. (2004), 'Third generation new product processes', *Journal of Product Innovation Management*, 11, 3–14.

Cope, J. (2005), 'Researching entrepreneurship through phenomenological inquiry', *International Small Business Journal*, 23(2), 163–189.

Cope, J. (2011), 'Entrepreneurial learning from failure: An interpretative phenomenological analysis', *Journal of Business Venturing*, 26(6), 604–623.

Drejer, I. (2004), 'Identifying innovation in surveys of services: A Schumpeterian perspective', *Research Policy*, 33(3), 551–562.

Edvardsson, B. (1992), 'Service breakdowns: A study of critical incidents in an airline', *International Journal of Service Industry Management*, 3(4), 17–29.

Edvardsson, B. (1998), 'Causes of customer dissatisfaction: Studies of public transport by the critical-incident method', *Managing Service Quality*, 8(3), 189–197.

Fagerberg, J., M. Fosaas, and K. Sapprasert (2012), 'Innovation: Exploring the knowledge base', *Research Policy*, 41(7), 1132–1153.

Flanagan, J.C. (1954), 'The critical incident technique', *Psychological Bulletin*, 51(4), 327–358.

Fuglsang, L. (2007), 'Critical incident teknikken', in L. Fuglsang, P. Hagedorn-Rasmussen, and P.B. Olsen (eds.), *Teknikker i samfundsvidenskaberne*, Frederiksberg: Roskilde Universitetesforlag, pp. 260–277.

Fuglsang, L. (2010), 'Bricolage and invisible innovation in public service innovation', *Journal of Innovation Economics*, 5(1), 67–87.

Fuglsang, L., and F. Sørensen (2011), 'The balance between bricolage and innovation: Management dilemmas in sustainable public innovation', *Service Industries Journal*, 31(4), 581–595.

Glaser, B.G., and A.L. Strauss (1967), *The Discovery of Grounded Theory: Strategies for Qualitative Research*. Chicago, IL: Aldine.

Gremler, D.D. (2004), 'The critical incident technique in service research', *Journal of Service Research*, 7(1), 65–89.

Helkkula, A., and M. Pihlström (2010), 'Narratives and metaphors in service development', *Qualitative Market Research: An International Journal of Advertising*, 13(4), 354–371.

Hernes, T. (2014), *A Process Theory of Organization*. Oxford: Oxford University Press.

Hoffman, K.D., S.W. Kelley, and B.C. Chung (2003), 'A CIT investigation of servicescape failures and associated recovery strategies', *Journal of Services Marketing*, 14(4), 322–340.

Johnston, R. (1995), 'The determinants of service quality: Satisfiers and dissatisfiers', *International Journal of Service Industry Management*, 6(5), 53–71.

Langley, A. (2007), 'Process thinking in strategic organization', *Strategic Organization*, 5(3), 271–282.

Langley, A., C. Smallman, H. Tsoukas, and A.H. Van de Ven (2013), 'Process studies of change in organization and management: Unveiling temporality, activity, and flow', *Academy of Management Journal*, 56(1), 1–13.

Meuter, M.L., A.L. Ostrom, , R.I. Roundtree, and M.J. Bitner (2000), 'Self-service technologies: Understanding customer satisfaction with technology-based service encounters', *Journal of Marketing*, 64(3), 50–64.

Price, L.L., and E.J. Arnould (1999), 'Commercial friendships: Service provider–client relationships in context', *Journal of Marketing*, 63(4), 38–56.

Ramseook-Munhurrun, P. (2016), 'A critical incident technique investigation of customers' waiting experiences in service encounters', *Journal of Service Theory and Practice*, 26(3), 246–272.

Roos, I. (2002), 'Methods of investigating critical incidents: A comparative review', *Journal of Service Research*, 4(3), 193–204.

Sørensen, F., J. Sundbo, and J. Mattsson (2013), 'Organisational conditions for service encounter based innovation', *Research Policy*, 42(8), 1446–1456.

Toivonen, M. and T. Tuominen (2009), 'Emergence of innovations in services', *The Service Industries Journal*, 29(5), 887–902.

Urquhart, C., A. Light, R. Thomas, A. Barker, A. Yeoman, J. Cooper, C. Armstrong, R. Fenton, R.E. Lonsdale, and S. Spink (2003), 'Critical incident technique and explicitation interviewing in studies of information behavior', *Library & Information Science Research*, 25(1), 63–88.

Van de Ven, A.H. (1999), *The Innovation Journey*. New York: Oxford University Press.

Welch, C., and E. Paavilainen-Mantymaki (2014), 'Putting process (back) in: Research on the internationalization process of the firm', *International Journal of Management Reviews*, 16(1), 2–23.

4. The laddering method in service innovation research

Niels Nolsøe Grünbaum

4.1 INTRODUCTION

In this chapter it is advocated that the so-called laddering method can serve as an interesting and novel methodology in service innovation research. Laddering is a qualitative interview technique applied in a situation with one interviewer and one informant (Reynolds and Gutman, 1988). More specifically, the method draws on Gutman's (1982) means–end theory. That is, the goal of laddering is to create an understanding of the value that Business-to-Consumer (B2C) customers extract from product attributes. Thus, laddering theory depicts a mental or cognitive map of the consumer pertinent to buying and consumption of specific goods. This is done through the means–end theory.

This is indeed rather interesting for B2C companies, because it creates an understanding of the values consumers extract from products and services that a given business offers to the market. Moreover, this knowledge can guide service and product innovations and thereby optimize the efficiency in R&D cost. The insights in values are also interesting for firms on the Business-to-Business (B2B) market, because they will get a better understanding of how their offerings can increase the value for partly the buying organization, and partly for the final end user. Furthermore, actors on the public market will also benefit from grasping user value structures related to innovation of services. Hence, it is suggested in this chapter, that the laddering method can serve as an interesting qualitative technique to efficiently create value throughout the value chain.

The rest of the chapter is structured in the following way; first the laddering method is explained more specifically and the historical and contemporary research in values, and means–end theory are elaborated. Second, an example of applicability of the laddering method is offered based on a study of consumers' political intentions and values when buying organic food products and the application of the method in services is discussed. Finally, the chapter's main points are summed up.

4.2 LADDERING METHOD – PARADIGMATIC ANCHORAGE, WHAT IT IS, AND HOW IT IS APPLIED

Values have been given much attention across many different fields, for example, in trying to understand thoughts and feelings when consumers buy products and services. More specifically, aiming to tap into the deeper motivations consumers pursue when buying products and services. Pertinent to this, marketing researchers have adapted a specific qualitative methodology called laddering (Reynolds and Gutman, 1988). Clinical psychologists first developed the laddering method in the 1960s. The method was used to understand the unapparent reasons for a patient's discontent. Marketers, however, are not interested in personal root problems but in understanding what consumers value and what the relationship is between these values and consumers' purchase of goods and services. The laddering method has proven to be robust in creating insights in this mental process. Instead of just understanding the more obvious reasons for buying and consuming, the laddering method thus generates insights into the deeper and more unconscious reasons for consumers' buying behaviour. Hence, a more complex, multifaceted, detailed and true understanding is obtained. Figure 4.1 below depicts the method. This novel understanding based on a micro-level (i.e. psychological) approach has in the field of management and marketing been used to profile consumers, to position current

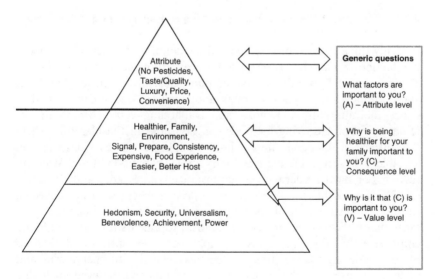

Figure 4.1   The iceberg analogy

products on the consumers' mental map, to develop and position strategies for new products, to evaluate sellers ethical/unethical behaviour, to create brand value, to benefit segmentation, to link motives to buying behaviour, to craft efficient and relevant market communications, to understand risk perception and buying behaviour and lastly to map motivation profiles (Gutman, 1982; Reynolds and Gutman, 1988; Pitts et al., 1991; Botschen et al., 1999; Günther et al., 1999; Parry, 2000; Fotopoulos et al., 2003; Reynolds and Olson, 2001; Phillips and Reynolds, 2009; Rosario, 2014; Menvielle et al., 2014). Nonetheless, the laddering methodology has so far not been applied to service innovation. The idea being vindicated in this chapter is that values indeed play an important role in relation to service innovation. First, when contemplating to innovate, it might be appropriate to probe: innovate what? And will there be a need for this innovation? Second, insights into and understanding of what the receiver (i.e. customer, user, client pending on market situation) values will help to guide what to innovate, how to innovate and cost–benefits of a given innovation process. Third, what if the customers' choice behaviour and motivation structure is ruled by unconscious values? If the latter is the case, uncovering these unconscious values seems to be a valuable voyage related to service innovation. That is, in unconscious values lies the opportunity to surprise the customer and thereby exceed the customers' expectations. The latter is a precondition for customer satisfaction, customer retention, customer loyalty, value creation and ultimately profitability, especially in services.

4.2.1   Streams of Research Related to Means–End Theory and Laddering

Roughly three streams of research can be identified in means–end theory and laddering, namely: a) one related to marketing and management strategy (see above); b) one related to methodological advancement (Woodside, 2004; Phillips and Reynolds, 2009); and finally c) one stream related to conceptual alternatives (Bagozzi and Dabholkar, 2000). Moreover, different types of laddering methods can be found in the literature where the softness of data collection technique applied serves as a classification variable. For soft laddering see, for example, Parry (2000) and Wansink (2003). For hard laddering see, for instance, van Rekom and Wierenga (2007). Hard laddering refers to an approach where data are collected through a questionnaire or a survey format, thereby discarding the advantages that a face-to-face interview entails. Proponents for hard laddering emphasize that this data-collection approach overcomes the difficulties of soft laddering, such as time and cost associated with interviewing and coding activities, possible geographic constraints and the need for highly skilled interviewers. Types of laddering related to service innovation are interesting because they will enhance the possibility of targeting types of laddering method with service innovation.

4.2.2 How Does Laddering Work?

Laddering draws on the means–end theory (Gutman, 1982; Reynolds and Gutman, 1988). According to the means–end theory, consumers construct and have constructed many mental hierarchical maps when consuming products. These mental maps consist of three abstraction levels, namely the attribute level, the consequence level and the value level (i.e. A–C–V), where values are related to the self (i.e. according to Rokeach, 1973). If consumers are probed about products, they have a tendency to respond to the obvious and concrete attribute level – characteristics that all products or services possess. For example, an informant would respond that they prefer organic food over conventional food because it tastes better, the quality of the food is perceived to be higher or the food products do not contain pesticides, etc. These responses can all be classified as attributes of organic food. Hence, they are at the concrete and low abstraction level. The purpose of the laddering method is thus to uncover the mental maps by directly probing using "why" questions, which uncover the meaning consumers assign to products. By using this continuous "why" probing technique related to responses given by the informant, consequences of the identified attributes will be clarified. Hence, the consequence level will arise from the interview. Lastly, the informant is probed about why the identified consequences are important. Moreover, this will lead to the end values the consumer enunciates from the consequences. A concrete example of the laddering technique exposing an A–C–V map of a high purchase organic consumer is offered below based on a study of the political consumer (n = 12):

Attribute level

Which factors influence your decision to buy organic food?

Because organic foods taste better, the quality is better, pesticides are not used, etc.

Consequence level

Why is it important that the food tastes good?

Because I can prepare tastier food (C)

Why is that important to you?

So I can be a better hostess (C) and a better wife (C)

Value level

Why is it important to be a better hostess?

I suppose, I am ambitious (V – Achievement)

In the example above the purpose of the first question is to get the informant to name as many attributes of organic food as possible. The "taste good" response is pursued. In the actual study all named attributes were examined further. Based on the interview one A–C–V ladder can be elicited, namely, taste better (A) → prepare tastier food (C) → be a better hostess (C) → be a better wife (C) → I am ambitious (V – Achievement). The achievement value is elaborated in Table 4.1 below, that is, demonstrating

Table 4.1   Schwartz's value system

Term	Encompasses the following values/domains
Self-direction (I)	Being able to choose own goals in life (creativity, freedom, independent)
Stimulation (I)	Novelty in life (a varied life, an exciting life, daring)
Hedonism (I)	Gratification for oneself (pleasure, enjoying life)
Achievement (I)	Demonstrating personal accomplishment matching to social norms (ambitious, successful, capable, influential, intelligent)
Power (I)	Demonstrating individual social status and prestige (authority, wealth, social power, preserving my public image, social recognition)
Security (I & C)	Safety and stability of society and of relationships to perceived important peers and safety of the self is focal here (social order, family security, national security, reciprocation of favours, clean, sense of belonging, healthy)
Conformity (C)	Control impulses that might upset others and social norms (obedient, self-discipline, politeness, honouring parents and elders)
Tradition (C)	Understand and respect traditions related to culture and religion (respect for tradition, humble, devout, accepting my lot in life, moderate)
Benevolence (C)	Preservation of welfare in one's own society (helpful, loyal, forgiving, honest, responsible, mature love)
Universalism (I & C)	Preservation, consideration, gratefulness of welfare for all people and nature (broad-minded, social justice, equality, a world at peace, a world of beauty, unity with nature, wisdom, protecting the environment)

personal accomplishment matching social norms (ambitious, successful, capable, influential and intelligent).

4.2.3 Data Collection and Analysis via the Laddering Method

Data are collected as demonstrated above and, when collected, the data are analyzed. Reynolds and Gutman (1988) provide good guidelines for the data analysis: first, a content analysis is performed based on summary content codes of the attributes, the consequences and values in a given data set. This analysis leads to an implication matrix which points to a map of hierarchical values, and thus the content codes are rather important in creating new knowledge. An example of how a content code is actually created follows (Grünbaum and Stenger, 2015). Point of departure is taken in the content code "no pesticides". In the collected data material, several comments were identified in relation to negative consequences of using pesticides in conventional food production. For example, "I don't like that they are sprayed, and I just think about a picture of an airplane flying over a field and spraying a lot of chemicals out". That statement and similar statements express the same content, namely that organic foods are deliberately chosen over conventional food products because organic foods are free of chemicals. Therefore, all statements that articulate this content are assigned as an attribute under the content code "no pesticides". When this work is done the implication matrix is created.

The implication matrix represents a summary of the number of times a specific response causes another response. The enumeration is done by listing how often, for example, a response such as (1) "no pesticides", leads to the response (9) "better for the environment". Finally, this results in a matrix expressing the aggregated ladders for the group of informants. The implication matrix illustrates the relations between the stated responses. The relationship of responses is composed of both direct relations and indirect relations. The direct relations are established when there is a direct connection between the responses. The hierarchical value map is then constructed based on the implication matrix. Figure 4.2 below sets out the steps that have been elaborated.

The hierarchical value map thus portrays a graphical representation of relations in the consumer's mind. Reynolds and Gutman (1988) note that the hierarchical value map is an important contribution in a laddering study because it gives a fast visual presentation of the findings. Figure 4.3 illustrates a value map for organic food buyers (Grünbaum and Stenger, 2015).

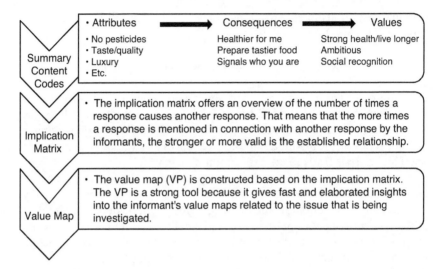

Figure 4.2   From data collection through data analysis to visual mapping of findings

4.3 VALUES, MEANS–END THEORY, LADDERING AND SERVICE INNOVATION

Values are important in means–end theory and in the laddering method. It is assumed and accepted in the literature that values guide human behaviour and by understanding these values it will be possible to predict human behaviour, for example, decision-making, motivations and intentions (Grunert and Juhl, 1995; Audenaert and Steenkamp, 1997; Steenkamp et al., 1999). Moreover, values have been given a lot of attention in several fields, for example, in marketing. The importance of values was coined by Rokeach (1973). Rokeach operates with two types of values: instrumental and terminal. The latter refers to a desired end state that individuals strive for (for example, freedom, happiness and inner harmony). The instrumental level serves as an auxiliary to achieve a terminal value (for example, ambitious, intellectual, responsible, self-control). Rokeach operates with 18 instrumental and 18 terminal values. This rather large number of values and hence difficulties with categorizing responses from informants has led to suggestions from other researchers to reduce the number of values and skip the distinction between types of values, i.e. instrumental and terminal (Schwartz and Bilsky, 1987, 1990; Schwartz, 1992). Thus, Schwartz's value theory has gained most acceptance in contemporary research (Steenhaut and Kenhove, 2006; Siltaoja, 2006). Schwartz and Bilsky (1987, p.551)

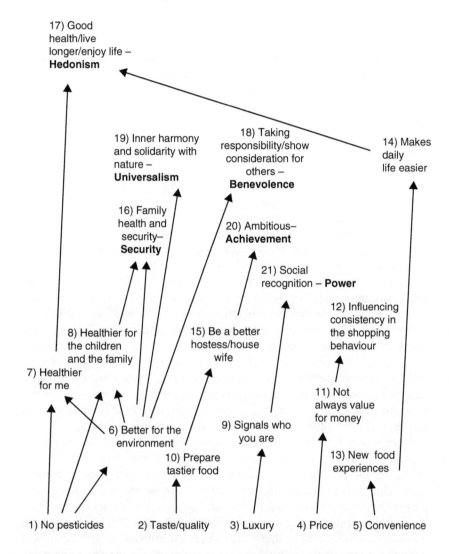

Figure 4.3   Value map for the boycott of organic food (Grünbaum and Stenger, 2015)

define personal values as: "concepts or beliefs about desirable end states or behaviors that transcend specific situations, guide selection or evaluation of behavior and events, and are ordered by relative importance". Schwartz (1992) further argues that his value systems are constant because they are derived from basic human circumstances. Moreover, the structure of Schwartz's value system has found empirical support based on studies from over 60 countries (Schwartz, 1992, 1994; Schwartz and Bardi, 2001). Accepting this argumentation makes values as a unit of analysis interestingly pertinent to service innovation, because the retrieved understanding will help guide what to innovate, how to innovate, how to communicate the innovations, and how to implement the innovations. More specifically, Schwartz (1992) argued for a taxonomy consisting of ten value systems. These are depicted in Table 4.1 above.

Based on Schwartz's ten value types, it is argued that ladders or chains of mental maps retrieved from users of service innovations can be understood and interpreted by Schwartz's value types. That is, the values apply to "all" consumers across geographical areas and transcend specific situations. The laddering method then serves as a procedure to retrieve these value hierarchies that are hidden to some degree for the informants themselves. These value types, and chains of mental maps, are also highly relevant for services. Additionally, because services are intangible, laddering and the different value types may in many cases be even more important for service innovation than for innovation of physical products. In services it is often the value that becomes the end product because nothing but the memory of consumption is left after consuming intangible services. Furthermore, some of the mentioned value types may be more relevant for some service sectors than for others. For example, value types such as self-direction, stimulation, hedonism, achievement, power and security are all fundamental in various leisure, tourism and experience services, but the different values may be important to varying degrees for different segments (for example, for adventure seeking versus ethnocentric tourists).

As mentioned, Rokeach argued for two superior types of values: instrumental and terminal. Opposed to this, Schwartz put forth that human activity could be motived by individual interest or by collective interest. The values of self-direction, stimulation, hedonism, achievement and power are purely self-serving, individual interests. The values of conformity, tradition and benevolence serve collective interests. The last two values, universalism and security, have dual interest purposes. In services, there may be a particularly interesting (but not perfectly clear) divide between collective interests, served predominantly by public organizations, and individual interests, served mainly by private companies. However, while public services mostly aim to serve collective interests, private service companies can also benefit from listening to their customers' collective interests, for example, banking or insurance businesses.

4.3.1 How Can Schwartz's Value System, Means–End Theory and Laddering More Specifically be Applied in Service Innovation?

Service innovation has been given much attention over the last two decades. It is a complex phenomenon that is applied in different contexts. Hence, defining service innovation is not a straightforward and easy task. Rubalcaba et al. (2012, p. 698) for example, distinguish between innovation in services, service innovation networks and service-oriented innovation in business all under the umbrella innovation through services. Nonetheless, it seems that there is consensus in the literature, that service innovation is best understood as a conceptual integrative framework (den Hertog et al., 2010; Rubalcaba et al., 2012). Den Hertog et al. (2010) thus note that service innovation should be understood and investigated as a multidimensional phenomenon (p. 492). More specifically, den Hertog et al. (2010) identify six dimensions in a business where service innovation can evolve, namely: a) new service concepts; b) new customer interactions; c) new business partner; d) new revenue model; e) new delivery system (personal, organization, culture); and f) new delivery system (technological). Hence, the meaning of innovation according to den Hertog et al. (2010) is embedded in the word "new". That is, it must be novel, strange or unfamiliar in the industry. Various dimensions suggested in the literature represent the complexity of framework perspective.

Because services are intangible and their consumption often highly driven by different value types (as mentioned above), service organizations, when innovating, may benefit from knowing about the value types and the related chains of mental maps of their (potential) customers. This counts, of course for the development of new service concepts but is also important when developing service interactions (during which services are often both produced and consumed) and it can also be relevant, for example, for choosing business partners and developing new revenue models (with values matching those of the consumers). Conversely, any change in a service or a business set-up which is "out-of-sync" with customers' inner value types may lead to frustrated customers seeking other service suppliers.

4.3.2 Implications of the Value Map Presented in Figure 4.3

Both practical and theoretical implications can be conveyed based on the value map above (i.e. Figure 4.3). First, it is important to understand that buyers of organic food attribute different values to product aspects. That is, some buyers are interested in organic food because they perceive it to be healthier for them and because they ultimately want to live longer.

Note that this is a value that has an individualistic motivation according to Schwartz's value system (i.e. Table 4.1). Other buyers are more concerned about environmental issues and are ultimately interested in living in harmony with nature. This is, according to Schwartz, a dually motivated value. Relating this understanding to innovation and in particular to service innovation, it would be helpful to segment the customer portfolio of a given company. Grünbaum and Stenger (2015) argue that values should be classified in three different analytical intensities, namely, society, group and individual. This leads to three segments classified as S, G and I, where each segment is demarcated by its own special characteristics. If this was not the case they would, of course, not be a segment. Now based on this typology a string of strategic decisions regarding innovation can be made in a more efficient manner, because the value classification scheme makes it possible to align service innovation decision with specific values held by a specific group of customers. Moreover, if alignment between type of value and type of segment is not the case, the resources invested in innovative efforts will be far less effective. This particular situation is graphically demonstrated in Figure 4.4 by the sloping arrow departing from value type group to segment I.

Segment S (i.e. society) is mainly driven by values, benevolence and universalism. This can be exploited when it is decided what specific service attributes should be innovated. In like manner, it will be possible to communicate the new aspects and benefits of the service to the segment if benevolence and universalism aspects are advocated. More specifically, segment S will value and thus find the green and environmental aspect highly relevant and important. Segment S could be called true political consumers. They are well educated and are more likely to live in the larger cities than in the countryside. They desire to "change" the world and if possible they will do this by proxy via their consumption of products and services. Services and products that help segment S to achieve the vision of sustainable consumption and production, a more environmentally balanced planet for their descendants, and security of equality and a fair welfare for all humans will be highly valued. Hence, demand for these kinds of services will be inelastic, making it possible to follow a premium pricing strategy.

Segment G (i.e. group) is contrary to segment S driven by the value "security". Segment G will typically focus on the nearest family but also on a broader concept of family. This extension of the family could be a large group that shares a strong common passion, for example, the fan club of the soccer team Manchester United or the Harley Davidson owners club. Segment G displays a strong loyalty to the "family". They value services and products that will insure the demand of belonging and of securing

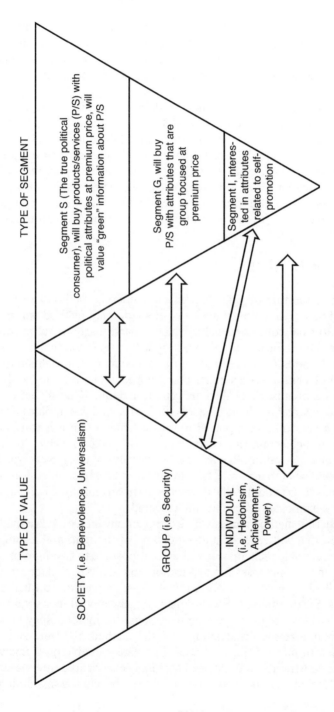

TYPE OF SEGMENT

Segment S (The true political consumer), will buy products/services (P/S) with political attributes at premium price, will value "green" information about P/S

Segment G, will buy P/S with attributes that are group focused at premium price

Segment I, interested in attributes related to self-promotion

TYPE OF VALUE

SOCIETY (i.e. Benevolence, Universalism)

GROUP (i.e. Security)

INDIVIDUAL (i.e. Hedonism, Achievement, Power)

Figure 4.4   G-S value classification scheme (Grünbaum and Stenger, 2015)

the well-known social order found in the family and society. Segment G is, however, also interested in environmental issues both for quite other reasons than segment S. For example, segment G is motivated by actions that lead to a stable, conservative and safe society without too many disruptions.

Segment I (i.e. individual) values freedom, an exciting lifestyle, being successful and displaying their success to peers. Segment I has a strong focus on themselves. They, moreover, value individualistic pleasure, a daring lifestyle and a joyful life. They work hard to get success and power. Segment I is money-driven and rather astute, although they are more likely to hold a BA than a Masters degree. Portraying success and power to perceived peers is rather important. Thus, segment I values services and products that can convey this self-perception to the surrounding entourage.

4.4   CONCLUSION

Attending to the title of this chapter, the laddering method can indeed be applied in service innovation. Using the laddering method will create insights into what consumers value which is particularly useful in service innovation. This information is interesting within several domains – on the B2B market, the B2C market and on the public market. Insights into the value level of consumers are particularly appealing because research has supported the premise that values are generic in nature. That is, they can be generalized to larger populations across industries and geographic borders. Since it is assumed and supported in various studies that it is values that guide human behaviour, (for example, decision-making), values are relevant in service innovation. Realizations of the value of consumers will help to understand what to innovate, how to innovate, how to communicate and sell the innovations and, finally, how changes in organizational procedures caused by the innovations can be implemented.

The laddering method comes with a string of advantages. It is a qualitative method that will generate understandings of thoughts and feelings of the informant's value schemas. It will make it possible to cast light on why questions and the premises for application and analysis of data are very well described. The latter, is often not the case in relation to qualitative techniques. Furthermore, the technique is largely applied in several fields and there has been a great focus on developing the methodology in ways that will minimize the disadvantages of the method: the time and cost associated with interviewing and coding of data; possible problems with geographic constraints; and the need for highly experienced interviewers.

The laddering method was first developed by clinical psychologists in the 1960s in order to understand root causes of patients' discontent. Marketers later adopted the method in marketing, in order to try to understand and predict consumers' buying behaviour, based on the values that consumers extract from the services and products they buy. Thus, marketers have applied the laddering method differently and in another analytical setting to that which was originally intended. Applying laddering in service innovation in like manner is yet a new area. The leap, however, is smaller than from the psychologist's couch. In service innovation we are still interested in what consumers value and the relationship between service attributes, the consequences thereof and how these consequences are related to the values of the individual consumer and sections of consumers. The starting point of the laddering interviews, however, needs some alteration since we might probe about matters that are not yet developed. Thus, in service innovation, the questions need to be more abstract in nature with the purpose of getting the informant to imagine the attributes and also the consequences of something that is not yet there.

LEARNING POINTS

- The chapter has introduced what the laddering method is and the historical background of the laddering method, as well as how to apply the laddering method.
- The method focuses on the importance of values in service innovation and in business and management in general.
- The method emphasizes the importance of coherence in values and innovation of services.
- The chapter has introduced the concept of a value schema and the values and characteristics of segments S, G and I.

DISCUSSION TOPICS

- Why is the laddering method useful in service innovation?
- Discuss the limitations of the laddering method in relation to service innovation.
- Discuss examples of service innovations tailored to segments S, G and I.

REFERENCES

Audenaert, A. and J.E.M. Steenkamp (1997), 'Means–end chain theory and laddering in agricultural marketing research', in B. Wierenga, A. van Tilburg, K. Grunnert, M. Wedel, and J.E.M. Steenkamp (eds.), *Agriculture Marketing and Consumer Behavior in a Changing World*. Amsterdam: Kluwer, pp. 217–232.

Bagozzi, R.P. and P.A. Dabholkar (2000), 'Discursive psychology: An alternative conceptual foundation to means–end chain theory', *Psychology & Marketing*, 17, 535–586.

Bieke Z., K. Geurden, R. De Cock, B. De Schutter, and V. Vanden Abeele (2014), 'Motivation profiles of online Poker players and the role of interface preferences: A laddering study among amateur and (semi-)professionals', *Computers in Human Behavior*, 39, 154–164.

Botschen, G., E.M. Thelen, and R. Pieters (1999), 'Using means–end structures for benefit segmentation', *European Journal of Marketing*, 33 (1/2), 38–58.

den Hertog, P., W. van der Aa, and M.W. de Jong (2010), 'Capabilities for managing service innovation: Towards a conceptual framework', *Journal of Service Management*, 21 (4), 490–514.

Fotopoulos, C., A. Krystallis, and M. Ness (2003), 'Wine produced by organic grapes in Greece: Using means–end chains analysis to reveal organic buyers' purchasing motives in comparison to the non-buyers', *Food Quality and Preferences*, 14, 549–566.

Grünbaum, N.N. and M. Stenger (2015), 'Uncovering consumers' political intentions and values when buying and consuming organic food products', *Business and Management Quarterly Review*, 6 (2/3), 41–56.

Grunert, S.C. and H.J. Juhl (1995), 'Values, environmental attitudes and buying of organic foods', *Journal of Economic Psychology*, 16 (1), 39–62.

Günther B., E.M. Thelen, and R. Pieters (1999), 'Using means–end structures for benefit segmentation', *European Journal of Marketing*, 33 (1/2), 38–58.

Gutman, J. (1982), 'A means–end chain model based on consumer categorization processes', *Journal of Marketing*, 46, 60–72.

Menvielle, L., W. Menvielle, and N. Tournois (2014), 'Purchasing behavior of consumers for foreign medical services', *Qualitative Market Research*, 17 (3), 264–282.

Parry, M.E. (ed.) (2000), *Strategic Marketing Management: A Means–End Approach*. New York: The McGraw-Hill Executive MBA Series.

Phillips, J.M. and T.J. Reynolds (2009), 'A hard look at hard laddering: A comparison of studies examining the hierarchical structure of means–end theory', *Qualitative Market Research: An International Journal*, 12 (1), 83–99.

Pitts, R.E., J.K. Wong, and J.D. Whalen (1991). 'Consumers' evaluation structures in two ethical situations: A means–end approach', *Journal of Business Research*, 22, 119–130.

Rekom, B.V. and B. Wierenga (2007), 'On the hierarchical nature of means–end relationships in laddering data', *Journal of Business Research*, 60 (4), 401–410.

Reynolds, T.J. and J. Gutman (1988), 'Laddering theory, method, analysis and interpretation', *Journal of Advertising Research*, 28, 11–31.

Reynolds, T.J. and J.C. Olson (eds.) (2001), *Understanding Consumer Decision Making: The Means–End Approach to Marketing*. Abingdon: Routledge.

Rokeach, M. (ed.) (1973), *The Nature of Human Values*. New York: Free Press.

Rosario, G.M., D. Carmen, and S. Biagio (2014), 'Values and corporate social initiative: An approach through Schwartz theory', *International Journal of Business and Society*, 15 (1), 19–48.

Rubalcaba, L., J. Sundbo, S.W. Brown, and J. Reynoso (2012), 'Shaping, organizing, and rethinking service innovation: A multidimensional framework', *Journal of Service Management*, 23 (5), 696–715.

Schwartz, S.H. (1992), 'Universals in the content and structure of values: Theoretical advances and empirical tests in 20 countries', *Advances in Experimental Social Psychology*, 25, 1–65.

Schwartz, S.H. (1994), 'Are there universal aspects in the structure and contents of human values?', *Journal of Social Issues*, 50 (4), 19–45.

Schwartz, S.H. and A. Bardi (2001), 'Value hierarchies across cultures: Taking a similarities perspective', *Journal of Cross-Cultural Psychology*, 32, 268–290.

Schwartz, S.H. and W. Bilsky (1987), 'Toward a universal psychological structure of human values', *Journal of Personality and Social Psychology*, 53, 550–562.

Schwartz, S.H. and W. Bilsky (1990), 'Toward a theory of the universal content and structure of values: Extensions and cross-cultural replication', *Journal of Personality and Social Psychology*, 58, 878–889.

Siltaoja, M.E. (2006), 'Value priorities as combining core factors between CSR and reputation: A qualitative study', *Journal of Business Ethics*, 68 (1), 91–111.

Steenhaut, S. and P.V. Kenhove (2006), 'An empirical investigation of the relationships among a consumer's personal values, ethical ideology and ethical beliefs', *Journal of Business Ethics*, 64 (2), 137–155.

Steenkamp, J.-B.E.M., F. Hofstede, and M. Wedel (1999), 'A cross-national investigation into the individual and national cultural antecedents of consumer innovativeness', *Journal of Marketing*, 63 (4), 55–69.

Wansink, B. (2003), 'Using laddering to understand and leverage a brand's equity', *Quantitative Market Research: An International Journal*, 6 (2), 111–118.

Woodside, A.G. (2004), 'Advancing means–end chains by incorporating Heider's balance theory and Fournier's consumer–brand relationship typology', *Psychology & Marketing*, 21 (4), 279–294.

5. Narratives as driver for co-creating new stories of service

Anne Vorre Hansen

5.1 INTRODUCTION

Both the past and the future are experienced in the present, and thus, Hernes argues, we live in an ongoing present. This is what a process perspective is about – both as a disposition and as a way of studying organizations (Hernes, 2014). The chapter is based on this explicit temporal understanding of process, which is why the narrative methodology has been applied to unfold value (co-)creation and innovation perspectives within the field of service innovation research. This is illustrated by a case study carried out in the non-profit housing sector in Denmark, as the housing associations are characterized by a longitudinal service relationship between residents and organizations based on facility service offerings. In the case, temporality plays a crucial role in understanding how services are experienced from a resident's (customer's) point of view and how past experiences influence future expectations. In this chapter, service is understood as "a *process of doing something beneficial for and in conjunction with some entity*" (Lusch and Nambisan, 2012, p. 10). This process view on service implies a focus on relationships and interactions. Accordingly, it is relevant to analyse how value is co-created in the relationships between actors and how this relational aspect is part of service development. Narratives support such an exploration since narratives allow for interpretations of how these interactions manifest themselves at both an individual and a social level (Uprichard, 2011).

Narrative methodology is widely used and cross-disciplinary; within fields such as psychiatry, criminology, organizational studies and interaction design, narratives are used to gain insight on subjective experiences and understandings (Alvarez and Urla, 2002; Polletta et al., 2011). The theoretical stand is that narratives are closely linked to perceptions of past and present and can constitute future expectations and/or behaviour. As such narratives also have the ability to change experience since narratives become a vehicle to organize perceptions and symbolically rearrange experience (Jackson, 2013). The chapter is based on the same assumption, that stories or narratives (the terms are used interchangeably throughout the chapter) open up the social world of customers and that understanding how value is created and negotiated in the sphere of customers is a central aspect when engaging in service innovation. Therefore, narrative methodology has been applied as both an underlying mindset and as a concrete method to analyse interviews, and by the use of storytelling and story creation as the foundation and objective for an innovation workshop. In the chapter, the main focus is on the workshop, which will act as an empirical illustration of such a narrative approach.

To sum up, the chapter employs a process view on service innovation and value co-creation. This leads to a discussion on how customer insight supports companies in facilitating value creation processes, in this sense understood as "innovation". In the following, the chapter is positioned in the overall framework of the book and subsequently, narrative methodology, especially as related to service innovation, is introduced.

5.2   TELLING STORIES

The focus on what a story is and what a story does began with Aristotle's study of the Greek tragedy and his understanding of stories as representations of the world (Riessman, 2008). In *Metaphysics*, Aristotle pinpoints that, "Now from memory experience is produced in men; for the several memories of the same thing produce finally the capacity for a single experience" (Aristotle, Book 1, part 10). As such, Aristotle from the very beginning, acknowledged the intertwined relationship between individual and shared experiences. Narrative methodology is based on the same assumption that narrating is a condition for humans, being in the world among others, and that individual narratives open up an understanding of social worlds (Holstein and Gubrium, 2002; Riessman, 2008). To focus on stories, and the stories we tell, is to take the lived life of people, and in this specific case the residents, as a point of departure.

Within the wide range of research in service innovation, the present case study is positioned in the stream that focuses on service innovation management on a micro level, and furthermore, with a distinct focus on customers. Sundbo and Toivonen (2011) state that the view of users as a foundation for service innovation is, in the field of service research, now acknowledged as crucial. The claim rests on the service characteristic that the customer, or user, benefits from both the service outcome and the service process itself. Therefore, the customer is essentially the co-producer of the service.

In line with the focus on the customer in service research, there has been a continuing conceptual discussion on the customer role in value creation processes and how and where value co-creation takes place (Gummerus, 2013; Mattelmäki and Visser, 2011; Tronvoll et al., 2011). The service-dominant logic (SDL) perspective has set the agenda within service marketing research by emphasizing the proposition that customers are *co-creators of value*. The focus is not on the product or the service per se, but rather, on the experienced value. Integrating the concept of experience opens up a more context-dependent understanding of value creation. Vargo emphasizes this through refinement of the former concepts, value-in-use and value-in-exchange to value-in-context (Lusch and Vargo, 2014; Vargo, 2008). In the same vein, the customer-dominant logic (CDL) perspective (Voima, Heinoken, and Strandvik, 2010) seeks to integrate the longitudinal aspect of value creation based on a phenomenological approach. The CDL perspective places the customer in the centre of value *formation* by taking the experience and the lived life of the customer into account. Value is therefore deeply embedded in and defined by past experiences and the present state of mind (Heinonen et al., 2013). This is an aspect that places the company in the role of value *facilitator* as companies can only facilitate value, not create value (Grönroos, 2008; Voima et al., 2010). Along the same lines, a specific way to perceive service innovation, or any type of innovation for that matter, is to define innovation as refining and/or developing new value propositions (Lusch and Vargo, 2014). This understanding of innovation is based on service marketing and is an attempt to apply SDL to service innovation literature. The view is that companies can only offer value propositions and not create value (in terms of SDL), which leads to the understanding of companies as value facilitators (in terms of CDL). Hence, the locus of innovation becomes the relationship between user and supplier and the way their interaction is facilitated (Miles, 2012). The marketing stand on innovation has come to the innovation discussion quite late and is narrow in the sense that it does not take new streams (e.g. employee-driven innovation and bricolage) into account (Hasu et al., 2014). But, as a supplement to existing approaches in service innovation studies, the broad perception of value as inherently co-created seems especially relevant when the emphasis is on customer/ user-driven innovation, having a main focus on "value for whom?".

The increased focus on customer lifeworlds and the move towards value in the experience have caused current service researchers to call for paradigmatic discussions and new methods based on interpretative sciences (Helkkula et al., 2012; Tronvoll et al., 2011). Hence, it is acknowledged that the field of service research needs supplemental approaches since the relational and process-oriented nature of service and service innovation calls for increased qualitative knowledge on the sphere of the customer and the relationship between the customer and the company. As a methodology rooted in an interpretative and hermeneutic tradition, focusing on lifeworlds and social interaction, narrative methodology is proposed.

Within organizational studies, the grip on narratives is related to strategy, organizing and innovation. In research on strategy, the focus is on storytelling, for example, how narratives can be useful in "re-storying" the self-perception of organizations (Barry and Elmes, 1997; Boje, 1995). In addition to applying the change aspect of narratives, it is recognized that stories are part of human organizing (Boje, 1995; Rosile et al., 2013). In the context of innovation, the change perspective is particularly interesting since the focus on narratives as a vehicle for understanding the past to prepare for the future is based on the supposition that stories are constitutive of future behaviour, and as such, can be drivers for change (Becker and Müller, 2013). To sum up, the narrative approach is concerned with meaning, on an individual, a social or a societal level, as well as how these levels are deeply entangled.

5.3 NARRATIVES AND SERVICE INNOVATION

Within service innovation research, there are studies on both the micro and the macro levels. The macro level focuses on innovation systems and on measuring innovation, whereas the micro level focuses on how innovation is achieved relative to management, strategy and organizing (Sundbo, 2014). To employ narrative methodology is to take the particular as the departure. Although, as mentioned, the use of narrative methodology is common in organizational research, exploring the applicability of narratives to micro-level service innovation processes is still quite a new field within innovation, and service innovation studies (Helkkula and Pihlström, 2010; Helkkula et al., 2012; Pedersen and Johansen, 2012). There are different approaches, but it seems that most research either focuses on innovation stories (i.e. how stories of innovation create, support and sustain an innovative culture) (Bartel and Garud, 2009; Halliday, 2008; Pedersen, 2013), on narrative inquiry as an instrument in research on the innovation processes (Makkonen, Aarikka-Stenroos, and Olkkonen, 2012; Rosile et al., 2013), or on narratives as a method to engage customers in the innovation process itself (Helkkula and Pihlström, 2010; Mitchell, 2013). Furthermore, the initial state of innovation is acknowledged as being especially challenging to approach. As Müller argues, often the "beginning of the story" is not taken into account when companies enter the process of innovation. The spillover effect involves fluffy ideas of the future that are not rooted in the present (Müller, 2013). In spite of these different takes on a narrative approach, the framework of narrative methodology seems to be a shared focus on temporality, on the relational aspect of narratives and on the constitutive role of storytelling.

To exemplify the stream of research that employs narratives as a tool for customer-centred innovation, Helkkula and Pihlström (2010) present the event-based narrative inquiry technique (EBNIT). Their method is situated within projective techniques and the objective is to generate ideas along evaluating existing service (Helkkula and Pihlström, 2010). As such, narrative inquiry is used to approach the experiences of the storyteller, which in this case is the customer. Accordingly, Helkkula and Pihlström apply the understanding of service as a holistic experience, transcending the distinction between goods and services. Helkkula and Pihlström argued for narratives and metaphors as being triggers for generating ideas in service development, and in the research presented, they, for example, use the metaphor of a magic wand to make customers think beyond what is currently possible and to come up with new ideas. The EBNIT is centred around the interviewees' experience of a service phenomenon, critical events related to the phenomenon, the stories related to these events in a broad sense and the introduction of metaphors to support the interviewees' creation of imaginary events (Helkkula and Pihlström, 2010). Through three empirical cases, the authors elucidate how stories can generate context-specific insights to be used in further research and development. Besides finding metaphors and storytelling fruitful in idea generating, the study reveals that metaphors must be familiar to the interviewees to make sense. Thus, Helkkula and Pihlström underscore that the technique needs to be contextualized (Helkkula and Pihlström, 2010).

As mentioned and exemplified, narratives have been applied to innovation studies in different ways. But, a general framework of the use of narrative methodology within organizational studies, and service innovation specifically, is yet to be developed. The argument in this chapter is that relative to service innovation, where the aim of the innovation is to create new value propositions not connected to products or objects, the mindset of narrative methodology might clarify the focus on context, social relations and experience. Hence, this study applies narratives, not only as an idea-generating method or technique, as Helkkula and Pihlström illustrate, but also as a way to develop the relationship between the service provider and beneficiaries. The underlying assumption is the understanding of stories as a social kit, which supports meaning making at both an individual and a social level, an understanding that makes the narrative approach relevant when exploring and refining service relationships embedded in time and context.

5.4 EXAMPLE: INNOVATING THROUGH NEW SERVICE STORIES

The example departs from a service innovation process in the non-profit housing sector in Denmark, where narrative analysis has been applied to gain insight into residents' perspectives, in addition to being used as a tool to integrate this insight in developing future stories of service. As such the research is an example of a user-based service innovation process insofar as user insights are the foundation for a development process where the users act as "co-developers" of service (Sundbo and Toivonen, 2011).

5.4.1 The Case

The non-profit housing sector is unique insofar as approximately 20 per cent of the Danish population lives in dwellings of non-profit housing associations, and this way of living, to a large extent, is for ordinary incomes (Kristensen, 2006). In the seventies, the non-profit housing sector was seen as a driver for development of housing policy in Denmark. However, the sector is now struggling with a tarnished reputation, associated with unattractive architecture and offering housing for the socially excluded. This is only a half-truth, but this societal meta-story is a millstone around the necks of the housing associations. They are non-profit administrative organizations delivering facility services, in addition to administering the budget of each housing department. The housing departments are economically autonomous units based on resident democracy. In collaboration with the housing association, an elected board of residents discuss and present the yearly budget to the other residents at an annual budget meeting. Hence, the service encounters between the residents and employees are related to both everyday problem-solving and to more strategic matters. The specific case company, Boligselskabet Sjælland, is, within the non-profit housing sector in Denmark, a medium-sized association managing approximately 13 000 dwellings in the region of Zealand (www.bosj.dk). Along with the rest of the sector, Boligselskabet Sjælland faces two major challenges: to future-proof the buildings at a low cost and to secure heterogeneity among residents, keeping the more socio-economically advantaged people in the sector – which is intertwined with the above-mentioned reputation of the sector. Furthermore, the latter challenge is closely related to the residents' perception of the services offered and to the quality of the collaboration among the residents and the housing association. Hence, Boligselskabet Sjælland seeks to refine their service, but is facing challenges in the process due to a lack of knowledge of the majority of residents and how they perceive the service given. Accordingly, the following innovation process is based on a wish from the top management to obtain insight on this specific group of residents and to involve residents in the development of their service relationship. Even though the case departs from a de-commercial sphere, it seems relevant when exploring service relationships. Because the presented relationship is both longitudinal and characterized by a daily customer-to-customer interaction, it exemplifies how service is experienced and negotiated relative to the past, present and future.

5.4.2   Identifying Stories

The research process consists of two parts: conducting interviews and conducting an innovation workshop. The first part is based on 12 in-depth interviews with residents. The interview guide was semi-structured, being flexible and relatively broad to make room for individual stories and to go back and forth in time (Alvesson, 2011). Furthermore, the interview guide supported storytelling by posing questions like, "Can you exemplify that?" and "What happened next?" Narrative analysis is concerned with both intention and language, which is why the analysis of the transcribed resident interviews focused on both content and how and why the stories were told in the way they were (Riessmann, 2008). The analysis identified prevailing narratives about the relationship between the housing association and residents and clarified how different types of narratives flourished concurrently. The narratives fell into three main categories:

1.   Individual stories that were especially centred on moving. Motivations for moving are related to changes in life situations and are, as such, characterized by a high degree of chance. What is perceived as valuable for residents is, therefore, tenancy due to associated advantages, such as flexibility and financial security.
2.   Collective stories based on residents' social and interactive behaviour with other residents. Some stories are experienced while others are learned, but the dominating stories about Boligselskabet Sjælland are mainly negative, and there is a shared understanding of the past that is referred to as "in the good old days".
3.   Stories based on the universal plot of "the little man against the system". This is especially apparent in the overall story of "Us vs. Them" (Boligselskabet Sjælland), which was also a theme in the interviews with employees.

After identifying the three different types of narratives in the interview material, the prevailing topics that related specifically to the service relationship between residents and Boligselskabet Sjælland were categorized.

It became clear that most stories of service were centred on four major themes: moving, problem-solving, resident democracy and living within the non-profit housing sector. The next part of the process was to conduct an innovation workshop for both residents and employees. The identified narratives and the overall themes in the resident interviews acted as a point of departure in the co-creation of new stories since the four themes became the scaffold of the innovation workshop design. Moreover, the "universal" story of Us versus Them was addressed, because the acknowledged division between employees and residents was perceived as frustrating to both parties. Hence, the innovation workshop aimed to serve as both an instrument for re-storying the service encounters and the relationship between the two parties and as an example of co-creation on equal terms. In the following, the process is presented.

5.4.3 Creating New Stories

The overall aim of the workshop was to get employees and residents to create new stories of service. To ensure that the process was anchored in the findings of the resident interviews, it was necessary to transmit knowledge from the interview phase to the story-creating phase. Thus, short citations were identified in the interview material and made into four sets of citation cards, one for each of the mentioned themes: moving, problem-solving, resident democracy and living in the non-profit housing sector. Thus, a design game called "Citation Scrabble" was developed prior to the workshop. The objective of the game was to give the participants a shared understanding of what is at stake in the life of residents and also to lift the participants out of their own experiences by relating and reflecting on other people's understandings. The workshop was held in a tenants' house in order to deal with the inherent asymmetry in the power relation of employees and residents. To place the workshop out of the headquarters was to underscore the informal set-up and to support a safe environment for knowledge-sharing. Six residents from three different departments and six employees from the front desk, middle management and the communication department participated. Two researchers facilitated the workshop.

On the day of the workshop, the tables were already placed in groups and the participants were divided into four groups of three beforehand, with both employees and residents in each group. The workshop began with a short introduction of the research and the background for conducting the workshop. The facilitator presented the game "Citation Scrabble" and each group received a deck of 40 citation cards. The citations related to the four overall themes identified in the resident interviews, but the themes were not introduced to the participants. Instead, the participants were

Figure 5.1   Boundary objects at play

instructed to choose three citations at a time and make up a category representing what the participants believed the cards concerned. Subsequently, the next player chose three new cards that could be partly related to the prior category. When all of the citations were brought into play, the groups formulated unifying themes for their game. After the games had been played, the groups visited each other and presented their reflections and discussions related to the identified categories and the formulation of the overall theme.

After playing with the citations, the facilitator presented a story template and gave all four groups a concrete situation as a point of departure for their story. Moreover, the facilitator underscored that the citation game was to be used as inspiration (the process is illustrated in Figure 5.1 above). The story template was divided into "beginning", "middle" and "end", in addition to a table for obstacles. The objective of introducing obstacles was to allow the participants to reflect on what could go wrong in their story and how this could be dealt with. Subsequently, the groups started creating stories. Some used the story template, while others used a whiteboard folio and toy figures as part of their presentation. The groups had half an hour to develop their stories, and afterwards, each group presented their story. Even though the frame for the developed stories was to make ideal narratives of the future, one group was not able to come up with something new. Therefore, the story to a large extent, was about present practices. The reason given was that the group did not believe anything would change within a five-year period. In another group, they made both a happy ending and a tragedy – it seemed that they needed to make the story fail in order to turn it around and come up with a positive counterpart. In the presentation round, the other participants further developed and refined the stories, which is why the final stories were based on both group work and the subsequent joint discussion. An informal evaluation revealed that the participants were positive towards the process and several commented that the collaborative aspect especially, which is where the employees and residents jointly created stories, was a good experience. Shortly after the workshop, the data were analysed. Based on the stories each group had presented, along with the joint discussions that had been videotaped, the data were typed out into four coherent stories. The co-created stories of new service relationships became part of the strategy work in the organization. To exemplify, one of these stories is presented in Table 5.1.

5.4.4 Main Findings

For the housing association to qualify their value propositions based on the obtained knowledge, the four service stories pointed towards a focus

Table 5.1   Example of a future scenario related to the theme "moving"

Beginning	Middle:	Ending:	Obstacles:
• Who is in the story? • Where does the story take place? • What do the actors want to accomplish?	• What happens? • What choices do the actors make? • Why do they make these choices?	• Do the actors obtain what they intended or did they not succeed?	• What might go wrong in the story you created?
Actors: Hans, his girlfriend Grete, neighbours in the department, the BSS database, the trade organization BL. Place: Hans' home and the housing department. Over time, Hans would like a larger home, with room for their children from previous marriages. Hans would like to know which big apartments in his own department would be available within a period of years.	Hans asks for the person in the housing department who could provide an overview of those who might move out in the near future. As such, he begins his search in the department itself. Hans also checks out the national database via BL and then visits the database of his own housing association to look for exchange flats. The three levels of search shall be accessible the moment Hans and his girlfriend start talking about moving in together. That is referred to as an emergent stage.	Hans has the experience of the housing association delivering the service he needs. They give him an overview of the apartments that might be available within the next year. Furthermore, the board of residents in his department have, together with the resident who manages the local database "Who is interested in what?", given him feedback. Meanwhile, a new possibility has emerged – now it is possible to either turn two apartments into one or split a big apartment into two smaller ones. Hans considers combining his existing apartment with the one above via the creation of, for example, circular stairs.	The legislation might not allow for flexible dwellings. The legislation makes it more difficult for Hans and others in his situation by tightening the rules concerning internal moving. The employees who manage the legislation might be rigid.

Notes: The story is based on the following situation: Hans lives in an apartment in one of the housing departments of Boligselskabet Sjælland (BSS). Hans has a new girlfriend and they would like to move in together in Hans' apartment. They have four kids altogether. Hans is 52 years old.

on what is possible within existing legislation; transparency and trust as parameters for collaboration; an increased focus on the association's role as a supporter for the social kit in the departments; and an increased understanding of the conditions for engaging in resident democracy from the perspective of the residents. These main focal points will form the basis of idea generation and further development. In the following, the findings of the study that are related to the use of storytelling and story creation are presented. The first paragraph is concerned with the process, whereas the latter focuses on drivers and barriers for the outcome.

The creation of the new service stories is based on the narrative structure – that the beginning, middle and end are based on, and driven by, the plot of the story (Labov, 1997; Müller, 2013). The participants found the story template easy to access, since they are familiar with the main structure of the stories. The stories are concrete and engaging, making developing a story seem like an intuitive task. This supported the group work and the creativity of each participant. As such, both the design game and the story template acted as boundary objects that facilitated the process of creating a shared neutral point of reflection (Bødker and Christiansen, 1994; Fuglsang and Scheuer, 2012; Star, 2010). To take resident citations as a point of departure reinforced the participants in transcending their subjective experiences and relating to the underlying constructs of the interviews. The process of working with stories underscores the same, since the participants managed to save their own subjective experiences for the following discussion. Furthermore, the process of co-creating stories became a platform for the participants to reflect upon and further develop their relationship. To sum up, the workshop enabled a room where the boundary between employees and residents vanished and where they acted as collaborators in realizing the task given – creating new stories of their service relationship.

In addition to the above mentioned, the context of non-profit housing framed the process and the possibility for innovation. To some extent, the stories never really left the present to approach the future. The finding is that the context of both the non-profit housing sector in general and the housing association specifically outlined the innovation process. First, the sectorial constraints of legislation frame what is actually possible to do within legal requirements. The legislation seemed hard to assess for both employees and residents, which is why the participants came to discuss the legal requirements with no common understanding of what was possible within existing laws. Therefore, the process revealed that the organization would benefit from increased knowledge on legislation among employees, both to qualify their communication with residents and to meet the needs and ideas of residents and employees, respectively. Moreover, the *history* of collaboration narrowed the out-of-the-box thinking. The workshop exposed the fact that residents shared an experience of not being met or listened to when introducing new ideas for development to the housing association. Consequently, they, to some extent, dismissed their own ideas before they were thoroughly discussed. Hence, doing idea generation without decision-making authority proved difficult in this context, and for this reason, a relationship of trust between residents and the housing association is needed when engaging in processes of service innovation.

5.5 DISCUSSION

In the example given, narrative methodology has been applied as an analytical strategy and as a concrete tool for service innovation. The introduction of the method in the field of service research is based on the increased focus on the sphere of the customer (Lusch and Vargo, 2014) and the facilitating role of the company in service innovation processes (Grönroos, 2008). This broad perception of service and the understanding of value, as contextualized and situated, initiate a need to expand the scientific toolbox and ontological approaches in knowledge production on service. The narrative approach in the present research refines the understanding of context and customer insight as essential aspects of service innovation. In the following section, these issues will be discussed, followed by reflections on the method's relevance for practice and academia.

5.5.1 Context

That context is a crucial factor in value co-creation and innovation is widely acknowledged within service research, but the implication of integrating a contextual perspective is still a bit vague. It might be that context needs to be further specified since context can both refer to the sphere of the customer (as in research on value co-creation) and to the perspective of the company. The point in this specific study is that context is the sphere where company and customer meet. Grönroos and Voima stated that it is the *joint sphere* of value co-creation that needs to be addressed when doing service innovation (Grönroos and Voima, 2013, p. 136). Applying a story form is a way to look into and play with how elements are related to each other, be that oral or textual accounts or actors (Makkonen et al., 2012). Thus, the story form is inherently about context. Creating stories is a way to approach context, since, for example, the participants related their stories to contextual knowledge instead of being urged to come up with isolated ideas framed by designers or managers within an organization.

Even though the stories created in the introduced workshop are not ready-made solutions to the challenges of the housing association, they can act as a qualified foundation for further service development. In Müllers' perspective, the stories ensure that the forthcoming idea generation is anchored in existing understandings (Müller, 2013). In addition, the study highlighted how the case of non-profit housing framed what was possible to achieve, since the history of collaboration and the legislative conditions of the non-profit housing sector influenced the innovation process. Consequently the use of stories in the case presented brought context to the fore and nuanced the understanding of what is to be understood and addressed as context in this specific setting. The use of narrative methodology in the example concerned has, as such, added to existing knowledge within the field of service research on how value is co-created and how the process of value co-creation can be facilitated.

5.5.2 Customer Insight

One of the main challenges within service innovation research and practice is how to approach the front-end of innovation, and the phase of obtaining customer insight seems especially tricky and complex. As underscored in the introduction, this chapter focuses on the stream of research that addresses service innovation concerning relationships and interactions – an understanding of service, which implicates a change in research focus and triggers new questions such as how to embrace the sphere of the customer and how to innovate in the area of relationships (Heinonen et al., 2013).

In the present case, this emphasis might both create room for opportunities and be a barrier since it seems as if focusing the innovation process on a service relationship is more challenging than focusing on developing specific service encounters. In the given example from the non-profit housing sector, it is still too early to evaluate whether or not the process leads to better service. Nevertheless, the provisional findings indicate that the co-creation of stories in the innovation workshop gave the housing association perspectives on both their current relationship with their customers and input for refining their value propositions. As previously mentioned, knowledge was integrated in their strategy towards 2020. Instead of focusing merely on idea production, the process of creating stories thus broadened the understanding of the customers' sphere. These ideas tend to be anchored in the subject, whereas stories are negotiated among actors and hence have an essentially relational aspect. Additionally, the innovation workshop in and of itself can be seen as an innovative activity since it was the first of its kind, and the story of the process is diffused among both employees and residents. Therefore, this new story will act as a departure for and frame the expectations to innovation processes prospectively. In that sense, the constitutive aspect of narratives embraces the process-related nature of service. Accordingly, the method seems especially fruitful to apply in long-term service relationships where the relational character of service and the temporal aspect are especially stressed.

5.5.3   Relevance and Application of the Method

Narrative analysis is about approaching what is already there – to tell stories is a human condition, and stories are, in a sense, quite easy both to access and apply. Furthermore, the narrative methodology addresses the process view of service research, along with the social and temporal aspects of value creation. In that way, the narrative mindset releases a refined understanding of time, which is not only chronological, but is also referred to as narrative time (Pedersen, 2009; Ricœur, 1988). When we tell stories, time "collapses" insofar as both the past and the future are embedded in the present. Service research and service innovation research may especially benefit from this perspective, since relationships evolve over time and bring forward a history of past experience and future expectations. An increased understanding of this condition for human organizing of experience and digging into the social kit of stories and storytelling might be the entrance into the social world of customers, an insight that can help companies enhance their value propositions by attaching the development of future services to the history of relationships and experiences of both employees and customers. To service researchers, the narrative approach further supports theorizing on value co-creation and user-based innovation. In line with Helkkula and Pihlström's (2010) findings, the method needs to be translated into the specific context of use. As mentioned, the workshop had a dual purpose: the process in and of itself and the creation of future stories. The use of the narrative methodology seems to support the realization of both objectives since storytelling is intuitive and appealing. However, the study also reveals that the process needs to be structured and based on contextual knowledge. Therefore, the aim of the chapter is merely to introduce narrative methodology as a mindset and not a ready-made generic method in service innovation processes.

5.6   CONCLUSION

The underlying understanding of organizations frames the current study of value co-creation and service innovation. In Van de Ven and Poole's terms, the research is ontologically based on the understanding of an organization as a process of organizing and is epistemologically focused on narrating processes (Van de Ven and Poole, 2005). Applying an understanding of service and organizations as a process along the overall focus on value creation (which is inherently a process) makes room for interpretative methods (Helkkula et al., 2012). Narrative methodology is, among other methods rooted in interpretative science, one such suggestion. Hence, the aim of the chapter was to present the framework of narrative methodology and to apply this in a discussion specifically on the early stages of service innovation processes. Taking a case from the non-profit housing sector in Denmark, how narratives elucidate the social and temporal aspects of the relational character of service and service innovation was illustrated. The temporal aspect of narratives and the constituting factor of storytelling are especially pivotal in the argument for using narratives in this context. The time perspective has to do with how we retrospectively perceive the past and how this frames our understanding of the future. Linked to the literature on narratives and innovation, this implies that development cannot take place without integrating past perceptions and the accumulated knowledge inherent in the organization (Müller, 2013). Therefore, as the case makes clear, it is argued that value propositions need to be anchored in deep insight into customers and their sphere of value creation – hence removing the fuzziness of the so-called fuzzy front-end of innovation (Alam, 2006).

LEARNING POINTS

- An innovation workshop takes place *somewhere* with *somebody*. Hence before digging into theoretical considerations, it is important to reflect on which venue to choose, who is going to attend the workshop and how the workshop is presented to the participants. Setting the scene during the recruiting process helps to give a common ground where all participants enter the room of innovation on as equal a plane as possible.
- The development of scenarios, or short stories, is a way to talk about the future from a neutral third place. To co-create a story is to engage in a collaborative process of invention where the ideas of one participant trigger new ideas from the rest.
- To raise the level of thinking outside the box, it might be fruitful to support the story creation phase with different triggers, for example, introducing future scenarios based on general future trends or, in this case, telling an invented story of housing 20 years into the future.

DISCUSSION TOPICS

- The link between micro and macro studies within service innovation research might benefit from a narrative perspective, focusing on the meta-stories of society and how these frame the way innovation is unfolded on a micro level.
- It seems fruitful to further explore how narrative methodology can reveal perceptions of service encounters and how this contextual knowledge can be integrated into innovation specifically targeting service encounters.
- Since the connection between narratives and service innovation are still quite new, this chapter hopefully opens forthcoming discussion on narratives as a method for embracing the context of value co-creation as a foundation for new or refined value propositions.

REFERENCES

Alam, I. (2006), "Removing the fuzziness from the fuzzy front-end of service innovations through customer interactions", *Industrial Marketing Management*, 35 (4), 468–480.

Alvarez, R. and J. Urla (2002), "Tell me a good story: Using narrative analysis to examine information requirements interviews during an ERP implementation", *Database for Advances in Information Systems*, 33 (1), 38–53.

Alvesson, M. (2011), *Interpreting Interviews*. London: Sage.

Barry, D. and M. Elmes (1997), "Strategy retold: Toward a narrative view of strategic discourse", *The Academy of Management Review*, 22 (2), 429–452.

Bartel, C.A. and R. Garud (2009), "The role of narratives in sustaining organizational innovation", *Organization Science*, 20 (1), 107–117.

Becker, L. and A.P. Müller (2013), "Narrative and innovation", in L. Becker and A.P. Müller (eds.), *Narrative and Innovation*, Germany: Karlshochschule International University and Springer VS, pp. 11–31.

Bødker, S. and E. Christiansen (1994), "Scenarios as springboards in design of CSCW", *DAIMI Report Series*, PB-488, ISSN 2245-9316.

Boje, D.M. (1995), "Stories of the storytelling organization: A postmodern analysis of Disney as 'Tamara-land'", *The Academy of Management Journal*, 38 (4), 997–1003.

Fuglsang, L. and J.D. Scheuer (2012), "Public–private innovation networks: The importance of boundary objects, brokers and platforms to service innovation", in Macaulay, L., Miles, I., Wilby, J., Tan, Y.L., Zhao, B., and Theodoulidis, B. (eds.), *Case Studies in Service Innovation*. New York, Heidelberg, Dordrecht and London: Springer, pp. 209–231.

Grönroos, C. (2008), "Service logic revisited: Who creates value? And who co-creates?", *European Business Review*, 20 (4), 298–314.

Grönroos C. and P. Voima (2013), "Critical service logic: Making sense of value creation and co-creation", *Journal of the Academy Marketing Science*, 41, 133–150.

Gummerus, J. (2013), "Value creation processes and value outcomes in marketing theory: Strangers or siblings?", *Marketing Theory*, 13 (1), 19–46.

Halliday, S.V. (2008), "The power of myth in impeding service innovation: A perspective gained from analysis of service providers' narratives", *Journal of Management Inquiry*, 17 (1), 44–55.

Hasu, M., M. Toivonen, T. Tuominen, and E. Saari (2014), "Employees and users as resource integrators in service innovation: A learning framework", in R. Agarwal, W. Selen, G. Roos, and R. Green (eds.), *The Handbook of Service Innovation*. London: Springer-Verlag.

Heinonen, K., T. Strandvik, and P. Voima (2013), "Customer dominant value formation in service", *European Business Review*, 25 (2), 104–123.

Helkkula, A. and M. Pihlström (2010), "Narratives and metaphors in service development", *Qualitative Market Research*, 13 (4), 354–371.

Helkkula, A., C. Kelleher, and M. Pihlström (2012), "Characterizing value as experience: Implications for service researchers and managers", *Journal of Service Research*, 15 (1), 59–75.

Hernes, T. (2014), *A Process Theory of Organization*. Oxford: Oxford University Press.

Holstein, J.A. and J.F. Gubrium (2002), *The Self We Live By. Narrative Identity in a Postmodern World*. Oxford: Oxford University Press.

Jackson, M. (2013 [2002]), *The Politics of Storytelling: Variations on a Theme by Hannah Arendt*. Copenhagen: Museum Tusculanum Press, University of Copenhagen.

Kristensen, H. (2006), "Fremtiden for de almene boliger", in *Den gode bolig – Hvordan skal vi bo i fremtiden?* Akademiet for de Tekniske Videnskaber, ATV.

Labov, W. (1997), "Some further steps in narrative analysis", *Journal of Narrative and Life History*, 7 (1–4), 395–415.

Lusch, R.F. and S. Nambisan (2012), "Service Innovation: A Service-Dominant Logic Perspective", *MIS Quarterly*, 39 (1), Special Issue, 155–175.

Lusch, R. and S. Vargo (2014), *Service–Dominant Logic. Premises, Perspectives, Possibilities*. New York: Cambridge University Press.

Makkonen, H., L. Aarikka-Stenroos, and R. Olkkonen (2012), "Narrative approach in businesss network process research: Implications for theory and methodology", *Industrial Marketing Management*, 41, 287–299.

Mattelmäki, T. and F.S. Visser (2011), "Lost in co-x: Interpretations of co-design and co-creation", Diversity and unity: Proceedings of IASDR2011, the 4th World Conference on Design Research, 31 October–4 November.

Miles, I. (2012), "Introduction to service innovation", in L. Macaulay, I. Miles, J. Wilby, Y.L. Tan, B. Zhao, and B. Theodoulidis (eds.), *Case Studies in Service Innovation*. New York, Heidelberg, Dordrecht and London: Springer, pp. 1–19.

Mitchell, R. (2013), "Tangible business model sketches to facilitate intersubjectivity and creativity in innovation encounters", in L. Becker and A.P. Müller (eds.), *Narrative and Innovation*. Karlshochschule, International University. Germany: Springer, pp. 131–139.

Müller, M. (2013), "How innovations become successful through stories", in L. Becker and A.P. Müller (eds.), *Narrative and Innovation*, Germany: Karlshochschule International University and Springer VS, pp. 139–151.

Pedersen, A.R. (2009), "Moving away from chronological time: Introducing the shadows of time and chronotypes as new understandings of 'narrative time'", *Organization*, 16 (3), 389–406.

Pedersen, A.R. (2013), "Collaborative narrative innovation: A case of public innovation in Denmark", in L. Becker and A.P. Müller (eds.), *Narrative and Innovation*. Germany: Karlshochschule International University and Springer VS, pp. 57–69.

Pedersen, A.R. and M.B. Johansen (2012), "Strategic and everyday innovative narratives: Translating ideas into everyday life in organizations", *The Innovation Journal: The Public Sector Innovation Journal*, 17 (1), 1–18.

Polletta, F., P. Ching, B. Chen, B. Gardner, and M. Alice (2011), "The sociology of storytelling", *Annual Review of Sociology*, 37, 109–130.

Ricœur, P. (1988), *Time and Narrative*. Chicago and London: University of Chicago Press.

Riessman, C.K. (2008), *Narrative Methods for the Human Sciences*. New York: Sage Publications.

Rosile, G.A., D.M. Boje, D.M. Carlon, A. Downs, and R. Saylors (2013), "Storytelling diamond: An antenarrative integration of the six facets of storytelling in organization research design", *Organizational Research Methods*, 16 (4), 557–580.

Star, S.L. (2010), "This is not a boundary object: Reflections on the origin of a concept", *Science, Technology & Human Values*, 35 (5), 601–617.

Sundbo, J. (2014), *The Evolution of Service Innovation Research*. (PowerPoint slides). Presented 6 October, at a PhD course lecture at Lillehammer University College.

Sundbo, J. and M. Toivonen (2011), "Introduction", in J. Sundbo and M. Toivonen (eds.), *User-based Innovation in Services*. Cheltenham, UK and Northampton, MA, USA: Edward Elgar Publishing, 1–25.

Tronvoll, B., S. Brown, D. Gremler, and B. Edvardsson (2011), "Paradigms in service research", *Journal of Service Management*, 22 (5), 560–585.

Uprichard, E. (2011), "Narratives of the future: Complexity, time and temporality", in Williams, M. and Vogt, P.W. (eds.), *The SAGE Handbook of Innovation in Social Research Methods*. London: Sage, pp. 103–120.

Van de Ven, A.H.V. and M.S. Poole (2005), "Alternative approaches for studying organizational change", *Organization Studies*, 26 (9), 1377–1404.

Vargo, S. (2008), "Customer integration and value creation: Paradigmatic traps and perspectives", *Journal of Service Research*, 11 (2), 211–215.

Voima, P., K. Heinonen, and T. Strandvik (2010), "Exploring customer value formation: A customer dominant logic perspective", *Hanken School of Economics Working Papers*, 522.

6. Mapping innovation processes: visual techniques for opening and presenting the black box of service innovation processes

Anne Rørbæk Olesen

6.1 INTRODUCTION

Innovation processes are inherently messy, complex and confusing (Langley, 1999). Researchers immersing themselves in data from innovation processes risk being overwhelmed by endless chaos, in the worst cases suffering from 'drowning in a shapeless mass of information' (Langley, 1999, p. 693) or 'death by data asphyxiation' (Pettigrew, 1990). To avoid such tragedies, there is a need for analytical tools that can help open up, explore and present innovation processes without reducing their complexity too much.

The aim of this chapter is to present different visual mapping techniques useful for performing qualitative analysis of innovation process data in line with this need. The use of visual mapping techniques has previously been recognized as a valid approach to analyzing process data, and such techniques have been heralded for their ability to assist the researcher in both analytical development and presentation of findings (see Langley, 1999). The chapter further argues that certain visual mapping techniques are particularly relevant for contemporary service innovation research given their ability to explore and present complexities visually. Indeed, service innovation processes are exceedingly complex because they often lack systematization, teeter on the brink between production and consumption, and involve a multitude of different actors – public and private stakeholders, researchers, clients, users – participating in different ways and at different times.

The chapter is structured into three parts: First, general insight on using maps for qualitative research is presented with reference to sociologists Matthew Miles and Michael Huberman (Miles and Huberman, 1994), who have been highly influential in terms of developing mapping formats and have argued strongly for the usefulness of maps in qualitative research. Second, the chapter zooms in on the use of maps for framing and presenting innovation processes, drawing particularly on organizational researcher Ann Langley (Langley, 1999). Third, mapping techniques of the approach 'situational analysis' constructed by sociologist Adele Clarke (Clarke, 2003, 2005) are presented, as well as a recent development of these techniques under the rubric 'temporal situational analysis' (Olesen, 2015). This third part of the chapter is the most extensive because these mapping formats are particularly useful for researching service innovation processes, even though their usefulness is yet to be fully explored.

To illustrate the presented visual mapping techniques, concrete maps from an example research project will be displayed. The purpose of the research project was to explore how digital museum communication emerged in collaborative design interaction between staff at museums and digital designers. The project sought to answer three research questions:

- How are digital designers involved in these collaborative design processes?
- How is digital museum communication understood in these collaborative design processes?
- How is digital museum communication negotiated and co-designed across boundaries in these collaborative design processes?

The data consisted of ethnographic material, such as field notes, interviews and design materials, generated by following two cases for approximately one and a half years. One case took place at an art museum, the other at a cultural heritage museum (for anonymization purposes, these cases are called the Art Case and the Cultural Heritage case, respectively). Throughout the chapter, maps used to analyze and present the complex service innovation processes of one of the cases, the Art Case, are displayed. Because of the limited amount of space, these maps will not be explained and analyzed in detail.[1] The purpose of this chapter is merely to illustrate mapping techniques as research tools for exploring and presenting the complex emergence of service innovation.

6.2   VISUAL DISPLAYS IN QUALITATIVE RESEARCH

Philosophically, the present chapter is concerned with the use of visual mapping techniques for qualitative and, more particularly, constructivist research agendas. This is evident in the above-mentioned interest in complexities of service innovation processes and the use of ethnographic methods in the example research project. However, visual mapping techniques can and have been used within a multitude of philosophical approaches to analyze various forms of data material. They have actually been used most extensively for quantitative research – for instance for 'data visualization' (Tufte, 2001) – and are less commonly used in qualitative research (Miles and Huberman, 1994). In qualitative research, textual explanations or narrative accounts usually stand alone, a tendency criticized by Miles and Huberman (1994), who argue for supplementing text with displays:

> Using only extended text, a researcher may find it easy to jump to hasty, partial, unfounded conclusions. Humans are not very powerful as processors of large amounts of information; our cognitive tendency is to reduce complex information into selective and simplified gestalts or easily understood configurations. [. . .] In the course of our work, we have become convinced that better displays are a major avenue to valid qualitative analysis. (Miles and Huberman, 1994, p. 11)

Miles and Huberman (1994) define a display as 'a visual format that presents information systematically' (p. 91). In a display, data can be viewed in one carefully organized location, helping the researcher and the reader to draw conclusions and interpret data within and across cases. Thus, using displays can increase the analytical power of results as well as their readability (Miles and Huberman, 1994).

According to Miles and Huberman (1994, p. 93), generating display formats is 'fairly easy and enjoyable'. Formats can be made in various ways. However, making a good display format requires direction and experimentation, meaning that the format should be driven by the research questions and that the format should be developed iteratively. The shape and character of a display format will also depend on how far along the researcher is in his/her research project and what occupies his/her attention at the time of making the display (Miles and Huberman, 1994, p. 93).

Overall, Miles and Huberman distinguish between two different types of basic display formats: *Matrices*, which consist of rows and columns, and *networks*, which consist of different nodes or points connected by lines. All types of qualitative data can be plotted into such display formats, and displays can be useful in relation to both single and multi-case research projects, according to Miles and Huberman (1994). However, it takes a great deal of analytical work to condense the data in a manner that fits into the format. This is one of the greatest challenges of making displays, and Miles and Huberman (1994, p. 98) stress the need to not 'bully the data' into unworkable, superficial or confusing formats or formats that do not include all the relevant data.

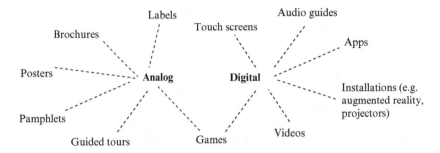

Figure 6.1   Simple network displaying analog and digital exhibition techniques

6.2.1   Example: A Network Display

Figure 6.1 illustrates a network that helps to give an overview of different exhibition techniques mentioned in the data material from the example research project. The data material was coded and displayed in relation to two categories, namely, analog and digital exhibition techniques. The network gives an overview of what is meant by digital museum communication – the central locus of the research questions – and how such communication relates to more classical, analog exhibition techniques.[2]

6.3   PROCESS MAPS

Drawing on Miles and Huberman (1994), Langley (1999) advocates using what she calls a 'visual mapping strategy' to analyze organizational processes, such as, for instance, innovation processes. She argues that such maps are particularly attractive for displaying temporal aspects such as 'precedence, parallel processes, and the passage of time' (Langley, 1999, p. 700). Langley points to the common use of process maps for planning and understanding work processes in practical organizational settings. She suggests that organizational researchers can use similar tools for data analysis, as has been done, for instance, by Meyer (1984, 1991), Meyer and Goes (1988) and Langley and Truax (1994). Also, organizational researchers interested in decision-making processes have had great success using visual process mapping, such as Mintzberg et al. (1976) and Nutt (1984).

   Data for mapping innovation processes can be constructed in two ways: By retrospectively tracing back an innovation process or by following it forward in real-time. If the process is studied retrospectively the researcher can use methods such as interviews and inspection of archival documents to gain insights into the process. If studied in real-time, the researcher can follow the ongoing emergence in details and with his/her own eyes (Bizzi and Langley, 2012), for instance, by using ethnographic methods, as done in the example research project.

In both cases, the innovation process data can be plotted into visual display formats to create 'an intermediary step between the raw data and a more abstract conceptualization' (Langley, 1999, p. 702). Taking this step can help the researcher 'produce useful typologies of process components' (Langley, 1999, p. 703). However, like Miles and Huberman (1994), Langley stresses the risk of producing a mechanical and superficial quality when making process maps and argues for supplementing them with other methods of analysis to take into account the emotions, cognitions, interpretations and 'underlying forces' (Langley, 1999, p. 703) driving processes. She frames this method as primarily suitable for multi-case research (5–10 cases preferably), probably on account of the weaknesses mentioned, in contrast to Miles and Huberman (1994) who describe displays as useful in multi-case and single-case research alike.

6.3.1   Example: A Process Map

A process map functions as a network display in which different nodes or points are connected by lines. However, the guiding framework is time. Thus, the point is to display central aspects in relation to temporal emergence. Figure 6.2 illustrates a simple process map that displays how the Art Case is framed as consisting of three different periods. The participants in the case got funding to develop three mobile apps for three

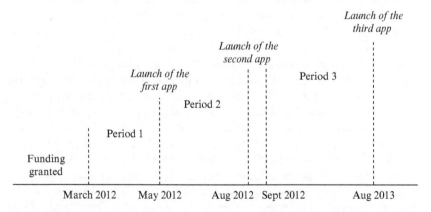

Figure 6.2   Simple process map displaying periods and milestones in the Art Case

different exhibitions and the framing is structured around these three outcomes: The first period corresponds to the development of the first app, the second period corresponds to the development of the second app, and the third period corresponds to the development of the third app. The map provides a simple overview of when the Art Case was initiated, which periods it consisted of and when the three apps were launched. Importantly, the process could also have been framed in other ways and in relation to other foci. Before this final version of the process map of the Art Case, a great amount of coding and experimentation took place, resulting in the selection of this particular framing. Scaling, relating and adjusting the data visually in different versions of the process map resulted in this particular framing of the situation, which would most likely have been different if performed only as written text. Furthermore, it provides a neat overview, helping readers/listeners to understand presentations of the research.[3]

6.4   TEMPORAL SITUATIONAL ANALYSIS

As mentioned in the introduction, more space will be used on the presentation of the third mapping format, since this format is arguably very useful for researching service innovation processes, thanks to its focus on complexities.

The classical version of situational analysis has recently been developed by American sociologist Adele Clarke (Clarke, 2003, 2005). Although it is a fairly new approach, it is used by many scholars across a variety of research fields (Clarke and Charmaz, 2014; Charmaz and Bryant, 2007; Kaldis, 2013; Outhwaite and Turner, 2007). The approach is intended as a supplement to grounded theory (Glaser and Strauss, 1967), providing 'fresh ways' (Clarke, 2005, p. xii) into the data by dealing more fully with complexities inherent in postmodernist thinking. Clarke is particularly interested in the analytical possibilities of maps and focuses less on presentational opportunities. According to Clarke, maps can support the researcher in seeing things differently, in noticing relations and in reworking/remapping conclusions. Furthermore, maps are more helpful in terms of moving around analytically in data than text and in terms of increasing methodological reflexivity (Clarke, 2005, p. 30; Clarke and Keller, 2014).

To enjoy the benefits of map-making, Clarke stresses that it is essential to *continually* make maps of the situation studied throughout the research process. The point is thereby to 'systematically' (Clarke, 2005, p. 85; Clarke and Keller, 2014) avoid bullying, superficial and mechanical display formats, the pitfalls of map-making mentioned in earlier sections.

In addition, situational analysis maps can – to some degree – assist in the exploration and expression of the emotions, cognitions, interpretations and underlying forces driving processes, thereby providing a supplement to process maps.

Situational analysis proposes three different mapping techniques with different analytical foci: First, *situational maps* that focus on all elements in a situation (human, non-human, conceptual, discursive, physical etc.) and their relationships; second, *social worlds/arenas maps* that focus on the worlds and arenas in which different actors participate in a situation; third, *positional maps* that focus on major concerns negotiated in a situation (Clarke, 2005).

However, even though Clarke does not ignore processuality, her mapping techniques do not deal well with such perspectives. Under the rubric 'temporal situational analysis', Olesen (2015) has suggested expansions to Clarke's mapping approaches in a way that better serves analysis and presentation of innovation process data in which time and emergence are considered to be essential interest points (Hernes, 2014; Langley, 1999; Langley and Tsoukas, 2010). In temporal situational analysis, the fundamental idea is to make situational maps, social/worlds arenas maps and positional maps in accordance with different temporal periods of a process. In this way, the focus is on what happens temporally in a situation, and comparing the maps of different periods becomes the analytical anchor point. These temporal maps can be very useful for presenting analytical points and should thus be perceived as presentational tools as much as analytical tools (Olesen, 2015).

Again, the Art Case will serve as an example to illustrate the mapping format. As pointed out in the process map presented in the previous section (Figure 6.2), the Art Case can be framed as consisting of three periods. Maps can thus be constructed in accordance with these periods, as will be visualized in the following sections, which present, first, social worlds/arenas maps and, second, situational maps and positional maps.

6.4.1   Examples: Social Worlds/Arenas Maps

In the research project example, social worlds/arenas maps were used to answer research question 1: How are digital designers involved in these collaborative processes?

Figure 6.3 illustrates an early and quite messy social worlds/arenas map of the Art Case. To make this map, a lot of basic coding took place, as well as a great deal of experimentation with different mapping formats and framings.

The map is a classical, non-temporal social worlds/arenas map that

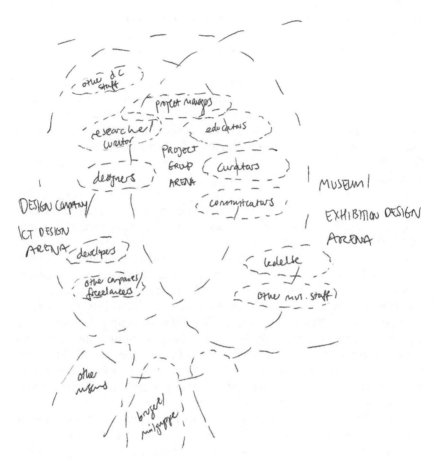

Figure 6.3   Messy social worlds/arenas map of the Art Case[4]

considers the overall situation and includes a multitude of worlds and perspectives to focus on in the reading. It is one out of many attempts to frame
the situation of the Art Case and it visualizes how different social worlds
(e.g. designers, other design company staff, curators and educators) might
be understood as part of different arenas (the design company/ICT arena,
the museum/exhibition design arena and the project group arena). Making
social worlds/arenas maps like Figure 6.3 was a helpful exercise for understanding the complexity of the service innovation process studied. Such
maps were also steps on the way to making maps that were more focused
and that could be useful for answering research question 1. Figure 6.4 illustrates the final social worlds/arenas maps of the research project example.

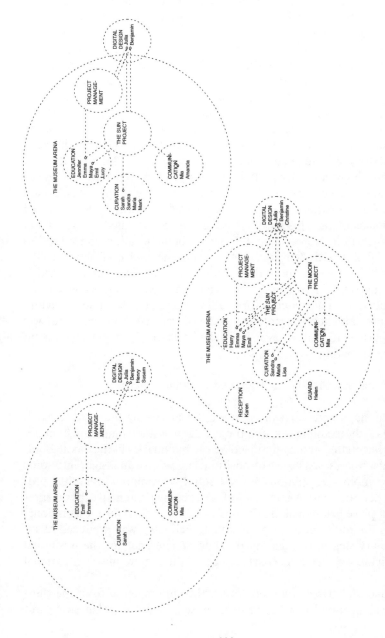

Note: The first period is displayed in the top left, the second period in the top right and the third period in the bottom middle.

Figure 6.4 Final social worlds/arenas maps of the Art Case[5]

103

These maps are temporal maps, displaying framings of the three periods of the Art Case. They are centered on what is termed 'the project group arena' in Figure 6.3, but 'the museum arena' is now framed as the central arena to emphasize that the project was anchored in the museum. In addition, concrete participants are now displayed in the maps. They are grouped in accordance with different social worlds, and their connections with other worlds are highlighted by the straight dotted lines. In this way, the number of participants and how their interrelations vary throughout the process are displayed, providing a visual overview of the answer to the research question concerning how digital designers were involved in the process. Most notably, the digital designers become increasingly connected to the museum arena (signified by the straight dotted lines). However, the number of museum staff and museum worlds participating increase while the designers are fewer in number in the last period than in the first one. Interestingly, a similar pattern was visible in the social worlds/arenas maps made of the other case of the research project example, the Cultural Heritage Case, a pattern that would not have been noticed without social worlds/arenas maps. This pattern turned out to be related to the second research question: How is digital museum communication understood in these collaborative design processes? During the course of action in the two cases, the dominating understanding of technology among participants changed from a techno-centric to a more context-centric conception. This resulted in an increased prioritization of museum-based ideation and discussions about how technology could be developed in a meaningful way for this particular context, explaining the heightened number of museum worlds participating.

6.4.2   Examples: Situational Maps and Positional Maps

Positional maps were particularly useful for answering the third research question of the example research project: How is digital museum communication negotiated and co-designed across boundaries in these collaborative design processes? The use of positional maps gave an insight into some of the positions (i.e. opinions, attitudes and viewpoints) driving the processes of the Art Case. Again, a lot of basic coding and map experimentation took place before making the positional maps used for presentational purposes. In addition, a range of situational maps was produced as an intermediary step in condensing the data of relevance for the positional maps. Figure 6.5 displays a part of one of these quite messy situational maps.

To make this messy situational map, the data material from the third period was analyzed in relation to a chosen focal point that stood out

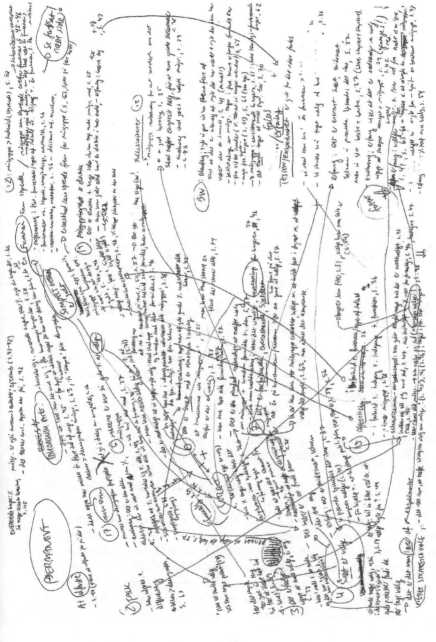

Figure 6.5   Messy situational map of the design negotiations on targeting in the third period of the Art Case[6]

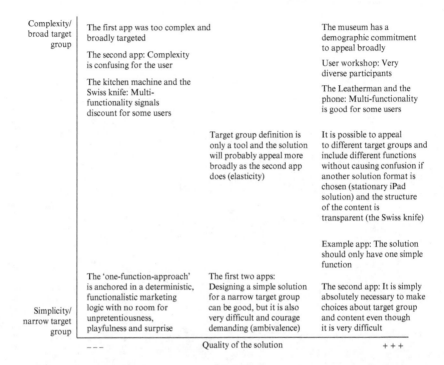

Complexity/ broad target group	The first app was too complex and broadly targeted		The museum has a demographic commitment to appeal broadly
	The second app: Complexity is confusing for the user		User workshop: Very diverse participants
	The kitchen machine and the Swiss knife: Multi- functionality signals discount for some users		The Leatherman and the phone: Multi-functionality is good for some users
		Target group definition is only a tool and the solution will probably appeal more broadly as the second app does (elasticity)	It is possible to appeal to different target groups and include different functions without causing confusion if another solution format is chosen (stationary iPad solution) and the structure of the content is transparent (the Swiss knife)
			Example app: The solution should only have one simple function
Simplicity/ narrow target group	The 'one-function-approach' is anchored in a deterministic, functionalistic marketing logic with no room for unpretentiousness, playfulness and surprise	The first two apps: Designing a simple solution for a narrow target group can be good, but it is also very difficult and courage demanding (ambivalence)	The second app: It is simply absolutely necessary to make choices about target group and content even though it is very difficult
	– – –	Quality of the solution	+ + +

Figure 6.6   *Final positional map of the design negotiations on targeting in the third period of the Art Case*[7]

as central to the case in initial coding, namely, design negotiations on targeting. More specifically, the discussions centered on controversies between positions that favored targeting a design solution broadly and making a complex solution, and positions that favored targeting a solution narrowly and making a simpler solution. The messy situational map was further analyzed to determine connections between data entries, visualized in Figure 6.5 by the lines between different parts of the map.

In Figure 6.6, the situational map of Figure 6.5 has been condensed into the final positional map of the research project example (third period).

On the vertical axis, the positions are placed in accordance with a continuum of the central opposition mentioned above (complexity/broad target group vs. simplicity/narrow target group). On the horizontal axis, the positions are placed in accordance with the quality of the solution. Thus, the positions are related to two dimensions, namely, whether choosing the one or the other design strategy (the vertical axis) will result in a good or a bad solution (the horizontal axis). For instance, the positions in the bottom right corner maintain that the solution will be good if it has only one simple function and choices are made about target group and content.

When the positional map of the third period is compared with positional maps of the two previous periods, in line with the idea of temporal situational analysis, it becomes clear that positions change and new positions arise. This exercise provided insight into some of the positional emergence that has great relevance in terms of the products developed in the Art Case. Moreover, these positional maps can be further interpreted, for instance, in terms of which positions are conceptualized by participants as the most powerful; in terms of their relation to concrete events and artifacts; in terms of what positions are not represented in the data; in terms of which social worlds favor which positions; in terms of how this favoring potentially changes, and so on. Experimenting with positional maps resulted in the conclusion that three features had particular significance for the emergence of digital museum communication in the Art Case: Being reflexive about ambivalence in terms of design choices, involving the positions of potential users in negotiations and developing concrete prototypes and artifacts to explore negotiations materially (Olesen, 2015).

6.5   DISCUSSION AND CONCLUSION

Hopefully, one conclusion is clear at this point: Maps for qualitative research can be constructed in many ways and for many research purposes. This chapter has presented different mapping formats: Matrices, networks, process maps, situational analysis maps and temporal situational analysis maps. For the purpose of researching service innovation processes, the three latter approaches are particularly interesting. Process maps can help to give an overview of different periods and milestones in a process in one carefully organized location. Situational analysis maps and temporal situational analysis maps can help open up complexities of service innovation processes, as well as close them down.

Indeed, the research project example was a very complex and fuzzy project, lacking systematization and involving a multitude of different actors. As documented in the chapter, making maps helped to open up the data not only by providing visual overviews of this complexity and ideas about how to frame the fuzzy situation studied, but also by giving attention to unnoticed relations and patterns in the data, both within and across cases. Furthermore, the maps were useful for closing down the data in the sense that they provided reflexive and systematic ways to condense and present the complexity visually. Thus, temporal situational analysis arguably holds great but as yet largely unexplored potential to support existing conclusions of service innovation research and to reach new ones. At least, this is the case if the research objective is to explore and/or take account of the complexities of service innovation processes. Otherwise, making maps may not be worth the effort. By way of conclusion, it is appropriate to close with a brief discussion of the limitations and pitfalls of using visual mapping techniques for qualitative research and constructivist research agendas, the focus of the present chapter. If a researcher chooses to work with these techniques, he/she should be mindful of at least three things.

First, maps cannot stand alone. They need to be supplemented with careful explanation or narrative accounts. In this chapter, the reader may have experienced confusion when looking at some of the maps presented, because the focus has been on the maps as research tools and not on the analysis related to the maps as such. In actual analytical texts, the maps would have been presented and discussed more carefully. Importantly, a central point is that the visualization in the maps and the actual analysis are closely intertwined. In the research project example, basic coding and analysis was used to build the maps that furthered the analysis by challenging initial insights and framings. In addition, the research questions of the research project example were not fully evolved before the mapping exercises were initiated, even though they may appear as such in the presentation. On the contrary, the mapping exercises greatly helped to construct and sharpen the research questions because the maps provided new insight about the situation researched and the interests of the researcher. Thus, using maps for constructivist analysis is not a stepwise process but an iterative journey of experimentation. This does not mean that maps cannot be useful for other, more stepwise research processes undergirded by other philosophical approaches, but in a constructivist perspective, insights and conclusions are reached by continual experimentation and iteration.

Secondly, as has been mentioned several times, basic coding and experimentation is essential when making maps. In these efforts, the researcher should be very attentive to making multiple pieces of paper with maps instead of erasing or changing existing maps. He/she should also remember to save all maps to reap the benefits of methodological reflexivity on how the data condensation took place and resulted in certain conclusions.

Third, in a constructivist perspective, maps should not be treated as neutral. As Turnbull (2000) has indicated, maps lie. They are metaphors, representing data and conclusions in specific, often highly convincing ways, due to their neatness. Obviously condensing thousands of pages of data into a couple of maps is a troublesome task that erases many details and specificities. One has to be very circumspect about how this is done and if the chosen format makes sense. Again, it is therefore advantageous to save all maps in order to see the intermediary steps. Moreover, the maps constructed should be tested against the entire dataset by reading through the data and checking for problematic deficiencies or interpretations. Having said this, the main strength of map-making is precisely its metaphorical character and ability to represent data and conclusions visually in one place, thus rescuing the researcher from potentially 'drowning in a shapeless mass of information' (Langley, 1999, p. 693) or 'death by data asphyxiation' (Pettigrew, 1990).

LEARNING POINTS

- Maps for qualitative research can be constructed in many ways and for many research purposes.
- Process maps are particularly useful for framing and presenting service innovation process data.
- Situational maps and temporal situational analysis maps can further help to open up and close down the complexities of service innovation process data.

DISCUSSION TOPICS

- Think about a current or earlier research project or study assignment. Which mapping format(s) would be particularly helpful in that situation?
- How would you construct a map?
- How do you think the map would evolve if you made multiple maps?
- What would the benefits be of making multiple maps?
- What would the limitations be of using maps for analytical and/or presentational purposes?

NOTES

1. Please see Olesen (2015) for more details.
2.. For other and more complex examples of matrices and networks, please see Miles and Huberman (1994) and Dahler-Larsen (2008).
3. For other and more complex examples of process maps, please see references in Langley (1999) and Bizzi and Langley (2012). In terms of framing these different periods, temporal bracketing can be a helpful strategy: See Langley (1999, pp. 703–704).
4. The map derives from Olesen (2015). Permission to reprint granted by the author. Parts of the map are in Danish, the native language of the mapmaker, but the entries in the

map are of no importance because the point is merely to give an example of how such a map might look. Details have been edited out for anonymization purposes. For closer inspection, please see Olesen (2015).
5. The maps derive from Olesen (2015). Permission to reprint granted by the author. The intention is not for the reader to assess these maps in detail but to provide a visual overview of the changing maps. 'The sun project' refers to the first period, 'the moon project' to the second period (see Figure 6.2). For closer inspection, please see Olesen (2015).
6. See note 4.
7. The map derives from Olesen (2015). Permission to reprint granted by the author.

REFERENCES

Bizzi, L. and A. Langley (2012), 'Studying Processes in and around Networks', *Industrial Marketing Management*, 41, 224–234.

Charmaz, K. and A. Bryant (eds.) (2007), *Handbook of Grounded Theory*. London: Sage.

Clarke, A. E. (2003), 'Situational Analyses: Grounded Theory Mapping After the Postmodern Turn', *Symbolic Interaction*, 26 (4), 553–576.

Clarke, A. E. (2005), *Situational Analysis: Grounded Theory After the Postmodern Turn*. Thousand Oaks: Sage Publications.

Clarke, A. E. and K. Charmaz (2014), *Grounded Theory and Situational Analysis*. London: Sage.

Clarke, A. E. and R. Keller (2014), 'Engaging Complexities: Working Against Simplification as an Agenda for Qualitative Research Today. Adele Clarke in Conversation With Reiner Keller', *Forum: Qualitative Social Research*, 15 (2).

Dahler-Larsen, P. (2008), *Displaying Qualitative Data*. Odense: University Press of Southern Denmark.

Glaser, B. G. and A. L. Strauss (1967), *The Discovery of Grounded Theory: Strategies for Qualitative Research*. Chicago: Aldine Publishing Company.

Hernes, T. (2014), *A Process Theory of Organization*. Oxford: Oxford University Press.

Kaldis, B. (ed.) (2013), *Encyclopedia of Philosophy and the Social Sciences*. Thousand Oaks: Sage.

Langley, A. (1999), 'Strategies for Theorizing from Process Data', *The Academy of Management Review*, 24 (4), 691–710.

Langley, A. and J. Truax (1994), 'A Process Study of New Technology Adoption in Smaller Manufacturing Firms', *Journal of Management Studies*, 31, 619–652.

Langley, A. and H. Tsoukas (2010), 'Introducing "perspectives on process organization studies"', in T. Hernes and S. Maitlis (eds.), *Process, Sensemaking and Organizing*. Oxford: Oxford University Press, pp. 1–26.

Meyer, A. D. (1984), 'Mingling decision making metaphors', *Academy of Management Review*, 9, 6–17.

Meyer, A. D. (1991), 'Visual data in organizational research', *Organization Science*, 2, 218–236.

Meyer, A. D. and J. B. Goes (1988), 'Organizational assimilation of innovations: A multilevel contextual analysis', *Academy of Management Journal*, 31, 897–923.

Miles, M. B. and M. Huberman (1994), *Qualitative Data Analysis: An Expanded Sourcebook*. Thousand Oaks: Sage.

Mintzberg, H., D. Raisinghani, and A. Théorêt (1976), 'The Structure of

Unstructured Decision Processes', *Administrative Science Quarterly*, 21, 246–275.

Nutt, P. C. (1984), 'Types of organizational decision processes', *Administrative Science Quarterly*, 29, 414–450.

Olesen, A. R. (2015), *Co-designing Digital Museum Communication*, PhD thesis. Roskilde: Roskilde University.

Outhwaite, W. and S. P. Turner (eds.) (2007), *Handbook of Social Science Methodology*. Thousand Oaks: Sage.

Pettigrew, A. M. (1990), 'Longitudinal Field Research on Change: Theory and Practice', *Organization Science*, 1, 267–292.

Tufte, E. R. (2001), *The Visual Display of Quantitative Information* (2nd ed.). Connecticut: Graphics Press.

Turnbull, D. (2000), Masons, Trixters, and Cartographers: Comparative Studies in the Sociology of Scientific and Indigenous Knowledge. Amsterdam: Harwood Academic.

7. Interpretivist analyses of social networks of service innovation

Jørn Kjølseth Møller and Flemming Sørensen

7.1 INTRODUCTION

Service innovation studies applying social network analysis (SNA) are rare. Furthermore, a few influential studies of social networks of businesses have applied qualitative approaches (Uzzi, 1997) but SNA mostly applies positivist and mathematical graph approaches when analysing structures of inter-organizational networks and their outcomes. Such approaches are supported by computers and software that facilitate calculations and illustrations of social network properties. This is also the case for SNA in innovation studies which have related networks' mathematical structural characteristics to companies' innovativeness or to aspects related to innovation processes (e.g. Tsai and Ghoshal, 1998; Ahuja, 2000; Gilsing et al., 2008). So prevalent is the mathematical approach in modern SNA that SNA is typically defined as relying on mathematical and/or computational models (Freeman, 2004). However, SNA originally grew out of ethnographic and anthropological approaches relying on observations and interviews (see Freeman, 2004). This chapter calls for a (re)turn to such in-depth, interpretivist, qualitative and constructivist approaches to SNA in the study of service innovation processes. We argue that interpretivist SNA is an important complementary approach to more positivistic studies and that combining positivist and interpretivist approaches using mixed methods can provide more complete knowledge about social networks and their role in innovation and innovation processes in service companies.

Typically SNA involves mapping and measuring relationships and flows between various entities such as people, groups, organizations or computers (Hanneman and Riddle, 2005). In an organizational context it can visualize relationships within and outside organizations, to identify who knows 'who' and 'what' and to show connections, isolated participants and knowledge bottlenecks. As such, the general focus of SNA is on implications of relationships among entities (Wasserman and Faust, 1994) and SNA assumes that the patterns of social ties have consequences for actors and their potentials (Freeman, 2004). In relation to innovation, SNA includes studies explaining the innovative performance of individual actors (companies) based on the characteristics of their networks (Salman and Saives, 2005) as well as descriptive studies of network structures (Balconi et al., 2004). Other studies have attempted to explain network development (Wagner and Leydesdorff, 2005). Generally research on SNA in relation to innovation has indicated that different measures of, for example, centrality, density and strength of network relations, that is, measures of how organizations are integrated and positioned in networks, relate to innovation and innovation processes in statistically significant ways (Tsai and Ghoshal, 1998; Ahuja, 2000; Lin et al., 2014). Due to their positivist inclination, the studies typically aim at testing hypotheses about how different properties of network structures relate to innovation in generalized terms.

The purpose of this chapter is to discuss when and how more interpretivist approaches can be beneficial for SNA in service innovation research. The chapter starts with a brief introduction on the basic ideas and concepts of SNA. Next it gives an overview of how SNA in general has been used in the field of innovation studies. The benefits of qualitative approaches to SNA in service innovation studies will then be discussed after which an example of a relatively simple qualitative interpretivist network analysis of a service innovation network is introduced. This will be followed by a discussion of the benefits and limitations of interpretivist approaches to SNA for service innovation.

Note that we apply the term interpretivism as an umbrella concept that covers different qualitatively oriented research approaches and philosophies, including constructivism and hermeneutical approaches, research that orients itself towards ontologies that generally perceive reality as multiple and socially constructed and epistemologies that accept (participant) observations, qualitative interviews and other qualitative methods as the foundation for interpretations of studied phenomena.

7.2   SNA AND ITS BASIC CONCEPTS

In SNA, a network is a set of nodes connected by a set of ties. The nodes can include a variety of entities, for example persons/individuals, teams, organizations, patents etc. but they typically include organizations or individuals. SNA can focus on different levels of analysis, especially full networks and ego networks. Full networks include relations between all entities with connections to each other, while ego networks include only the ties of one entity (the 'ego') and the ties among the entities (referred to as 'alters') directly related to this ego. Data related to the ties of a set of nodes is termed relational data (see Scott, 2000). Consequently, several levels or units of analysis can be embedded in the network including the node-level, the group (or local-level) and the network level. Furthermore, networks can be one, two or higher-modes (Wasserman and Faust, 1994). Networks which only comprise one type of node are called homogeneous, otherwise they are heterogeneous. One-mode networks include similar entities only (for instance organizations), whereas two- and higher-mode networks include different sets of entities (for instance firms, individuals, organizational units etc.). By choosing appropriate measures, different types and aspects of networks may be studied (Coulon, 2005). Furthermore, a distinction is made between information about social actors and information concerning the social structures existing between these actors. This reflects two different approaches to SNA: one that focuses on structures to interpret behaviour and one that focuses on structure and actor-diversity to interpret behaviour (Wellman, 1988).

As indicated in the introduction, SNA typically operates with a number of computed variables or measures. The four most important concepts used in SNA are network *density* (the number of ties in a network expressed as a proportion of the maximum possible number of ties), *centrality* (how centrally an actor is situated in a network), *betweenness* (the extent to which a particular node lies 'between' the various other nodes in the network) and *centralization* (the degree to which the network is organized around particular focal nodes). Additionally, a number of measures related to network performance are applied, of which the most common are *robustness* (an estimate of the tendency of individuals in networks to form local groups or clusters), *efficiency* (concerning how many other nodes a node can access through a relatively small number of ties), *effectiveness* (concerning the clusters of nodes that can be reached through non-redundant contacts) and *diversity* (concerning the diversity of nodes that can be reached) (Burt, 1992; Scott, 2000). All such measures are applied to calculate the structural characteristics of particular networks or the position and structural integration of different actors in different networks. They may then be used to test hypotheses about how such network characteristics have implications for different outcomes of networks or the possibilities of actors to achieve various goals in the networks.

7.3 SNA AND INNOVATION STUDIES

According to Van Der Valk and Gijsberg (2010), in the field of innovation studies the contribution of SNA includes three different domains. First, research on *collaboration networks* includes studies explaining the innovative performance of individual actors by relating these to the characteristics of their networks. Second, research on innovation in *communication networks* aims to describe communication flows in networks and their structure. Third, SNA of *technologies and sectors* aims to gain insight about structures of technology networks and their implications for management and policy. In such SNA, nodes are considered technological (sub)fields while linkages between the nodes can be, for example, patents, publications or firms (Van Der Valk and Gijsberg, 2010).

Generally in SNA, networks are argued to sustain innovation of actors, companies or networks themselves for several reasons. First, social networks can overcome certain uncertainties, costs as well as risks that are often related to processes of innovation, for example, because social networks increase the chance of an innovation being successful if it is supported by a number of interconnected actors and, if it is less successful, the loss is shared among a number of actors. Second, social networks connect different actors with different resources and sustain the organization and coordination of development activities. Third, social networks sustain information distribution and development, which are crucial elements of innovation processes. All these functions may be sustained by different social network structures, making them more or less efficient (Kolleck, 2013).

In particular, studies on the role of social networks for innovation have focused on the role of information distribution and knowledge development. Such innovation studies using SNA have focused on, for example, the role of density and strengths of relations in networks for information distribution and knowledge development in innovation processes, for example, in terms of exploration and exploitation (Ahuja, 2000; Lin et al., 2014; Sørensen and Mattson, 2016). Initially Granovetter (1973) introduced the distinction between strong and weak ties, demonstrating that network benefits do not arise mainly from densely and strongly interconnected networks but more so from weak ties between individuals who frequently do not know each other that well and who possess different knowledge and relations to other actors. This argument was further developed by Burt (1992, 2000), who argued that actors spanning structural holes in sparse networks have particular information benefits. Both arguments contradicted Coleman (1988) who argued that information and network benefits arise from cohesive and dense networks that facilitate trust and, thus, individuals' and companies' inclination to collaborate and share information. These contrasting views have been combined and innovation studies have shown that sparse networks facilitate exploration of new opportunities while dense networks and strong relations support exploitation of opportunities (Rowley et al., 2000; Sørensen, 2007).

Furthermore it has been argued that a combination of the two types of networks supports ambidextrous approaches to information access, knowledge development and innovation and thus sustains both incremental and radical innovation (Sørensen and Mattsson, 2016). These discussions indicate how the positions in networks of actors and the structures of networks have implications for the innovation of actors and networks, for example, in terms of network centrality, density, strength, effectiveness and diversity.

In studies of networks related to innovation, a crucial element to take into account is the networks' dynamism. Innovation is a dynamic phenomenon and networks related to innovation processes are also inherently dynamic. Yet often SNA takes a snapshot approach to network analysis. Because of such static approaches, the understanding of networks and their outcomes suffers (Ahuja et al., 2012). Watts (2003) identified two relevant types of dynamics of networks: dynamics *of* the network and dynamics *on* the network. Dynamics *of* the network refer to the evolving or changing structure of the network itself, for example, the making and breaking of ties. Dynamics *on* the network refer to individuals (persons or firms) in the network doing something that affects the network, for example, searching for information, learning, spreading ideas, making decisions etc. In real life networks, both dynamics (*on* and *of* networks) will be taking place simultaneously and be interdependent (Watts, 2003): an actor can do something and thereby affect the structure of the network or, conversely, the changing structures of the network can make an actor do something he/she may otherwise not have done.

A focus on network dynamics provides insights about longitudinal perspectives on networks and innovation. Different typical processes have been argued to characterize such network development. According to Barabási and Albert (1999), large networks can be characterized as scale free, which implies that new linkages are typically formed with nodes that are already highly linked, resulting in a denser and more cohesive network. In this respect, relationships are self-reinforcing and so-called repeated ties are common (Gulati and Gargiulo, 1999). Alternatively over time, networks start to show 'small world' characteristics, which means that they possess a combination of numerous local ties and a few distant ties making knowledge transfer in the network very efficient (Watts and Strogatz, 1998). Often new relations are built with partners that tend to be similar to previous partners, or through imitation, meaning that new partners are chosen based on the choices made by others in the sector. Alternatively new relations may be established through multiconnectivity processes, implying that new partners are chosen so that the diversity of the network increases (Powell et al., 2005). Thus, different dynamics can lead to

different network structures and they may (depending on theoretical arguments) be assumed to lead to inertia or, conversely, to diversity and new
knowledge development. For example, one risk is that network dynamics
over time reduce the openness of the network and, thus, its potential to
absorb 'new variety of content' (Gilsing and Nooteboom, 2006), while
other network mechanisms may increase the variety of information that a
network can distribute and process, which an individual in a network may
receive from others (Powell et al., 2005).

The dynamics of social networks have also been demonstrated to be
important in specific innovation processes during which networks develop
towards stronger and denser relations as the innovation process changes
from idea-generating phases to more development and implementation-
oriented phases (e.g. Sørensen and Fuglsang, 2014; Sørensen and Mattsson,
2016). Additionally, the dynamism of social networks of entrepreneurs has
been shown to develop during entrepreneurial start-up processes from
networks of sparse and weak relations to stronger and denser network
relations or conversely from strong to weaker relations depending on the
type and process of the start-up company (spin-off or not) and its related
innovation (incremental or radical) (Elfring and Hilsink, 2003). However,
it has also been demonstrated how such processes of network dynamics are
more complex and show less obvious traits when innovation processes are
parallel rather than sequential (Sørensen and Mattsson, 2016).

While this chapter focuses mainly on the benefits of SNA in innovation
research, in addition to providing academic knowledge about innovation
processes, SNA can also be used by organizations in practice to induce
changes and promote innovation processes. According to Kolleck (2013),
SNA has the capacity to promote innovation processes through: 1) identification of innovation networks (existing or potential) and investigation
of actors, structures and network boundaries; 2) revelation of where and
how structural conditions enable innovations and development processes;
3) identification and promotion of coordination, information and motivation by, for example, providing insights into knowledge transfer processes,
illustrating where they exist and how efficiently they function; and 4) developing strategies to reduce uncertainties related to innovation processes
(Kolleck, 2013).

7.4 INTERPRETIVIST SNA OF SERVICE INNOVATION

In spite of the mainly quantitative approach to SNA there are, for a
number of reasons, various potential benefits of more qualitative and

idiosyncratically focused SNA studies. For example, they can provide 'insider' views of networks and support complex interpretations of the roles of networks and of actors within them (Jack, 2010). In other words, quantitative approaches typically attempt to draw general models of relations between network characteristics and innovation or innovation-related processes and conditions but suffer in terms of detailed accounts of the more complex network characteristics. Qualitative approaches on the other hand seek to gain deep knowledge about the development and functioning of networks, and of particular relations between actors in networks, and their roles for network development and benefits. Additionally, qualitative methods facilitate inclusion of the context in the analysis of innovation networks and can emphasize the change in relations and their meaning over time. Because networks are discursive formations that are constituted through communicative interactions (Mische, 2003), to understand networks and their more complex dynamics there is a need to understand their cultural and communicative processes. In relation to this and whereas quantitative data is 'uni-dimensional', there is a need for more 'bi-focal' (Coviello, 2005) and exploratory approaches to innovation network analysis.

Such idiosyncratic and often more exploratory SNA approaches are particularly relevant for investigating various aspects of service innovation processes which are varied and increasingly complex, knowledge intensive and open, thus often involving many different actors. Services include both small and large companies, knowledge intensive and manual, as well as many different sectors (e.g. banking, hospitality, retailing etc.). Such different companies and sectors (and their sub-sectors) may for different reasons engage in, and benefit differently from, many different types of networks and network structures. For example, in tourism the innovation networks of attractions are typically different from, say, hotels' innovation networks, in terms of geographical spread of network relations and in terms of types of collaborative partners and the strength of relations with such partners. Additionally, within the same sub-sectors of tourism – for example, hotels – large hotels belonging to international franchises engage in social networks with other structural characteristics, rather than small locally based hotels and attractions (Sørensen, 2007). Furthermore, innovation networks in some tourist destinations appear to be different from those of other tourist destinations because of contextual conditions, and such networks seem to develop over time as destinations develop (Sørensen and Fuglsang, 2014). Thus in services such as tourism, complex spatial, historical, material, production, consumption, organizational and cultural conditions lead to the development of different networks and result in different (rather than generalized) structures of networks and related benefits.

Furthermore, understanding the more complex dynamism and networks of heterogeneous actors seems particularly relevant for service innovation studies as service innovation often relies on collaboration of multiple actors (including private and public actors, individuals, companies and other organizations) in reflexive and dynamic interactive processes. For example, the dynamism of tourism companies' innovation networks has been demonstrated to be related to the companies' innovation strategies and to be important for their long-term survival (Sørensen and Fuglsang, 2014). Additionally social networks related to specific service innovations have been illustrated as dynamic and this dynamism depends on the nature of the service innovation process (Sørensen and Mattsson, 2016).

Interpretive SNA of specific service innovation processes may be relevant for other reasons as well and they may show how other aspects of innovation are important when compared to other sectors. As discussed in the introduction of this book, innovation in services often occurs on an ad-hoc basis, as bricolage and/or as un-systematized processes and, at times, may be recognized only in hindsight (Toivonen and Tuominen, 2009; Fuglsang and Sørensen, 2011). In such cases, the networks associated with innovation are not necessarily systematically organized by the service companies and it may thus not even be realized how networks influence innovation. Even the existence of the networks and their potentials may not be recognized by the service organizations. In such cases a qualitative SNA approach may be the most appropriate way to identify and analyse relevant networks in the past and the present, for example, by using various approaches such as critical incident technique (see Chapter 3 in this book), narrative methods (see Chapter 5) or mapping techniques (see Chapter 6).

Thus, the above suggests how SNA is relevant for understanding innovation and innovation potentials of service companies. Furthermore, it indicates that to understand the more complex dynamics, structural complexities and their conditions interpretivist studies of social networks and their varied roles for different service sectors and actors can benefit knowledge development about service innovation processes. Such studies can provide thick descriptions of networks and deep insights and understandings of the functioning and innovation benefits of networks. However, interpretivist SNA bears no possibility to generalize results in a positivistic sense. Nevertheless idiosyncratic interpretivist approaches can be used in, but are not limited to, exploratory studies. They may, like case studies, be exemplary, unique or typical (Yin, 2003; Flyvbjerg, 2006) and may thus lead to theoretical generalization (Yin, 2003) or transferability of results (Morgan, 2007) as well as illustrating theoretical positions.

In the following section we provide a simple example of an exploratory interpretivist analysis of a service innovation network in which traditional qualitative interviewing was applied. The example illustrates the potential contribution of interpretivist SNA in terms of the development of knowledge about service innovation processes.

7.5   EXAMPLE

The example concerns a public–private network responsible for developing an event, a fruit festival, in a small Danish town. The fruit festival became a success and is now an annual event. Data were collected by interviewing central actors in the network in qualitative semi-structured interviews. The interviews covered aspects such as the background of the innovation project, the type of actors involved in the network and their roles, the development of relations and structures in the network, problems and issues that occurred in the network and the benefits of the network. The aim of the analysis was to gain an understanding of how the network developed during the innovation process and how different aspects of the network, its dynamism and its participating actors, influenced and depended on the innovation process. This included dynamic aspects related to network strength and density, the actors and their activities and roles, and the related barriers and potentials of the network. Thus the aim was to develop a longitudinal account of the dynamics *of* and *on* the network and to gain an in-depth understanding of the relation between network development, collaboration and innovation in the specific context, and concerning the specific type of innovation.

7.5.1   Case Description

The network was initiated by three local fruit-growing and wine-producing entrepreneurs. The most prominent of these entrepreneurs is a well-known chef, food producer and trendsetter, Claus Meyer. The three entrepreneurs initially invited local actors to a public meeting to present their idea and gain support. In the meeting, participants included a number of fruit-growers, representatives of the municipality as well as the municipal tourist organization, the business association of the town and a local priest, plus a few additional actors. At the meeting the tourist organization offered their assistance in applying for funds. This resulted a few months later in the project receiving funding from the Danish Ministry of Food, Agriculture and Fisheries.

After the funding was received and as the idea phase turned into a design and planning phase, the tourist organization complemented the entrepreneurs by providing an event secretary who coordinated the logistics of the event. This was done in close cooperation with the three entrepreneurs. At an early stage of the planning process the municipal Department of Business and Employment also became involved. The department additionally used their internal network of the municipal authorities to develop relations between the tourist organization and other actors from the municipal organization, including the Department of Infrastructure and Environment who, among other things, supported the process by providing needed infrastructural resources and allowances for the use of the public space. The business association of the town also joined the developing network, providing a work force and organizational activities. As they had prior experience with hosting smaller events in the town they possessed local 'event knowledge' and a network that they could mobilize, consisting especially of voluntary organizations that assisted with the practical activities at the event. After the public meeting, a local priest got involved. She became closely involved in the design and planning process and, apart from helping with the logistics at the actual event she was, for example, responsible for making a special 'fruit ceremony' in the church and she mobilized volunteers of the church community who participated in different activities. A number of other actors who would be interested in participating in the event were also contacted. Also, the tourist organization made use of their extensive network within the local community. Furthermore, the three entrepreneurs possessed extensive networks with food producers and used these to invite Danish and foreign producers of cider, vinegar and the like in addition to the local fruit growers.

7.5.2   Main Findings

Several characteristics of the network, which were important for the innovation process became evident in the analysis of the network. These are briefly summarized below.

First, the network was entrepreneur-driven but assisted by the tourist organization, which acted as a process manager and involved a large number of other actors and their networks. Thus, the innovation network and the related innovation process may, on the one hand, be considered a top-down process as it was driven, to a large extent, by the three entrepreneurs. However, because it included a number of other actors who provided inputs and supported a number of activities, the process can also be considered a more participatory process or collaborative network. This participatory character of the network was crucial because it helped anchor the event in the local community and it facilitated the success of the event as, in this way, a number of important actors came to be included in and shaped the event.

Second, the mobilization of this large number of actors was efficiently done as the central actors in the network had their own networks, which complemented each other and could quickly be mobilized for a specific purpose. Thus, the central actors in the network acted as network brokers or network entrepreneurs, eliminating structural holes, that is, making the link between otherwise unconnected actors (cf. Burt, 2000). Most of these relations could originally be considered weak ties and this weakness was exactly their strength because the weak ties linked to actors who were not already connected (cf. Granovetter, 1973) just as weak ties make it possible to have access to a larger number of relations (Uzzi, 1999).

This means, *third*, that in terms of network structures, the network can be described as consisting of an inner core with the three entrepreneurs, an outer core consisting of the actors taking part in the design and planning of the event (including the tourist organization, the municipality, the priest and the business association), and the rest of the network consisting of other actors who were mobilized by the actors in the inner and outer core who participated in the event. Consequently, the network consisted of a relatively large number of relations but these were centred around a few nodal actors, among whom relations were dense and strong (i.e. cohesive). Thus, the distances in the network were short, that is, there were only a few links between the actors in the core and other actors in the network. This was possible because the network developed in a relatively close-knit, local community characterized by small 'distances' – economically, culturally as well as spatially (cf. Lundvall, 1992) – between the actors in the local community. Such closeness is generally argued to facilitate networking in local communities (e.g. Maskell and Malmberg, 1999) as also seen in this case.

Fourth, the common goals of the actors facilitated the quick mobilization of the local network. Thus, one important success factor was that all actors had mutual goals and interests in the project. The common goals, or missions, consisted of making the fruit production more locally known and helping not only to market and sell fruits non-locally but more importantly to brand the geographic area (locally and non-locally) and to show its potential. As these broader and geographical social, cultural and economic aims could go hand-in-hand with fruit marketing and its growers, all actors, private and public, could see the benefits of the event. Therefore, instead of various actors having different short-term economic interests (which could lead to conflict in the network) the common interests in the long-term benefits of the event secured a favourable cooperative milieu being established in the network.

However, *fifth*, the local foundation of the network and of the event was combined with the external networks and the inspiration of the three entrepreneurs behind the event. This combination of local and non-local networks and inspiration sustained the creation of an innovative event based on the combination of something locally unique and on new external inputs. This combination of local and non-local networks has also, in other cases, been observed to facilitate innovation of experiences and the creation of unique new experiences (Sørensen, 2008; Sørensen and Fuglsang, 2014). All in all, the combination of strong and dense relations and of weaker relations, as well as of local and non-local relations facilitated access to varied information and resources, and promoted trust and coherence in the central part of the network among the central actors. This supported the network development and facilitated the innovation.

Sixth, evidently the network was not a static one, but instead one that developed and expanded rapidly, and continually included new actors. Again this was possible due to the localized nature of the network in which relations could quickly be mobilized. Thus, during the innovation process more and more actors were included in the network while also the activities of the network intensified, as did the interactions in the network. More weak ties were continually included in the network while other ties grew stronger as closer cooperation was needed. The expansion of the network occurred as the actors of the core of the network searched their networks to include new actors. As such, the central part of the core of the network was created first (in the idea phase), then the rest of the core (in the design phase) and then the rest of the network (in the planning phase).

Seventh, an important aspect of the network was its combination of private, semi-public, public, voluntary and even religious organizations/ actors. These different actors' knowledge and information as well as their different networks and activities were combined and supported each other (cf. Gulati, 1998). The municipality, for example, could supply resources, channels and relations that were different from those of private actors. The voluntary organizations maintained that the activities were anchored in the local community and the private actors, for example, contributed an entrepreneurial drive and their business networks.

Finally, *eighth*, different interviewed actors in the network told different stories of the network, its development, its other actors and of their activities. These varied perceptions can be seen as a result of the social construction of social networks. Emphasizing such social constructions can provide additional knowledge about networks and their development. This will be further discussed in the following section.

All in all, the analysis demonstrates the dynamism of the network and indicates how the network developed during the innovation process in terms of density and strength, and how this development was related to different actors, their activities and resources, including their existing networks, as well as to the historical and contextual conditions within which the network developed and, not least, to the type of innovation in question. Thus the brief summary of the analysis indicates the complexities associated with network development and the knowledge and understanding about collaborative innovation processes that idiosyncratic and interpretivist SNA can provide.

7.6   DISCUSSION

The example of an interpretivist SNA, presented above, illustrates the wealth of information that even a rather simple qualitative SNA can provide about a service innovation social network. It is evident that, while the strength of relations, network density, positions and centrality of actors are all relevant aspects to take into consideration, to understand a single service innovation process none of the constructs can on their own explain the network and its innovative strength. Instead the network and the innovation were a result of complex patterns of relationships, heterogeneous actors performing a variety of activities, and of contextual factors. Thus, the example illustrates how a qualitative SNA approach can provide understandings about service innovation networks, their dynamism and their innovative outcomes.

First, the approach can provide explorations and illustrations of the dynamism of specific innovation networks and can indicate the complex determinants of such dynamism thus complementing more positivist studies on network dynamism. In the example above, relevant factors included individual actors acting as network entrepreneurs and network brokers, the existence of various networks in the local community that could be mobilized, and so on. Second, in relation to the above, the approach can illustrate the importance of the context. In this specific case this included the role of the close-knit community and the public–private set-up. Combined with the other emphasized aspects, this shows that innovation networks have certain 'local' characteristics and determinants. Thus, while statistical SNA may enable generalizations to populations of networks, 'generalizing' from populations to particular cases is not possible. This is also illustrated in the presented case because it focused on the innovation of an event. The innovation network related to such an experience innovation will be different from the innovation networks related to other types of service innovations, for example, in home banking or transportation. Third, interpretivist approaches can illustrate the complexity of actors, their resources and activities within networks. For example, in the case above, actors consisted of individuals, organizations, public, semi-public, private, voluntary and religious actors who each played different roles in the network and in the service innovation process. Different actors had access to different resources, including knowledge and capabilities, and they performed different activities. The combination of these actors, activities and resources characterized the network and its development as well as sustaining its outcomes.

Fourth, a significant characteristic of the network, or rather characteristic of the interpretations of the network, which requires specific attention concerns, as indicated, that the different actors in the network told rather different stories about their own and other actors' roles in the network. This shows how social networks are social constructions and, therefore, that interpretivist studies of networks can provide important knowledge about such social constructions of social networks. Generally, in the presented case, when comparing across the interviews, the actors seemed to overestimate their own initiatives, work and interest in the network. For example, actors described by other actors as reluctant to participate in the network were not at all so in their own stories of the network. The varying stories and interpretations of the network and its actors, their activities and the resources put into the event, may be driven by 'everybody wanting to be part of a success', that is, the success of the event means that everybody retrospectively wants to share in this success which (perhaps unintentionally) influences the stories told about the network. However, it also indicates that some conflicts existed in the network and that these conflicts can be attributed to culturally dependent entrepreneurial differences between the actors. The positive account of this problem is that the network turned out to be an organizational tool for breaking these cultural barriers. In this way the network not only facilitated innovation, it also included actors who were shown new ways of doing things. However, from a methodological point of view, the different stories told about the network call for taking into account such different stories. One may (from a positivistic perspective) suggest that these, at times highly subjective, accounts of the network which are provided by qualitative data collection techniques are a limitation to this type of SNA because it limits the validity and reliability of the study. However, as indicated, this type of interpretation of networks brings new insights and knowledge about the network including how it is perceived from different positions within the network. The benefits of such subjective accounts may be particularly interesting and relevant when networks involve different types of public and private actors who possess different goals and perspectives. In this way the interpretivist approach acknowledges that there is no objective reality of networks, only subjective accounts, each depending on individual actors' positions in the network, their cultural background, social relations, power relations, earlier experiences with other actors, etc. This is particularly so when not only (apparent) facts about the network (e.g. density, strength, centrality etc.) are sought but when also interpretations of more complex causes and effects in the network need to be taken into account. Thus, insights about the social construction of social networks bring a complementary perspective to that of more positivistic and objective accounts of networks.

In sum, the simple example illustrates how a complex combination of network structures and dynamics, of existing networks, of actors and resources, and of contextual elements and success factors were related to the innovation network and its development. Thus, instead of relating a single or a few measures, such as density or strength of relations, to innovation outcomes, this interpretivist study illustrated the complexity of multiple factors that shape innovation networks and affect their outcomes. Positivist approaches to SNA have primarily attempted to establish cause–effect relations between single network measures and innovation which may, given the illustrated complexity of social networks, lead organizations in individual innovation networks to make false assumptions about the relevance of generalized statements about network structures and innovation.

While there are clear benefits to interpretivist SNA, this of course does not mean that quantitative approaches to SNA are of little value. On the contrary, from a pragmatic philosophical (Morgan, 2007) point of view there will be advantages in combining qualitative interpretivist and quantitative positivist SNA in mixed methods approaches to SNA. This can provide a number of the benefits emphasized by mixed methods literature; for example, taking advantage of the benefits of both quantitative and qualitative data can provide enhanced evidence for conclusions and increase the generalizability of results and produce more complete knowledge (Johnson and Onwuegbuzie, 2004; Teddlie and Tashakkori, 2009). Such approaches may also benefit from CIT-based data sources, such as communication through e-mails or on social media and from the quantitization (Sandelowski et al., 2009) of such data as demonstrated by Sørensen and Mattsson (2016).

7.7 CONCLUSION

This chapter has discussed the potential of interpretivist approaches to SNA for analysing service innovation processes. The complementary benefits of such SNA approaches when compared to the more typical positivist, mathematical and computational approaches have been highlighted. The chapter has discussed and illustrated how interpretivist-oriented SNA can identify, emphasize and explain the development of innovation networks and how this dynamism is related to service innovation. Furthermore, the chapter has discussed how interpretivist SNA can emphasize the differences in service innovation processes and in related network collaboration in different sectors and places. It can illustrate the role of actors, their activities and resources and how these interact in service innovation processes and are related to specific contexts. Thus, cultural historical and other aspects of the context for service innovation can be detected and included in interpretivist SNA and turn out to be of central importance in such analyses. From this perspective it is also acknowledged that accounts of social networks surrounding service innovations are social constructions rather than single truths. This can bring new knowledge about the development of such social networks and about their character and importance for service innovations as seen from different actors' perspectives – knowledge that can be complementary to that typically provided by traditional SNA. It can show how and why different actors perceive these complexities in similar or different ways. Thus, the in-depth analysis of specific networks of particular innovative processes which interpretivist SNA can sustain provides new and varied knowledge about service innovation processes, their development, potential and barriers.

Thus, interpretivist SNA can show and highlight how a complex combination of factors is important for network development and for related service innovation processes. This also includes factors such as network density, centrality, diversity etc. (i.e. the typical measures employed by positivist-inclined SNA), which are all observed to influence network development and innovation processes, however, not individually but in concert. Interpretivist SNA approaches have the potential to include considerations about how such complex combinations of factors influence network dynamics, both *on* and *of* the network. Thus, they can explore the longitudinal development of particular service innovation networks and how this development influences innovation processes and innovation potentials in service companies, places and sectors; and further, they can complement positivist studies on network dynamism, by providing more complex, however less generalizable (in a positivist sense), accounts of such dynamism.

Evidently we do not suggest, either, that interpretivist SNA should stand alone or that they are per se a better choice than positivist-inclined SNA. Instead, the value of combining quantitative and qualitative SNA to better understand how and why innovation processes develop and impact innovation must be emphasized. Quantitative techniques of SNA can identify innovation networks, compute and measure strength, densities, centrality etc. and relate these statistically to innovation capabilities or innovation process-related factors. A combination of qualitative and quantitative SNA techniques in mixed methods research may thus provide a fruitful path for future service innovation research by taking advantage of the benefits of both approaches to produce more complete and robust knowledge.

LEARNING POINTS

- Interpretivist SNA can illustrate and investigate the dynamics *on* and *of* social networks of service innovation and the complexities associated with the development of such networks.
- Interpretivist studies of social networks can account for and illustrate the complexity of multiple factors that shape service innovation networks and affect their outcomes and can explore the complex combinations of network structures, of actors and resources, and of contextual elements and success factors.
- Interpretivist SNA can illustrate how social networks and their outcomes are social constructions and, thus, how and why they are perceived differently from different network actors' perspectives.
- Mixing and combining qualitative interpretivist and quantitative positivist SNA can provide enhanced evidence for conclusions, increase the generalizability of results and produce more complete network knowledge.

DISCUSSION TOPICS

- When may positivist, interpretivist or mixed approaches to SNA be more beneficial?
- Which data collection and analysis techniques may be relevant in interpretivist SNA and for what purposes?
- How can 'measures' such as centrality, density etc. be applied or discussed in qualitative SNA and how may they be relevant?

REFERENCES

Ahuja, G. (2000), 'Collaboration networks, structural holes, and innovation: A longitudinal study', *Administrative Science Quarterly*, **45** (3), 425–455.
Ahuja, G., G. Soda, and A. Zaheer (2012), 'The genesis and dynamics of organizational networks', *Organization Science*, **23** (2), 434–448.
Balconi, M., S. Breschi, and F. Lissoni (2004), 'Networks of inventors and the role of academia: An exploration of Italian patent data', *R&D Management*, **37** (3), 179–196.

Barabási, A.L. and R. Albert (1999), 'Emergence of scaling in random networks', *Science*, **286** (5439), 509–512.

Burt, R.S. (1992), *Structural Holes: The Social Structure of Competition*. Boston, MA: Harvard University Press.

Burt, R. (2000), 'The network structure of social capital', *Research in Organizational Behavior*, **22**, 345–423.

Coleman, J. (1988), 'Social capital in the creation of human capital', *American Journal of Sociology*, **94**, 95–120.

Coulon, F. (2005), 'The use of social network analysis in innovation research: A literature review', Paper presented at 2005 Druid Conference 2005.

Coviello, N.E. (2005), 'Integrating qualitative and quantitative techniques in network analysis', *Qualitative Market Research: An International Journal*, **8** (1), 39–60.

Elfring, E. and W. Hilsink (2003), 'Networks in entrepreneurship: The case of high-technology firms', *Small Business Economics*, **21**, 409–422.

Flyvbjerg, B. (2006), 'Five misunderstandings about case-study research', *Qualitative Inquiry*, **12** (2), 219–245.

Freeman, L. (2004), *The Development of Social Network Analysis. A Study in the Sociology of Science*. Vancouver: Empirical Press.

Fuglsang, L. and F. Sørensen (2011), 'The balance between bricolage and innovation: management dilemmas in sustainable public innovation', *The Service Industries Journal*, **31** (4), 581–595.

Gilsing, V. and B. Nooteboom (2006), 'Exploration and exploitation in innovation systems: The case of pharmaceutical biotechnology', *Research Policy*, **35** (1), 1–23.

Gilsing, V., B. Nooteboom, W. Vanhaverbeke, G. Duysters, and A. Van Den Oord (2008), 'Network embeddedness and the exploration of novel technologies: Technological distance, betweenness centrality and density', *Research Policy*, **37** (10), 1717–1731.

Granovetter, M.S. (1973), 'The strength of weak ties', *American Journal of Sociology*, **78**, 1360–1380.

Gulati, R. (1998), 'Alliances and networks', *Strategic Management Journal*, **19**, 293–317.

Gulati, R. and M. Gargiulo, M. (1999), 'Where do interorganizational networks come from?', *American Journal of Sociology*, **104** (5), 1439–1493.

Hanneman, R.A. and M. Riddle (2005), 'Introduction to social network methods', available at faculty.ucr.edu/~hanneman/nettext/ (accessed 15 March 2015).

Jack, S.L. (2010), 'Approaches to studying networks: Implications and outcomes', *Journal of Business Venturing*, **25**, 120–137.

Johnson, R.B. and A.J. Onwuegbuzie (2004), 'Mixed methods research: A research paradigm whose time has come', *Educational Researcher*, **33** (7), 14–26.

Kolleck, N. (2013), 'Social network analysis in innovation research: Using a mixed methods approach to analyze social innovations', *European Journal of Futures Research*, **1** (1), 1–9.

Lin, Z., H. Yang, and I. Demirkan (2014), 'The performance of ambidexterity consequences in strategic alliance formations: Empirical and computational investigation theorizing', *Empirical Investigation and Computational Theorizing*, **53** (10), 1645–1658.

Lundvall, B.-A. (1992), 'User-producer relationships, national systems of innovation and internationalisation', in B. Lundvall (ed.), *National Systems of*

Innovation: Toward a Theory of Innovation and Interactive Learning. London: Pinter, pp. 45–67.

Maskell, P. and A. Malmberg (1999), 'Localised learning and industrial competitiveness', *Cambridge Journal of Economics*, **23** (2), 167–185.

Mische, A. (2003), 'Cross-talk in movements: Reconceiving the culture–network link', in M. Diani and D. MacAdam (eds.), *Social Movements and Networks: Relational Approaches to Collective Action.* Oxford: Oxford Scholarship Online, pp. 258–280.

Morgan, D.L. (2007), 'Paradigms lost and pragmatism regained: Methodological implications of combining qualitative and quantitative methods', *Journal of Mixed Methods Research*, **1** (1), 48–76.

Powell W.W., K.W. Korput, and J. Owen-Smith (2005), 'Network dynamics and field evolution: The growth of interorganizational collaboration in the life sciences', *American Journal of Sociology*, **110** (4), 1132–1205.

Rowley, T., D. Behrens, and D. Krackhardt (2000), 'Redundant governance structures: An analysis of structural and relational embeddedness in the steel and semiconductor industries', *Strategic Management Journal*, **21** (3), 369–386.

Salman, N. and A.L. Saives (2005), 'Indirect networks: An intangible resource for biotechnology innovation', *R&D Management*, **35** (2), 203–215.

Sandelowski, M., C.I. Voils, and G. Knafl (2009), 'On quantitizing', *Journal of Mixed Methods Research*, **3** (3), 208–222.

Scott, J. (2000), *Social Network Analysis: A Handbook.* London: Sage.

Sørensen, F. (2007), 'The geographies of social networks and innovation in tourism', *Tourism Geographies*, **9** (1), 22–48.

Sørensen, F. (2008), 'The urban innovation network geography of leisure experiences', in J. Sundbo and P. Darmer (eds.), *Creating Experiences in the Experience Economy.* Cheltenham, UK and Northampton, MA, USA: Edward Elgar Publishing, pp. 134–156.

Sørensen, F. and L. Fuglsang (2014), 'Social network dynamics and innovation in small tourism companies', in M. McLeod and R. Vaughan (eds.), *Knowledge Networks and Tourism.* Abingdon: Routledge, pp. 28–45.

Sørensen, F. and J. Mattsson (2016), 'Speeding up innovation: Building network structures for parallel innovation', *International Journal of Innovation Management*, **20** (2).

Teddlie, C. and A. Tashakkori (2009), *Foundations of Mixed Methods Research: Integrating Quantitative and Qualitative Approaches in the Social and Behavioral Sciences.* Thousand Oaks, CA: Sage.

Toivonen, M. and T. Tuominen (2009), 'Emergence of innovations in services', *The Service Industries Journal*, **29** (7), 887–902.

Tsai, W. and S. Ghoshal, S. (1998), 'Social capital and value creation: The role of intrafirm networks', *Academy of Management Journal*, **41** (4), 464–476.

Uzzi, B. (1997), 'Social structure and competition in interfirm networks: The paradox of embeddedness', *Administrative Science Quarterly*, **42** (1), 35–67.

Uzzi, B. (1999), 'Embeddedness in the making of financial capital: How social relations and networks benefit firms seeking financing', *American Sociological Review*, **64**, 481–505.

Van der Valk, T. and G. Gijsberg (2010), 'The use of social network analysis in innovation studies: Mapping actors and technologies', *Innovation: Management, Policy & Practice*, **12**, 5–17.

Wagner, C.S. and L. Leydesdorff (2005), 'Network structure, self-organization, and the growth of international collaboration in science', *Research Policy*, **34** (10), 1608–1618.

Wasserman, S. and K. Faust (1994), *Social Network Analysis: Methods and Application*. New York: Cambridge University Press.

Watts, D.J. (2003), *Small World: The Dynamics of Networks between Order and Randomness*. Princeton, NJ: Princeton University Press.

Watts, D.J. and S.H. Strogatz (1998), 'Collective dynamics of "small-world" networks', *Nature*, **393** (6684), 440–442.

Wellman, B. (1988), 'Structural analysis: From methods and metaphors to theory of substance', in B. Wellman and S.D. Berkowitz (eds.), *Social Structures: A Network Approach*, Cambridge, UK: Cambridge University Press, pp. 19–61.

Yin, R. (2003), *Case Study Research: Design and Methods*. Thousand Oaks, CA: Sage.

8. The role of social media data for research on user-driven innovation

Ada Scupola

8.1 INTRODUCTION

Open innovation, defined as "a paradigm that assumes that firms can and should use external ideas as well as internal ideas, and internal and external paths to market, as the firms look to advance their technology" (Chesbrough, 2003, p. 26) is becoming an important paradigm within innovation research. In addition, the development of information and communication technologies (ICTs) in our society provides both potential and challenges when conducting open innovation at different points of the innovation process. Organizations that have proactively leveraged different forms of ICTs for open innovation include Procter and Gamble with the program Connect and Develop (Sakkab, 2002; Huston and Sakkab, 2006); InnoCentive, an online platform where money is offered in exchange for the solution to problems (Lakhani, 2008); Threadless, an Internet-based t-shirt company, whose designs are created, voted for and finally selected for print by users (Lakhani and Kanji, 2008); and Fiat Mio, an initiative begun by Fiat through which a car has been created following the suggestions of users.

As our society is transformed by new technology and especially ICTs (Scupola, 2002), new forms of qualitative and quantitative data to be collected by the researchers, as well as new ways and means in which qualitative researchers collect and analyze data, emerge (Hanna et al., 2011). This is especially true after the advent of the Internet, social media and big data. In fact, just as social media can be useful to organizations to get information and data from the customers (Larson and Watson, 2011; Malone et al., 2010), so it might also be useful for social science researchers to study online how organizations and their customers behave, and they can also use social media themselves to collect data or analyze social media data. In the field of marketing, for example, Kozinets (2002) developed "netnography" as an online marketing research technique for providing consumer insight. "Netnography" is ethnography adapted to the study of online communities. According to Kozinets (2002) "netnography" as a method is faster, simpler, and less expensive than traditional ethnography, and more naturalistic and unobtrusive than focus groups or interviews. Simultaneously "netnography" provides information on the symbolism, meanings and consumption patterns of online consumer groups. In the field of parallel innovation, Sørensen and Mattsson (2016) used qualitative and quantitative analysis of e-mails to identify new features of the network or other interesting issues related to the development of the network. At the annual symposium on statistical challenges in electronic commerce research (http://scecr.org) the question of how to use Internet data including social media data in both quantitative and qualitative research is often addressed. In addition, it is increasingly common among students to use social media such as Facebook to distribute online surveys and collect data concerning a specific research subject, or conduct analysis of companies' social media pages, for example, in studying open innovation or marketing strategies. Therefore, it is important that social science researchers, and especially service innovation researchers, explore how to use social media and user-generated content in service innovation research.

In this chapter, the use of a specific type of social media, namely blogs, as a means to collect ideas in open innovation processes for service innovation in engaged research, is presented and discussed (Van de Ven, 2007). The results of the study show that, from a practice point of view, blogs can contribute to the generation of service innovation ideas from the users, which are useful to organizations. From a research point of view, the study confirms that social media such as blogs can indeed be useful in service innovation research processes. However, the method also presents a number of limitations.

The chapter is organized as follows: The introduction above provides background and the purpose of the chapter. Section 8.2 provides a short overview of studies investigating ICT and social media in innovation research as well as providing some basic definitions of social media. Section 8.3 describes blogs as a method for engaged research in service innovation, while Section 8.4 presents an application of the method in the case of the Roskilde University Library (RUB). Finally, sections 8.5 and 8.6 present a discussion of the findings and some concluding remarks, respectively.

8.2   INNOVATION RESEARCH, ICT AND SOCIAL MEDIA

A number of studies have investigated the use of ICTs to support user involvement in open innovation processes for product and service innovations. Prandelli et al. (2006) have, for example, identified 28 different web tools that can be used in the different stages of product innovation. These web-based tools range from surveys and 'complaint areas' used in the idea-generation phases to 'virtual product tests' in the product test phases. In their study conducted in several industries Prandelli et al. (2006) detected that the web-based tools are mainly used by larger corporations and in the first and last stages of the innovation process. In addition they also show that the online tools are mainly used as substitutes for offline practices. Many of the tools highlighted by Prandelli et al. (2006) have been investigated in other studies. For example, Franke and Piller (2004) describe the use of simple toolkits to create the user-adjusted design of watches. The design made by users may additionally provide insight into different customers' tastes and trends. Some companies may use such a design for future production lines as in the case of design competition for t-shirts described by Ogawa and Piller (2006) or the design of skis described by Franke et al. (2008). Virtual communities are also another example where customers help organizations to innovate products or service development. Lego Mindstorm and online gaming are well-known examples (Jeppesen and Molin, 2003). These communities may be user or company initiated, as in the case of Lego Mindstorm or Starbucks. In both cases, user involvement is based on users' own interest and prestige in the community. Thus, the interaction among the customers of an organization can be an important source of knowledge regarding customers' challenges, discontent and needs relevant for new service or new product development.

8.2.1 Social Media

The advent of Web 2.0 has enabled social media and the social web to flourish. The concept of social media is top of the agenda for many business executives today (Kietzmann et al., 2011). Decision-makers, as well as consultants, try to identify ways in which firms can make profitable use of social media applications such as Wikipedia, YouTube, Facebook, Second Life, and Twitter (Kaplan and Haenlein, 2010).

According to Kaplan and Haenlein (2010) "social media is a group of internet-based applications that build on the ideological and technological foundations of Web 2.0, and that allow the creation and exchange of User Generated Content" (Kaplan and Haenlein, 2010, p. 61). The ideological concept of social media therefore encompasses the idea of allowing Internet access to users for sharing, collaborating, and updating web content (Parnet et al., 2011). Social media encompasses a wide range of digital channels: forums, blogs, micro-blogs such as Twitter,

Table 8.1   Classification of social media by social presence/media richness and self-presentation/self-disclosure (based on Kaplan and Haenlein, 2010)

		Social media presence/media richness		
		Low	Medium	High
Self-presentation/ self-disclosure	High	Blogs	Social networking sites (e.g. Facebook)	Virtual social worlds (e.g. Second Life)
	Low	Collaborative projects (e.g. Wikipedia)	Content communities (e.g. YouTube)	Virtual game worlds (e.g. World of Warcraft)

social networking sites such as Facebook, creative-work sharing sites such as YouTube, and business networking sites such as LinkedIn (Boyd and Ellison, 2007).

The era of social media, however, probably started around the beginning of the 1990s when Bruce and Susan Abelson founded "Open Diary," a social networking site that brought together online diary writers into one online community. The term "weblog" was first introduced at the same time, and later truncated as "blog" when one blogger changed the name "weblog" into the sentence "we blog." Twenty years earlier, in 1979, Tom Truscott and Jim Ellis from Duke University created the Usenet, a worldwide discussion system that allowed Internet users to post public messages. Today the growing use of the Internet has led to social networking sites such as Facebook and LinkedIn. According to Kaplan and Haenlein (2010) social media can be classified by social presence/media richness and self-presentation/self-disclosure as illustrated in Table 8.1.

8.3   THE USE OF SOCIAL MEDIA IN SERVICE INNOVATION RESEARCH

In service innovation research, researchers have used a variety of methods. Currently, the most popular qualitative methods in service innovation research are: personal interviews (e.g. Scupola and Nicolajsen, 2010; Nicolajsen and Scupola, 2011; Scupola and Zanfei, 2016), focus groups, workshops (e.g. Matthing et al., 2004) and recently experiments (Sørensen et al., 2010).

However, the Internet has created many opportunities for organizations to interact both directly and indirectly with their users (e.g. Prandelli and Swahney, 2008). Some of these Internet-based tools for innovation have been widely reported in the literature such as, for example, user toolkits (von Hippel, 2001; von Hippel and Katz, 2002) and idea competitions (e.g. Piller and Walcher, 2006). However, blogs have received rather limited attention as a technology to collect data and discuss ideas in service innovation so far, both from a practice-based and research point of view, even though a few studies have investigated the blogs' potential for innovation, especially concerning new product development (e.g. Droge et al., 2010).

Historically, blogs are special types of websites that display date-stamped entries in reverse chronological order (OECD, 2007 in Kaplan and Haenlein, 2010). They are the social media equivalent of personal web pages. Blogs are usually managed by one person or organization, but provide the possibility of interaction with others through the addition of comments. However, changes in the technology, growing experiences, combination with other tools such as video, easy access to free platforms as well as an increasing acceptance and use of user-created content has opened up opportunities for new use forms including professional, medical, political and industrial (see Droge et al., 2010).

Even though, due to their historical roots, text-based blogs are still the most common, blogs have also begun to take different media formats, especially the possibility to create comments, which has created a shift towards more interaction and discussion (Aharony, 2009). One of the new use forms is described as a specific theme with interactive comments or video clips (Aharony, 2009). For example, San Francisco-based Justin. tv allows users to create personalized television channels via which they can broadcast images from their webcam in real time to other users. Many other companies are also using blogs to inform employees, customers and shareholders on developments they consider to be important. For example, Jonathan Schwartz, CEO of Sun Microsystems, maintains a personal blog to improve the transparency of his company (Kaplan and Haenlein, 2010).

Despite the content and style of the blog (Aharony, 2009), other functionalities are also of importance. Blogs provide the means for "public" knowledge transparency (Kuhn, 2007), in a way that users' input may inspire later users, and documentation. The written input and the archiving function of the blog provide an easier way to consult and hold onto contributions without additional work compared to, for example, innovation ideas provided orally or sent by e-mail. Despite the fact that blogs provide interaction among users, and between users and organizations' members, it may be argued that this sort of interaction is limited compared to a real-life situation. The feedback mechanisms (comments) are there, but may be characterized as limited, as they are asynchronous and the number of participants might be many and somewhat unlimited. The communication may become impersonal, if the contributors are anonymous or if limited knowledge of the communicators exist. On the other hand, the blog and its written form accommodate for well-formulated thoughts and input, as nothing is published until the communicator decides to do so. Kuhn (2007), moreover, argues for blogs as promoting equality. Wishes for anonymity may be easily provided using blogs. This might result in more inputs, especially if the content concerns taboo subjects. On the other hand, anonymity, or lack of knowledge about the senders, might provide challenges such as difficulties in understanding the input, or it might result in irrelevant or harsh input.

Given the characteristics of blogs described above, we can see that blogs might have benefits in service innovation both from a practice- and research-based point of view. From a research point of view, by using blogs for idea generation and collection, we may learn, for example, about the value of users' inputs in the service innovation process, the value of interaction among users, and between users and organizations, in creating ideas (especially at fuzzy front end or later in the innovation process). In addition we may also learn about the value of different types of social media in idea generation. From a practice point of view the use of blogs in open service innovation can be characterized as a data collection method that can provide useful information around a topic, and is somewhere in-between idea competitions and online focus groups with an unlimited amount of potential participants. Blogs, as discussed above, may have different potentials but also present several challenges for providing inputs for service innovation, because of the type of communication that they promote. Blogs may favor heterogeneity as they can attract different users but the possibility of drawing on many users may, on the other hand, limit the trust and the engagement in the conversation.

However, using blogs also presents some risks. The first risk is that customers who—for one reason or another—turn out to be dissatisfied with or disappointed by the company's offerings may decide to engage in virtual complaints on the blogs (Ward and Ostrom, 2006), which may result in the availability of potentially damaging information in online space. Second, firm employees who actively contribute to the blogs may write information on the blog that the company, for one reason or another, might not want to be published there (Kaplan and Haenlein, 2010). Despite this, we can hypothesize that blogs may be a useful method for collecting data concerning user involvement in service innovations research that can benefit both the customer and the company. On the other hand this type of communication may pose limits to the types and the potential relevance of the inputs provided by blogs. This is especially relevant for service innovation research, as many services today are Internet-based (e.g. library services) so the Internet is the natural meeting place for users of the services, making social media the natural place for user-based and open innovation in services. In fact, social media data, such as that collected by using blogs, may be useful in engaged research processes as they may serve the dual purpose of generating ideas useful for the innovation process of the organization, while providing the researcher with data of relevance to the research. In addition, because there are benefits for practitioners and researchers, the blog data/methods have good potential for doing research that creates direct value for both researchers and practitioners. Given the way the use of blogs has been orchestrated in this study, it is argued that such a method relies on the critical realist philosophy of science. Critical realism in fact assumes that there is a real world out there, but that our understanding of such a world is limited. According to Van de Ven (2007), in critical realism all facts, observations and data are theory-laden; social science has no absolute, universal, error-free truths or laws; no form of inquiry can be value free and impartial; knowing and studying a complex reality demands use of multiple perspectives; robust knowledge is in common across multiple models; and finally, models that better fit the problems they are intended to solve are selected, producing an evolutionary growth of knowledge.

8.4   THE APPLICATION OF BLOGS IN THE IDEA-GENERATION PHASE OF THE SERVICE INNOVATION PROCESS AT ROSKILDE UNIVERSITY LIBRARY

In order to illustrate why and how blogs can be used to involve users in the idea-generation phase of the service innovation process, here the application of blogs in the context of a research study conducted at Roskilde University Library is presented. The setting of this study should be seen in the context of engaged scholarship, an important academic discourse initiated in the last decade, stressing the importance of conducting research that is of relevance to practice and that is conducted together with practice (Van de Ven, 2007). Van de Ven (2007) states in fact that often practitioners find little value in academic and especially social science research and that often practitioner and academic knowledge are unrelated. Therefore he identifies a dual challenge: academics need to put theories into practice and managers need to put practice into theory. This may be accomplished according to Van de Ven (2007) by studying complex problems *with* and/or *for* practitioners and other stakeholders, thus practicing what he defines as engaged scholarship. According to Van de Ven (2007) this form of scholarship should increase the likelihood of advancing knowledge for science and professions.

This research, by reflecting and following the guidelines for engaged research (Van de Ven, 2007), consisted of the following phases:

- Phase 1. Uncovering current service innovation practices at Roskilde University Library with a particular focus on user involvement and methods for involvement and establishing agreements with RUB about the research problem to be investigated and frames for collaboration.
- Phase 2. Using social media for involving users in the service innovation process. In this phase the researchers together with the library established a blog on the website of the library to collect ideas for new services and e-services development.

8.4.1 The Case—Roskilde University Library

There are two types of libraries in Denmark: public libraries and research libraries. Danish research libraries are government institutions and serve mainly higher education and research, but most of them are also open to the public at large. The purpose of public libraries is to promote information, education and cultural activity by placing books and other media at the disposal of the public at large. In Denmark there are 20 major research libraries connected to universities and other institutions of higher-level education. There are also a large number of smaller research libraries that are connected to educational institutions.

RUB is a research library serving the students and staff at Roskilde University. Roskilde University is an academic institution accounting for about 9,000 students, 650 teaching staff and about 430 workers with technical and administrative tasks. It is located in Roskilde, a city about 35 km from Copenhagen, the capital City of Denmark. The library was founded in 1971, as part of Roskilde University. As a research library, RUB is responsible for providing Roskilde University staff and students access to information and materials needed for research, teaching and learning. Since RUB is also a public library, regional research and educational institutions, businesses and citizens also have access to the library (www.ruc.dk). In 2001, the library moved into a new building, designed by Henning Larsen's Architects. Today the library counts 36 employees. The library consists of an 8,000 square meter building, of which 4,500 square meters are for public use, 930 for offices and 875 for closed stacks. In 2013, it had a collection of about 944,000 books and 218,000 AV media, while

RUB counted about 4 million downloads in 2013 (see http://rub.ruc.dk/en/about-library/noegletal/ for a detailed overview of the key figures of RUB over the last ten years). Over the last decade, RUB has conducted a library virtualization process, due to ICT evolution in this sector (e.g. Scupola, 1999) and initiated by the government in the mid-1990s, that has substantially changed the organization, the services and the service delivery process of many of RUB's services by substantially increasing e-services and self-service (Scupola, 2008; Scupola et al., 2009; Scupola and Nicolajsen, 2009).

In this chapter the "virtual library" is conceptualized as a library that facilitates users to search for needed information from sources worldwide, to browse and retrieve selected information and request help at any point in the process, instantly from users' own network-connected computers, anytime, anywhere (Maness, 2006). Examples of new services and service delivery processes are access to e-journals and e-books, a digital repository of all the student projects, and the ability to chat with a librarian. From an organizational point of view, the library has been reorganized several times over the last decade. In 2014, RUB organization consisted of top management (a director and a head of reader services) and four lines (departments), each of which have a number of staff and a head of department also called a line manager. Some employees might belong to different lines, thus creating a matrix organization.

As a consequence of the virtualization process of the research libraries initiated by the government at the beginning of the 1990s, Roskilde University Library (and the other Danish libraries as well) has been forced to innovate its service and e-services to its users (www.deff.dk). (Please refer to Scupola and Zanfei (2016) for a detailed overview of this process.) It was in this context that the collaboration between the researchers and the library took place in the form of engaged research (Van de Ven, 2007), in order to understand the extent to which the library involved the users in the innovation processes and also to intervene to help the library in the process of involving users in the innovation processes.

8.4.2   The Blog as a Platform for Idea Collection

In using blogs as a platform for both idea generation for practice and as a research method, we identify three main important phases of the process: the preparatory phase; the blog establishment and idea collection phase; and finally the follow up and evaluation phase.

The preparatory phase

In this phase, the researchers investigated and uncovered the service innovation practices at RUB with particular focus on user involvement and methods for involvement in order to understand what the library was doing in relation to innovation activities and how RUB was approaching them. This was done by conducting several explorative and semi-structured interviews with library employees, and management and document analysis. The results of this preparatory phase have been documented in several publications (see e.g. Scupola and Nicolajsen, 2009, 2010). In addition in this phase, RUB and the researchers established common objectives and expectations from participating in the project, and a plan for how to involve users in the innovation process by using ICT was discussed. After several meetings and discussions among the library's top management, the researchers, and the IT manager at RUB about several possibilities of involving users in service innovation at the library by using ICTs, the decision was made to use a blog. This was mainly due to the fact that RUB already had experience with blog technology, since they had already established one for internal organizational purposes and communication. RUB believed that this was relatively easy for them to establish and that it also fitted well with the library virtualization process and the use of social media by libraries that Danish libraries had undertaken since the policy program "An Information Society for All" was established at the end of the 1990s (see Scupola and Zanfei (2016) for more details about this virtualization process).

The blog establishment and idea collection phase

After having agreed with RUB's top management that the social media to be used to collect innovation ideas from the users had to be a blog, a small team was established to design and implement the blog. The team comprised four employees from different library departments, as well as two researchers. The team met on an ongoing basis for a period of six months. In this period the blog was designed and set up and a small test was conducted by inviting a small group of computer mediated communication experts to look at the blog and provide feedback before the launch of the blog to the public. This group of experts provided some suggestions that were incorporated into the final version. In addition, lengthy discussions were had on how to best meet and engage the users in order to make them contribute with innovative ideas.

Different blog names and layouts were discussed, inspired by similar blogs regarding content, tone etc. After several meetings and workshops, a decision was made to formulate four topics within which innovative ideas were solicited. Such topics were formulated by the library personnel based on their innovation needs.

The topics were formulated in order to get feedback on the face-to-face and web-based services provided by the library as well as to get feedback on the library physical settings. The topics were formulated as questions on the blog: 1) "Do we comply with your wishes?" 2) "If you should furnish the library. . .?" 3) "Is RUB your favorite library?" and 4) "The future of the library—give us your suggestions". It can be argued that the questions overlap, however, but the different formulations sought to motivate different answers. In addition to the questions, a small piece of text giving examples of the kind of input looked for was put on the first page of the blog to provide guidance.

The blog was advertised in several ways, both online and at the university campus. For example, a direct link to the blog was put at the Front Page of the RUB homepage; posters describing the blog were hung inside campus buildings and bookmarks with the blog address were handed out to the library users when they borrowed library books.

To motivate library users to participate in the idea collection process, two gift vouchers were promised at the end of the period to two randomly drawn blog contributors. This was advertised on the main page of the blog. The idea collection period lasted for a period of three months. To increase credibility of the initiative, the blog introduction also stated that the library would follow up on the ideas provided on the blog and report back to the users. During these three months, one library middle manager was designated as the blog administrator and had the responsibility to comment and respond to the users' postings, since the idea was that the blog should function as a web-based interactive platform between the users and RUB's employees.

The follow up and evaluation phase
The researchers followed up with RUB management on the content of the blog, the process, the value of the suggested ideas and the extent to which the ideas were implemented by RUB. At the end of the three-month period, there were about 25 ideas posted on the blog. These ideas were analyzed and discussed by library management in relation to their relevance and implementation potential at a management meeting. Most of them were suggestions for incremental innovations. All ideas were implemented by RUB in the following period. RUB management was very satisfied with the results obtained from the blog and they kept it on their web page for a long period until they switched to Facebook.

8.4.3   Findings

Most of the ideas generated by the blogs were incremental in nature. One idea was more radical (moving the library outside when the weather was nice in the summer). As promised in the blog's first page, RUB took the ideas very seriously and implemented them all within one year. In addition, the blog contributed at that point in time to give RUB the image of an innovative library. From a research point of view, the blog showed that users can be engaged in the open innovation processes through social media, but only to a limited extent. In fact, the study shows that it is difficult to generate a huge amount of ideas from the users as well as a huge amount of communication between the organization and the users on the blog. These findings support findings from similar studies (e.g. Jarvenpaa and Tuunainen, 2013).

8.5   DISCUSSION

Based on the experience with using blogs for open innovation in service innovation processes at RUB, a number of lessons have emerged. First of all, the case shows that blogs can be used for open innovation in services. This is important both from a research and a practice point of view. However, there are also some problems and issues with the application of the method in an engaged research context. For example, we would have expected much more interaction between RUB and the users, and among the users themselves. This was, however, not the case in our use of the blog. There was some interaction between RUB and the users in the form of clarifying issues. However, the interaction among the users (for example, for the refinement of ideas) was very low. Therefore, in our case we cannot really say anything about the value of interaction between the organization and the users or among the users. In addition, we found that it was very difficult to collect a large number of ideas through the blog. There could be several explanations for this. For example, it could be due to the fact that three months is a short time period to observe what is going on in the blogs. It could also be due to the fact that users are generally satisfied with RUB services; the library users might not be interested in providing ideas for innovating the library services since they are used to getting the services gratis. Or, finally, that the blog layout was not appealing enough to potential idea contributors.

Concerning the planning and implementation of the blog, several learning lessons have emerged. An important lesson is that finding the right title for the blog and formulating the subjects about which ideas are solicited for in a clear and interesting way might not be a trivial task. It is very important that the subjects are not too broad, but not too narrow either. In addition, it is important that the blog is placed centrally on the organization's website and that the layout is appealing but not complicated. Promoting the blogs to the potential user population is also a challenge. Finally, it might be a very good idea to keep in contact with the organization benefiting from the blog and take time to closely follow the implementation phase at the organization. We did this only to a limited extent with two follow-up interviews, and we feel that our research results would have been stronger if we had more closely followed this part of the innovation process.

8.6 CONCLUSIONS

The study shows that blogs can be a useful tool for open innovation in service, as they provide benefits for both research and practice. From a practical point of view, for example, users of the blog can put forward their ideas and recommendations in a way that the organization/company can use to innovate their services and service offerings. The researchers might get some useful insight into the extent to which social media such as blogs can be used in open innovation in services, and especially in the idea-generation phase of the service innovation process. This is especially relevant in engaged research, where collaboration between industry and academia is a prerequisite and it is important that the method is beneficial for both involved parties. The use of blogs and the data generated by it in this study have contributed to an understanding of the extent to which blogs and social media can be used to involve users in open innovation processes in the specific sector of library services.

However, the use and application of social media such as blogs as a research method requires also a strong commitment from both the research team and the collaborating organization as a lot of meetings and discussions are required to reach a common ground and agreement about the subjects for idea generation, blog layout, etc.

LEARNING POINTS

● It is important to carefully consider what type of social media is the most appropriate for the type of organization and users in question, and the type of innovative ideas that need to be elicited. In our study, for example, we have decided to use blogs based on the library's previous experience with a blog, but other types of social media such as collaborative projects or Facebook could well have been a good alternative choice or even a better one.

● The setup and design of the blog is very important for the type, amount and quality of ideas to be collected.

● It is important not to underestimate the amount of time and effort required both by the researchers and the organization when collaborating about engaged scholarship, as time and effort are key to the successful implementation of the common project.

DISCUSSION TOPICS

● Are there contexts, organizations or types of services in which the method is a better choice than in others? For example, would the method be better for investigating open service innovation in relation to electronic-based or knowledge-intensive services than manual services?

● Are there contexts and situations where the method should not be considered at all? For example, if we are interested in collecting a huge amount of ideas, would this method be appropriate?

● How can we engage a large number of users to provide ideas for service innovation by using social media tools such as blogs?

REFERENCES

Aharony, N. (2009), 'Librarians and information scientists in the blogosphere: An exploratory analysis', *Library & Information Science Research*, 31(3), 174–181.

Boyd, D.M. and N.B. Ellison (2007), 'Social network sites: Definition, history, and scholarship', *Journal of Computer-Mediated Communication*, 13(1), 210–230.

Chesbrough, H.W. (2003), *Open innovation: The new imperative for creating and profiting from technology*. Boston: Harvard Business School Press.

Droge, C., M.A. Stanko, and W.A. Pollitte (2010), 'Lead users and early adopters on the web: The role of new technology product blogs', *Journal of Product Innovation Management*, 27(1), 66–82.

Franke, N. and F. Piller (2004), 'Value creation by toolkits for user innovation and design: The case of the watch market', *Journal of Product Innovation Management*, 21(6), 401–415.

Franke, N., P. Keinz, and M. Schreier (2008), 'Complementing mass customization toolkits with user communities: How peer input improves customer self-design', *Journal of Product Innovation Management*, 25(6), 546–559.

Hanna, R., A. Rohm, and V.L. Crittenden (2011), 'We are all connected: The power of the social media ecosystem', *Business Horizon*, 54, 265–273.

Huston, L. and N. Sakkab (2006), 'Connect and develop: Inside Procter & Gamble's new model for innovation', *Harvard Business Review*, 84(3), 58–66.

Jarvenpaa, S.L. and V.K. Tuunainen (2013), 'How Finnair socialized customers for service co-creation with social media', *MIS Quarterly Executive*, 12(3), 125–136.

Jeppesen, L.B. and M.J. Molin (2003), 'Consumers as co-developers: Learning and innovation outside the firm', *Technology Analysis & Strategic Management*, 15(3), 363–383.

Kaplan, A.M. and M. Haenlein (2010), 'Users of the world unite! The challenges and opportunities of social media', *Business Horizon*, 53, 59–68.

Kietzmann, J.H., K. Hermkens, I.P. McCarthy, and B.S. Silvestre (2011), 'Social media? Get serious! Understanding the functional building blocks of social media', *Business Horizon*, 54, 241–251.

Kozinets, R.V. (2002), 'The field behind the screen: Using netnography for marketing research in online communities', *Journal of Marketing Research*, 39(1), 61–72.

Kuhn, M. (2007), 'Interactivity and prioritizing the human: A code of blogging ethics', *Journal of Mass Media Ethics*, 22(1), 18–36.

Lakhani, K.R. (2008), 'InnoCentive.com', *Harvard Business School Case Study*, 9, 608–170.

Lakhani, K.R. and Z. Kanji (2008), 'Threadless: The business of community', *Harvard Business School Multimedia/Video Case*, pp. 608–707.

Larson, K. and R. Watson (2011), 'The value of social media: Toward measuring social media strategies', *ICIS 2011 Proceedings*, Article 11.

Malone, T.W., R. Laubacher, and C. Dellarocas (2010), 'The collective intelligence genome', *MIT Sloan Management Review*, 51(3), 21–31.

Maness, J.M. (2006), 'Library 2.0 theory: Web 2.0 and its implications for libraries', *Webology*, 3(2).

Matthing, J., B. Sandén, and B. Edvardsson (2004), 'New service development: Learning from and with customers', *International Journal of Service Industry Management*, 15(5), 479–498.

Nicolajsen, H.W. and A. Scupola, (2011), 'Investigating issues and challenges for customer involvement in business services innovation', *Journal of Business and Industrial Marketing*, 26(5), 368–376.

OECD (2007), *Participative web and user-created content: Web 2.0, wikis, and social networking*. Paris: Organisation for Economic Co-operation and Development.

Ogawa, S. and F.T. Piller (2006), 'Reducing the risks of new product development', *MIT Sloan Management Review*, 47(2), 65.

Parnet, M., K. Plangger, and A. Bal (2011), 'The new WTP: Willingness to participate', *Business Horizon*, 54, 219–229.

Piller, F.T. and D. Walcher (2006), 'Toolkits for idea competitions: A novel method to integrate users in new product development', *R&D Management*, 36(3), 307–318.

Prandelli, E. and M. Swahney (2008), *Collaborating with customers to innovate: Conceiving and marketing products in the networking age*. Cheltenham, UK and Northampton, MA, USA: Edward Elgar Publishing.

Prandelli, E., G. Verona, and D. Raccagni (2006), 'Diffusion of web-based product innovation', *California Management Review*, 48(4), 109–135.

Sakkab, N.Y. (2002), 'Connect & develop complements research & develop at P&G', *Research Technology Management*, 45(2), 38–45.

Scupola, A. (1999), 'The impact of electronic commerce on the publishing industry: Towards a business value complementarity framework of electronic publishing', *Journal of Information Science*, 25(2), 133–145.

Scupola, A. (2002), 'The impact of electronic commerce on industry structure: The case of scientific, technical and medical publishing', *Journal of Information Science*, 28(4), 275–284.

Scupola, A. (2008), 'E-services: Definition, characteristics and taxonomy', *Journal of Electronic Commerce in Organizations*, 6(2), i–iii.

Scupola, A. and H.W. Nicolajsen (2009), 'Open innovation in research libraries—myth or reality?', *Proceedings of the VI Conference of the Italian Chapter of AIS (ITAIS)*, Costa Smeralda (Olbia), Italy, October 2–3.

Scupola, A. and H.W. Nicolajsen (2010), 'Service innovation in academic libraries: Is there a place for the customers?', *Library Management*, 31(4/5), 304–318.

Scupola A. and A. Zanfei (2016), 'Governance and innovation in public sector services: The case of digital library', *Government Information Quarterly*, in press.

Scupola, A., A. Henten, and H.W. Nicolajsen (2009), 'E-services: Characteristics, scope and conceptual strengths', *International Journal of E-Services and Mobile Applications (IJESMA)*, 1(3), 1–16.

Sørensen, F. and J. Mattsson (2016), 'Speeding up innovation: Building network structures for parallel innovation', *International Journal of Innovation Management*, 20(2).

Sørensen, F., J. Mattsson, and J. Sundbo (2010), 'Experimental methods in innovation research', *Research Policy*, 39(3), 313–322.

Van de Ven, A.H. (2007), *Engaged scholarship: Creating knowledge for science and practice*. Oxford: Oxford University Press.

von Hippel, E. (2001), 'Perspective: User toolkits for innovation', *Journal of Product Innovation Management*, 18(4), 247–257.

von Hippel, E. and R. Katz (2002), 'Shifting innovation to users via toolkits', *Management Science*, 48(7), 821–833.

Ward, J.C. and A.L. Ostrom (2006), 'Complaining to the masses: The role of protest framing in customer-created complaint web sites', *Journal of Consumer Research*, 33(2), 220–230.

USEFUL RESOURCES

www.deff.dk
http://rub.ruc.dk/en/about-library/noegletal/
www.ruc.dk
http://scecr.org

9. Using technology-oriented scenario analysis for innovation research

Francesco Lapenta

9.1 TECHNOLOGY AND SERVICE INNOVATION INEXTRICABLE LINK

> *Change is the law of life and those who look only to the past or present*
> *are certain to miss the future*
> (J. F. Kennedy, 1963)

Advancements in technology and service innovation have always been intertwined, with service always relying on technology as either an operational resource (Gallouj and Weinstein, 1997; Argyres, 1999) or a core service innovation dimension (Dewett and Jones, 2001). In both applications the strategic adoption of new technologies has always been considered an advantage (Gago and Rubalcaba, 2007). Its speedy evolution, however, has also transformed technology into an innovation challenge, created by the need for faster innovation cycles, and the constant threat of the loss of competitive advantage to other businesses better equipped to foresee, create, adopt, and adapt to this technological evolution and its attendant cycles. This chapter argues that any service innovation-oriented business strategy should take advantage of a number of existing methodological tools derived from the general area of innovation research. The chapter focuses on one such method, *technology-oriented scenario analysis*, and presents a combined theoretical and methodological model that describes how contemporary methods based on "future-oriented technology analysis" (FTA)[1] (Cagnin et al., 2008) can help to foresee these technological evolutions and prepare in time for their possible development and strategic adoption and integration. Scenario analysis is a common and normally integrated methodological approach used in many, if not most, business practices (Diffenbach, 1983). Technology-oriented scenario analysis shares some of its principles with FTA, but in the specialized application described in this chapter is based on a specific set of theoretical assumptions, subjects, data, and analytical approaches that set technology and future technologies' forecast and foresight at center stage. The chapter gives an overview of the theoretical and methodological rationale that informs future-oriented technology analyses and develops a general model that is then applied to service innovation.

The ongoing interrelation between technology and services has been strongly cemented by the development of new Information Technologies (Argyres, 1999; Dewett and Jones, 2001; Bygstad and Lanestedt, 2009; Gago and Rubalcaba, 2007). IT and associated applications have fundamentally transformed established service practices and their old business models. The IT-fueled service evolution started in retailing with new e-service providers such as Amazon and eBay and it evolved with the likes of PayPal in banking, Skype in communication, Wikipedia in education, Uber in transportation, and Airbnb in tourism. It continued with countless other platforms and applications that have quickly transformed service innovation into an imperative, even for business practices once mostly dominated by product development (consumer electronics, automotive and transportation, consumer goods, housing, etc.). In general it can be argued that there is no business or institutional practice or business model that has not been touched or affected by contemporary evolutions in IT and the increasing demand for service and support now associated with any of them. There is also very little chance of this process ending soon, with most areas of life moving towards a greater level of digital interconnectedness.

This well-known shift has generated a more sustained expectation for management to increasingly embed strategies of continuous service development in a sustained effort to transform services as they do with products. It also created a stronger demand for service innovation researchers and theorists to develop new methods and strategies specifically designed to maintain the pace with fast evolving technological evolutions. In this chapter I argue that methods and models adopted in FTA can and should be permanently implemented in service innovation. While introducing some of the most established methods in the field of technology forecast, foresight, and assessment, I specifically focus on one, technology-oriented scenario analysis.

9.2 TECHNOLOGY-ORIENTED SCENARIO ANALYSIS AND STRATEGIC DECISION-MAKING

The history of humankind, and our own human nature, has always been characterized by an interest in the future. This interest has created, throughout history, a number of practices, and their practitioners, who have claimed to be able to see and forecast the future. These ancient traditions, and their often gaudy practices, took a drastic turn at the beginning of the 19th century when a new modern tradition, started by the likes of Copernicus, Kepler, and Galileo, matured into the development of specific practices that wanted to reach a scientific understanding of the future. This understanding was based, on the one hand, on the observations of the laws of nature and their predictability, and on the other on the study of social patterns and behaviors. These scientific practices have soon turned their attention to the study of the significant social, economic, cultural, and behavioral shifts led by the evolution of technology, and the impact that developing and future technologies might have.

At the turn of the century and after the first and second world wars when the consequences of the wrong use of new technologies became painfully known, it quickly became clear that this forward thinking was a necessary condition for strategic decision-making. The core understanding was that: "Those who do not want to deal with the possibilities of the future were at far greater risk of being sidelined or being pushed towards possible futures they had neither desired nor chosen" (Kreibich et al., 2011).

The effort to control or guide the future became a strategic decision, and the ability to lead and govern technological developments became the tools to exert such control. For the past century this awareness has motivated a constant technological race in which different actors have continually competed for the definition of the future, and the social, economic, and political advantages created by the ability to control such futures by controlling technological developments and the adoption of new technologies. This constant effort has created extremely diverse fields of practice and diverse groups that, with different agendas, engage with one another, and try to influence diverse dimensions of technological developments and future scenarios for social, political, and economic advantage.

A byproduct of such an effort has been the creation of a fragmented technological timeline (well exemplified by the concept of the digital and energy divide) in which different groups' access, use and understanding of new or developing technologies has given them the advantage over other groups quite literally creating, in the same continuous time, a fragmented relative technological timeline where different groups live in the past, present, or future of one another. This is true for nation states as it is for different groups, businesses, and institutions within them. As Gibson (2003) stated very evocatively: "The future is already here, it's just not very evenly distributed".

At the forefront of this timeline there are the experts and the practitioners of the future: the innovators and researchers in their research facilities, scientists in their laboratories, the policymakers, artists, film makers, novelists, philosophers, economists, and business visionaries who are constantly "living in the future", or speculating about the possible futures that might be elicited by the advancement of specific technologies and the impact of their adoption. These groups are followed by the early technological adopters: the states, the public and private institutions, businesses, social groups, and individuals who, earlier than others, invest or speculate on the advantages that can be gained, or challenges that can be posed, by certain technological evolutions.

The economic, social and political advantage and the challenges created by these possible technological scenarios have created an increasing need to engage in forms of future scenarios analysis. These techno-centric analyses of the future have evolved into three different directions and practices: technology foresight, technology forecasting, and technology assessment. The difference among these interconnected approaches is somewhat slippery, but their different emphases are meaningful and can be exemplified through a basic review of their definition, and associated methods, to gain a sense of their history and trajectory.

Technology forecasting relates to a set of analytical and interpretative activities that aim at capturing the expected trend and growth rate of existing or developing technologies. This is a practice consistently used by businesses and organizations to assess and plan short- to medium-term strategies and is at times associated with the term "technological intelligence"; an activity that enables companies "to identify the technological opportunities and threats that could affect the future growth and survival of their business" (Mortara et al., 2007). Methods used in technology forecasting include, according to a categorization made by Louie (Louie et al., 2010): Judgmental or Intuitive Methods such as the Delphi method (Dalkey, 1967; Dalkey et al., 1969); Extrapolation and Trend Analysis based methods such as Trend Extrapolation (Moore, 1965); Gompertz and Fisher-Pry Substitution Analysis (Fisher and Pry, 1970; Lenz, 1970); Analogies (Green and Armstrong, 2004, 2007); Morphological Analysis (XWY); Models-based methods, based on the Theory of Increasing Returns (Arthur, 1996); Chaos Theory and Artificial Neural Networks (Wang et al., 1999); Influence Diagrams (Howard and Matheson, 1981); or methods based on Scenarios and Simulations (Kahn, 1960, 1962).

Technology foresight is described by Martin (1995) and Georghiou and Keenan (2006) as "the process involved in systematically attempting to look into the longer-term future of science, technology, the economy and society with the aim of identifying the areas of strategic research and the emerging generic technologies likely to yield the greatest economic and social benefits" (Martin, 1995) and assess the ones that might have the strongest "impact on industrial competitiveness, wealth creation and quality of life" (Georghiou, 1996). A significant number of approaches and methods have been developed or used for technology foresight. The well-known paper by the Technology Futures Analysis Methods Working Group (Porter et al., 2004) identified 51 methods divided into nine groups (13 groups according to Porter, 2010) that can and have been used for technology foresight. These are qualitative, quantitative, semi-quantitative (Popper in Georghiou et al., 2008) methods that have been divided by Porter in the following groups: Creativity Approaches, Monitoring & Intelligence, Descriptive, Matrices, Statistical Analyses, Trend Analyses, Expert Opinion, Modelling & Simulation, Logical/ Causal Analyses, Road-mapping, Scenarios, Valuing-Decision Aiding-Economic Analyses, Combinations (ibid.).[2]

Technology assessment (TA) is a "scientific, interactive and communicative process which aims to contribute to the formation of public and political opinions on societal aspects of science and technology" (Decker and Ladikas, 2004). The focus here is on the assessment of the socio, economic, political, and ethical consequences that the adoption of certain technologies might have for society at large. Methods used in TA include, according to Tran and Daim (2008): structural modeling and system dynamics, impact analysis, scenario analysis, risk assessment, decision analysis, environmental concerns and integrated TA, cost–benefit analysis, measures for technology, road-mapping, scenarios and delphi, surveying, information monitoring, new technology assessment, and mathematical and other synthesis methods.

Future-oriented technology analysis (FTA) has, since 2008, become one of the many banners representing these efforts, and the product of this scientific history. A scientific, speculative, theoretical, and methodological effort to study and assess technological development is one of the key drivers in the evolution of these possible future scenarios. One of the core understandings in FTA is that technology and technological evolutions are subjects of a complex dynamic system that entails the interaction of different forces and the participation of multiple stakeholders. In this interpretation, innovation and foresight activities are not strictly localized activities, closed in the laboratories, corporate, or individual companies, or institutions but part of a move towards an open innovation ecology in which more and more information is shared among different knowledge providers. FTA has come to represent the attempt to coordinate the efforts of this multitude of groups and interests that are now using different scientific methods and approaches to study, forecast, and evaluate possible future technology-based scenarios. In the context of innovation, and service innovation specifically, this field of research, its principles, and history are meaningful to focus the attention of innovation researchers and practitioners on a number of pivotal aspects: 1) technology and information technologies are inextricably linked with service and they represent both an opportunity and a challenge to service innovation; 2) technology has become an increasingly fundamental driver of change in service innovation, and reflections about the role of future technological developments cannot be excluded in any medium or long-term service innovation plan; 3) service innovation has to adapt and adopt new methods and strategies specifically designed for technology forecasting and foresight. Specifically, I argue, it needs to integrate future scenarios, and hypotheses generation methods, and analyses; and 4) Technology forecast and foresight methods and analyses should be understood as dynamic processes of organizational intelligence. They are designed to activate key and dependent actors to collaboratively participate in a systematic, methodologically structured, but open and creative analytical activity inspired by reflection on possible future scenarios.

To further illustrate the core thinking in the field and its motivations, the following elaboration by Schoemaker (1995) presents a particularly illustrative perspective for which it deserves to be quoted at length. He explains why future-oriented scenario analysis constitutes a key methodological approach among these analytical strategies:

Early in this century, it was unclear how airplanes would affect naval warfare. When Brigadier General Billy Mitchell proposed that airplanes might sink battleships by dropping bombs on them, U.S. Secretary of War Newton Baker remarked, "That idea is so damned nonsensical and impossible that I'm willing to stand on the bridge of a battleship while that nitwit tries to hit it from the air." Josephus Daniels, Secretary of the Navy, was also incredulous: "Good God! This man should be writing dime novels." Even the prestigious Scientific American proclaimed in 1910 that "to affirm that the aeroplane is going to 'revolutionize' naval warfare of the future is to be guilty of the wildest exaggeration." In hindsight, it is difficult to appreciate why air power's potential was unclear to so many. But can we predict the future any better than these defence leaders did? We are affected by the same biases they were. It was probably as hard for them to evaluate the effect of airplanes in the 1920s as it is for us to assess the impact over the next decades of multimedia, the human genome project, biotechnology, artificial intelligence, organ transplants, superconductivity, space colonization, and myriad other developments. The myopic statements in the sidebar remind us how frequently smart people have made the wrong assumptions about the future with great certainty. Managers who can expand their imaginations to see a wider range of possible futures will be much better positioned to take advantage of the unexpected opportunities that will come along. And managers today have something those defence leaders did not have – scenario planning. (Schoemaker, 1995, p. 25)

9.3　A COMBINED THEORETICAL AND METHODOLOGICAL MODEL FOR TECHNOLOGY-ORIENTED SCENARIO ANALYSIS

Technology-oriented scenario analysis can be described as a specialized, or focused, application of similarly scoped exercises in scenario analysis. Ultimately, all scenario analyses aim to create multi media "representations" of certain visions of the near- (5–10 years), medium- (10–20 years) or long-term future (20–50 or more years). Technology-oriented scenario analysis, as a sub-genre of scenario analysis, can be described as an approach that specifically speculates about possible technological scenarios and the social, economic, and political relations and structures these technological evolutions might support or favor. Depending on their timescale and scope these scenario analyses might rely on quantitative, qualitative, or mixed research tools. The complex nature of these scenario analyses and the variety of methods they might apply explains why a singular methodological approach is neither possible nor desirable. A brief research on the subject is going to lead to an enormous variety of approaches and methods. Despite this diversity, however, it is still possible to look at the process and the different stages involved in the design of a scenario exercise and some of the elements they have in common. In the specific case of a technology-oriented scenario analysis there are also a number of theoretical and empirical considerations that might help to structure what seems so complex and difficult to classify. I argue that two principles are specifically important and helpful. One I call the principle of dialogic consequentiality, the other multiple stakeholder technology foresight.

9.3.1　Technology-oriented Scenario Analyses as a Scientific Discourse Genre, Based on the Principle of Dialogic Consequentiality

Contemporary futures studies are based on the core understanding that future developments, although not entirely predictable, are based on a set of conditions established in the past and the present. These conditions constitute the background for future developments that, although uncertain, are not arbitrary but the product of a complex series of decisions and actors that can potentially give shape to a number of differently possible, probable, or desirable future scenarios. The relative openness of these future scenarios gives scope to the idea that the future can be influenced or designed. The realization that these future scenarios cannot be totally arbitrary gives scope to the study of the conditions that can contribute to their evolution.

Independently from the tools used in the process, scenario analyses, and technology-oriented scenario analyses, only produce *descriptions and narratives* that detail certain aspects of a possible future. They might be said to share some of the qualities and insights that belong to other future scenario genres – science fiction and art not excluded – but they differ from these other forms of speculation and narratives because of *the process that leads to their narrative constructions*. While other forms of future speculation might be free from the need to specifically explain the history or the rationale that brought about the construction of such scenarios, technology-oriented scenario analyses are limited by the scientific conditions of existence of any technology, and the requirement of a consequentiality between the different steps that describe their potential evolution. Technology-oriented scenario analysis should really be considered as a creative, albeit structured, exercise in the construction of possible future scenarios that, starting from known elements of the past and the present (the known) moves via a number of scientific approaches, and associated scientific discourse genres (Miller and Fahnestock, 2013) into the future (the unknown). This timeline, composed of a series of key steps and necessary conditions, although uncertain cannot be arbitrary, but needs to be anchored in a consequential discourse. Each key step of the timeline, and hypothesis, needs to account for and describe the conditions of what was before and what follows. This does not mean that all details of this possible evolution need to be described, but rather that what are believed to be key steps or conditions need to be highlighted and consequentially analysed. Because of the hypothetical, and multiple, nature of these scenarios any narrative timeline should always be considered as "dialogic" (Bakhtin, 1982), open to a continual dialog and to further elaborations, to alternative hypotheses, or challenges by alternative scenarios, discourses, and interpretations.

These speculative efforts can go outward towards the future, moving from a set of chosen conditions, or inward moving from a hypothetical future condition back to the present. If looking at the steps that could lead to a future scenario, this is known as an "exploratory" or "outward bound" (JRC European Commission) approach. The reverse is also possible. When starting from a hypothetical future, the analyses move backwards trying to investigate the precise line of events that might have led to that hypothetical future. This is known as a "normative" or "inward bound" (ibid.) approach. Both approaches have their purpose. What they do have in common is that they both have to rely on: a scientific discourse genre and a methodologically accountable, theoretically informed, data aware and data rich analysis and speculation about the past, present, and future; a systematic description and analysis of the necessary conditions and steps that might lead or cause such futures; and a dialogic openness to alternative hypotheses and interpretations. Practices that together combine in what I call the principle of "dialogic consequentiality".

9.3.2 An Integrated Theoretical Model for Technology Analysis and Foresight

Future-oriented Technological Analyses developed from the effort of creating a dialog between different practitioners and groups that share a common interest in technology, technology foresight, technology forecasting, and technology assessment. Cagnin and Keenan (Cagnin, Johnston, Keenan, and Barre, 2008) in their reconstruction of the various stages that characterized the field used Georghiou's (2001, 2007) five generations model to identify the key theoretical traditions and methodological approaches that characterized the history of the field. These five generations describe a process of increasing inclusion of actors and forces active in the process of technological development, and technology foresight. In the first generation the focus is on the experts, the developers of technology, and their forecasts. In the second generation a link is recognized between the financial markets and their speculations and technology. In the third generation the influence of user- and users'-based social trends are recognized as an influence. In the fourth generation technology foresight has reached a more distributed role in the science and innovation system, with many organizations conducting their own foresight activities. In the fifth generation, these efforts become distributed among many sites that focus on either the structures, actors of technological development, or "on the scientific-technological dimensions of broader social and economic issues" (Cagnin et al., 2008, p. 3). Of course many, if not most, projects exhibit characteristics of different generations that are not mutually exclusive.

There are a number of models and analyses that link one or more of these groups and forces to technological evolutions, for example, in the work of Melissa Schilling, Robert Burgelman, and Clayton Christensen on strategic management and technology and innovation. Or on user-driven innovation, such as in the work of Eric von Hippel. Increasing attention has been lately paid to the relations existing between politics and technology. These approaches either focus on selected forces and groups or claim the existence of different historical stages in which attention has been turned to one aspect or group, or the other.

Consistently with contemporary analyses that focus on multiple stakeholder processes, I suggest (Lapenta, 2013) an integrated model that sees technological evolutions as the product of the constant interaction of a number of key representative groups and interests (Lapenta, 2011). These stakeholder groups (and decision-makers), that for the sake of this discussion can be broadly defined as the "developers," "policymakers," "financial actors," "users and users' groups"[3] (Lapenta, 2013), that with their combined interactions, and driving forces, are responsible for the path of evolution and trajectory of any technology. The model also recognizes that "technology" itself, as well as being influenced by these groups and forces, once adopted will exert an influence of its own on the other groups and forces, social trends, their trajectories, and dynamics.

The recognition of these interlinked influences acknowledges that you cannot really understand the evolution of any technology without understanding and accounting for the interrelation of all these forces – forces and influences exercised, at different times and for different periods of time, by these different groups that, together, work in shaping a technology's trajectory and fate. It also understands that these groups are part of social trends and trajectories of their own, which are formed and extend in a time frame not necessarily consistent with the time frame of other groups' trends and trajectories, or to technology (and specific technologies' life cycles). These specific stakeholder groups' trends and trajectories, such as fashions among users, national and global policies for policymakers, financial market phases and inner dynamics; private or public investments' fashions or priorities; and policy groups' priorities and focus, are all characterized by unique time frames that vary in subject and duration, and exert a direct or indirect influence on specific technology's related evolution. A specific time frame might appear to give relevance to one group's influence or another's, at a specific time, for a specific technology, but in this interpretation and model *these forces are always all interrelated* and part of *any* technology's evolution, and their interactions and intersections can always be observed by narrowing or extending the time frame under observation. This time frame, and the underlying social trends and trajectories under observation, can start in the past and move to the present, as well as be extended into the future. One meaningful way to understand the evolution of any technology, I argue (Lapenta, 2013), is to position that technology within this system of different groups and forces, and their specific trajectories, and study and describe how and when they intersect and with what consequences (for an example[4]).

A limit of this model is that the reduction of the key actors to those four groups, although meaningful, can be seen as reductive, but this is beyond its function. The function of the simplification of this model is that it compels researchers to always consciously apply a basic multiple stakeholders' approach that at least accounts for these four fundamental forces (however defined in context). The model also helps to understand how to adopt a motivated and variable time frame for the analyses, that instead of focusing on the sole technology (as in a technology-based trend extrapolation and life cycle analysis) focuses and accounts for the long- and short-term social dynamics, and key actors' own social trends and trajectories, in which any technological evolution is embedded. These time frames are most likely going to be different from the ones of the very technology itself. This approach has an equal value when investigating the evolution and impact of existing technologies and also, although more complex, when evaluating the groups and conditions that might favor or hinder the development of a yet to be adopted technology, and the effects that that technology might have on the other groups and forces.

9.3.3   A Methodological Model to Conduct Technology-oriented Scenario Analysis

What is meaningful about the two theoretical dimensions and considerations outlined above is that they allow us to describe a set of theoretical and methodological guidelines that should help to initiate any form of technology-oriented scenario analysis. Scenario analyses can be divided in two main approaches: "exploratory" ("outward bound") or "normative" ("inward bound"). Scenario analysis speculative efforts can go outward towards the future, moving from a set of chosen present conditions, or inward, moving from a hypothetical future condition back to the present. Both approaches have their purpose, but they are not different in their underlying logic. What they do have in common is that they both have to methodologically rely on the principle of dialogic consequentiality to investigate the line of events that might lead to or have caused that hypothetical future. Both approaches have also to thoughtfully apply a defined multiple stakeholders' approach that moves towards the identification of the key actors and driving forces involved in the scenario. They both have also to use a motivated and variable time frame for the analyses, that instead of focusing on the sole technology's life cycle focuses and accounts for the long- and short-term trajectories or social trends that might characterize these key actors' hypothetical actions.

There are many different approaches that can be used to initiate, structure, and organize long- or short-term scenario exercises and scenario foresight activities and analyses. Scenario exercises can be long or short-term activities, organized as single workshops, or more long-term activities, and involve a variable number of different stages, and varying numbers of participants and stakeholders. Given this diversity, we are more interested in the methodological phases and functions that need to be accomplished by these activities than in the specific organizational aspects of these activities. One well-known model that describes the basic research phases of a scenario exercise is described by Schoemaker (1995, p. 29). Another that is specifically framed within the area of FTA is suggested by Kreibich et al. (2011, p. 19). Combined together they give a good sense of how a scenario exercise can be structured, its key phases, and their methodological function. Kreibich et al. describe six phases in a scenario exercise: *framing, scanning, forecasting, foresight, visioning, planning and action.* I will shortly describe them, combining them with Schoemaker's scenario while using an example, and possible application, in financial services innovation to contextualize them.

Framing

In this phase the scope of the scenario exercise is defined. Key elements are defined such as the key area of investigation, the time frame of the exercise, the main stakeholders involved, and an initial problem formulation that defines what areas of a certain technological development or possible evolution the researchers are interested in. (For example, what will be the future of online banking and financial services in relation to the development of mobile technologies and applications in ten years from now?)

Scanning

In this phase all kinds of relevant data and information are collected based on the themes identified in the framing phase. Those available such as published research and reports, historic analyses, and current research data and analyses, can be integrated by qualitative and quantitative research, interviews, surveys, expert opinions etc. (in the case of the online financial services and banking, for example, a meaningful amount of research and data is published by institutional organizations, such as in the Board of Governors of the Federal Reserve System report on consumers and financial services, or research institutes and think thanks).

Forecasting

In this phase the collected data are analysed to identify and discuss key trends, uncertainties, and drivers of change (for example, in the case of the financial services regarding mobile services development, security and privacy concerns associated with mobile applications, trends and challenges in privacy legislation, and technological developments in secure networks).

Foresight

In this phase, on the basis of the analysis and results of the forecasting phase, a number of hypotheses and possible future scenarios are explored, challenged, compared to alternative cases, and tested for relative consistency and plausibility (for example, what if cash payments were declared illegal? Or what if national currencies were all replaced by one single digital currency? What would be the consequences of such evolutions for financial infrastructures and services? While the former are somewhat utopian scenarios, they open the discussion for a possible multiple scenario analysis in which various scenarios, that account for intermediate possibilities, can be explored. Such as, for example, the case in which the use of cash was limited only to specific transactions or anyway somehow regulated, and digital currencies evolved in parallel to older monetary systems).

Visioning
In this phase the lead scenario or scenarios that have emerged from the framing, scanning, forecasting, and foresight phases are tested more in depth. A more strategic, detailed and articulated discussion of the necessary conditions, and the actors' necessary steps involved in a specific scenario, and their relative likelihood, are analysed and carefully evaluated. (Qualitative and/or quantitative models can be tested, for example, to evaluate the likelihood of cash transactions disappearing in 5, 10, 20 or 50 years' time, and/or new electronic currencies to take over in similar time frames.)

Planning and action
Following the insights of the analytical stage of the vision building phase, a number of strategies, options, agenda setting considerations, or actual development plans might be developed to act on the insights produced by all the previous phases (in our case, for example, it can be decided that a certain amount of resources will be assigned to the long-term development of financial services based on these new scenarios).

9.4   WHEN FORECASTS AND FORESIGHTS ARE WRONG, WHEN THEY ARE RIGHT, AND WHEN IT DOES NOT MATTER IF THEY ARE

Foresights and forecasts are predictably complex activities. A wealth of empirical evidence proves that very often attempts to predict future behaviors is incredibly complex, and often wrong. Political forecasts and economic analyses, and micro and macro economic modeling, are known to be often very imprecise, many times intentionally or unintentionally biased, regularly entirely wrong. While this is often the case even with theoretically more predictable dimensions (such as the ones governed by the laws of nature – weather forecasts, for example), it is even more common when dealing with human behavior, and human decision-making activities where their limitations become even more apparent and predictable (Schoemaker, 1998). These limitations might question the advantages that can be gained by such foresight activities, and the costs associated in running them, especially considering how many times these forecasts are wrong. A general answer to this question is that in many contexts it is not really important if the predictions were right or wrong, and the accuracy of these scenarios might really not be the main reason why these scenarios exercises are done:

> Many times the aim of these forecasting and foresight practices is not to be correct about their predictions of the future. Often their aim is to force decision-makers into a critical process of constant engagement with possible future scenarios. Rather than a tool for prediction, they are a tool to favor a process through which new insights emerge, new organizational skills are developed, medium- to long-term visions are conceived and tested, and strategic decisions are taken. So that future scenarios can be influenced and built, or as it might be the case, intentionally avoided. Having explored several scenarios and their possible consequences is also a resource in its own right. These scenario-building practices can be a very powerful tool to train decision-makers to quickly evaluate emerging scenarios, and react more effectively to otherwise unforeseen actual events.

9.5 BIG DATA AND ALGORITHMIC PREDICTIVE COMPUTING: EVOLVING PRACTICES OF FUTURE SCENARIO ANALYSES

The field of FTA and the scientific investigation of the future are in their relative infancy. Until very recently they were based as much on expert knowledge and science as they were on individual creative and analytical skills. Things are, however, changing very rapidly. Speculative foresight is more and more replaced or assisted by developing forms of "algorithmic predictive computing" (Lapenta, 2013) and more mathematically and statistically formalized forecast and foresight activities. As one of the fastest developing areas of research, these developments are influenced by parallel developments in big data collection, better and more sophisticated mathematical modeling, and the constant push towards an artificial intelligence-based analysis of an increasingly growing and diversified amount of data. Because of this consistent growth of foresight and forecasting activities, and projects and institutional investments, an increasing amount of data and tools are made available by many different authors and organizations, some small such as think thanks and research institutes, and others representing the articulated effort of national or international institutions. These research, data, tools, and applications, scenario analyses and reports are often provided with the hope of eliciting debate, discussion, speculation and further elaboration by the widest range of individuals, groups, and stakeholders. They constitute an invaluable resource. Despite these changing tools, and the certain evolution of new methods and tools, foresight and scenario analyses ultimately remain an intellectual exercise in understanding the forces that contribute to the future and its possible alternative evolutions. Foresight should be understood as a process for understanding the developing relations among key actors and their individual and collective contributions to the development of the future – a process to critically problematize the consequences of different actions, and the possible future scenarios that these actions and decisions might lead to or inspire. Technology foresight should really represent a checks and balances system in which the role of the intellectual and the researcher is to foresee the evolving and invisible structures of power established by technology, and question the values of their irresistible evolution. The role of the creative thinker and maker is to imagine these technological evolutions and make them possible. And that of the policymaker, in a combined effort, is to make sure that the sole purpose of technology and innovation will be to serve the evolution of humanity in its ethical quest for purpose and direction.

LEARNING POINTS

- Information Technologies and Technology have become structural drivers of change. Any medium- or long-term innovation plan cannot exclude reflections about probable and possible future technological developments.
- Innovation in Technology and Information Technologies are inextricably linked with service innovation. Their evolution represents both an opportunity and a challenge to service innovation.
- Technology forecast and foresight methods should be understood as new, necessary, and dynamic processes of organizational intelligence. They are designed to activate key and dependent actors to participate into a constant innovation process inspired by, and aware of, possible future technological scenarios.

DISCUSSION TOPICS

- What theoretical model can be used to understand the different forces that contribute to technological development and innovation?
- What methods and analytical tools can be adopted to forecast, evaluate, and influence possible future technological scenarios?
- How can technology-oriented scenario analysis be implemented and used for innovation, and service innovation, research and development?

NOTES

1. The origin of the term "future-oriented technology analysis" can be traced to the planning for the Institute for Prospective Technological Studies Seminar 'New Horizons and Challenges for Future-oriented Technology Analysis: New Technology Foresight, Forecasting and Assessment Methods' held in Seville, Spain in May 2004.
2. For an accessible overview I suggest reading Popper, R. (2008) "Foresight methodology." In L. Georghiou, J. Cassingena, M. Keenan, I. Miles, and R. Popper (eds.), *The Handbook of Technology Foresight.* Cheltenham, UK and Northampton, MA, USA: Edward Elgar Publishing, pp. 44–88. For a complete list of methods and references to each method I suggest looking at the original paper by the Technology Futures Analysis Methods Working Group (2004).
3. For an example of the application of this model you can watch my presentation at Re:publica 2013 in Berlin (https://www.youtube.com/watch?v=wJYtHBD0XbI) in which I adopted this model to speculate about emerging geolocational augmented visualization technologies against historical, technological, social and economic trends, and elaborate on the basis of these interpretations on the specific normative, and cognitive effects, that these technologies might acquire.
4. Kahn (1960) *On Thermonuclear War* and (1962) *Thinking About the Unthinkable* are notable examples. They are also the first two scenario exercises that defined the method.

REFERENCES

Argyres, N. S. (1999). "The impact of information technology on coordination: Evidence from the B-2 'Stealth' bomber." *Organization Science*, 10(2), 162–180.

Arthur, Brian W. (1996). "Increasing returns and the new world of business." *Harvard Business Review* (July–August).

Bakhtin, M. M. (1982). *The Dialogic Imagination: Four Essays.* Austin, TX: University of Texas Press.

Cagnin, C., R. Johnston, M. Keenan, and R. Barre (2008). *Future-Oriented Technology Analysis: Strategic Intelligence for an Innovative Economy.* Berlin, Heidelberg: Springer.

Dalkey, Norman C. (1967). *DELPHI.* Santa Monica, CA: RAND Corporation.

Dalkey, Norman C., Bernice B. Brown, and S.W. Cochran (1969). *The Delphi Method, III: Use of Self-Ratings to Improve Group Estimates.* Santa Monica, CA: RAND Corporation.

Decker, M., and M. Ladikas (eds.) (2004). *Bridges between Science, Society and Policy. Technology Assessment – Methods and Impacts*. Berlin: Springer.

Dewett, T. and G. R. Jones (2001). "The role of information technology in the organization: A review, model, and assessment." *Journal of Management*, 27(3), 313–346.

Diffenbach, John (1983). "Corporate environmental analysis in large US corporations." *Long Range Planning*, 16 (3).

Fisher, J. C. and R. H. Pry (1970). "A simple substitution model of technological change." *Technological Forecasting and Social Change*, 3(1), 75–78.

Gago, D. and L. Rubalcaba (2007). "Innovation and ICT in service firms: Towards a multidimensional approach for impact assessment." *Journal of Evolutionary Economics*, 17(1), 25–44.

Gallouj, F. and O. Weinstein (1997). "Innovation in services." *Research Policy*, 26(4–5), 547–556.

Georghiou, L. (2001). *Third Generation Foresight – Integrating the Socio-Economic Dimension*. International Conference on Technology Foresight – The approach to and the potential for New Technology Foresight, Science and Technology Foresight Center. National Institute of Science and Technology Policy (NISTEP). Ministry of Education, Culture, Sports, Science and Technology, Japan.

Georghiou, L. (2007). *Future of Foresighting for Economic Development*. UNIDO Technology Foresight Summit 2007. Budapest, September 27–29.

Georghiou, L. and M. Keenan (2006). "Evaluation of national foresight activities: Assessing national processes and impact." *Technological Forecasting and Social Change*, 73, 761–777.

Georghiou, L., J. Cassingena, M. Keenan, I. Miles, and R. Popper (eds.) (2008). *The Handbook of Technology Foresight*. Cheltenham, UK and Northampton, MA, USA: Edward Elgar Publishing.

Green, Kesten C. and J. Scott Armstrong (2004). "Structured analogies for forecasting." Working Paper 17, Monash University Department of Econometrics and Business Statistics. September 16.

Green, Kesten C. and J. Scott Armstrong (2007). "Structured analogies for forecasting." *International Journal of Forecasting*, 23(3), 365–376.

Howard, Ronald A. and James E. Matheson (1981). "Influence diagrams." In Ronald A. Howard and James E. Matheson (eds.), *Readings on the Principles and Applications of Decision Analysis*, vol. I (1984). Menlo Park, CA: Strategic Decisions Group, pp. 721–762.

Kahn, H. (1960). *On Thermonuclear War*. Princeton, NJ: Princeton University Press.

Kahn, H. (1962). *Thinking About the Unthinkable*. New York: Horizon Press.

Kreibich D. R., B. Oertel and M. Wölk (2011). "Futures Studies and Future-oriented Technology Analysis Principles, Methodology and Research Questions." HIIG Discussion Paper Series 201205. Alexander von Humboldt Institut für Internet und Gesellschaft: Berlin.

Lapenta, F. (2011). "Geomedia: On location-based media, the changing status of collective image production and the emergence of social navigation systems." *Visual Studies*, 26(1), 14–24.

Lapenta, F. (2013). "Life After the Screen. Mediated Life After Virtualization. A Critical Look at the Cognitive and Social Scenarios Forecast by Augmented Visualizations Technologies, Algorithmic Predictive Computing and Emerging Algorithmic Systems." Paper presented at the conference "Re:publica 2013" – May 2013, Berlin.

Lenz, R. C. (1970). "Practical application of technical trend forecasting." In M. J. Cetron and J. D. Goldhar (eds.), *The Science of Managing Organized Technology*. New York: Gordon and Breach, pp. 825–854.

Louie, G. G. et al. (2010). *Persistent Forecasting of Disruptive Technologies*. National Academy Press [B1] 12.

Martin, B. R. (1995). "Foresight in science and technology." *Technology Analysis and Strategic Management*, 7, 139–168.

Miller, Carolyn R. and Jeanne Fahnestock (2013). "Genres in scientific and technical rhetoric." *Poroi*, 9(1), Art. 12.

Moore, George E. (1965). "Cramming more components onto integrated circuits." *Electronics* 38(8).

Mortara, L., C. Kerr, R. Phaal, and D. Probert (2007). *Technology Intelligence: Identifying Threats and Opportunities from New Technologies*. Cambridge: University of Cambridge Press.

Porter, A. (2010). "Technology foresight: Types and methods." *International Journal of Foresight and Innovation Policy*, 6(1/2/3).

Porter, A. L., W. B. Ashton, G. Clar, J. F. Coates, K. Cuhls, S. W. Cunningham, K. Ducatel, P. van der Duin, L. Georghiou, T. Gordon, H. Linstone, V. Marchau, G. Massari, I. Miles, M. Mogee, A. Salo, F. Scapolo, R. Smits, and W. Thissen, (Technology Futures Analysis Methods Working Group) (2004). "Technology futures analysis: Toward integration of the field and new methods." *Technological Forecasting and Social Change*, 71, 287–303.

Schoemaker, Paul J. H. (1995). "Scenario planning: A tool for strategic thinking." *Sloan Management Review*, 36(2), 25–40.

Schoemaker, Paul J. H. (1998). "Twenty common pitfalls in scenario planning." In L. Fahey and R. Randall (eds.), *Learning from the Future*. New York: Wiley & Sons, pp. 422–431.

Tran, T. A. and Daim, T. (2008). "A taxonomic review of methods and tools applied in technology assessment." *Technological Forecasting and Social Change*, 75, 1396–1405.

Wang, Clement, Xuanrui Liu, and Daoling Xu (1999). "Chaos theory in technology forecasting." Paper MC-07.4. Portland International Conference on the Management of Engineering and Technology, Portland, Oregon. July 25–29.

10. Using Future Workshops for idea generation in engaged service innovation research

Ada Scupola

10.1 INTRODUCTION

User-driven innovation, co-creation and open innovation are all concepts emphasizing the potential of opening up organizational innovation processes by inviting external stakeholders to participate in innovation (Sundbo and Toivonen, 2011; Alam and Perry, 2002). The external stakeholders include suppliers, governmental agencies, competitors and customers. Involving these stakeholders in an organizational innovation process is a complex matter which requires quite some changes to the existing practices within the organizations, including new and different ways to communicate and collaborate with the external stakeholders (Chesbrough, 2003).

Customer involvement, especially, has often been argued to be fruitful in innovation processes (Chesbrough, 2006; Kristensson et al., 2003; Hennestad, 1999; von Hippel, 1986, 1989, 2001; von Hippel and Katz, 2002; Piller and Walcher, 2006). However, the involvement of customers in open innovation has also been questioned along the way. One main reason is that users are often too traditional in their thinking, therefore studies argue that they only provide incremental ideas for innovation processes and very limited radical, outside-of-the-box ideas. Another reason being that user or customer involvement demands time and effort from the organization, and also the users and the required resources in such a process might not outweigh the value of the innovation (Magnusson, 2003; Magnusson et al., 2003). Thus, open innovation is riskier due to less control of the process and the outcome.

Many models trying to explain and understand the process of innovation of new products or services have been developed in the literature over the last decades. They can be mainly divided into the linear or stage gate models and the interactive models, taking into consideration feedback loops between the different stages of the process. One well-known model is Rogers' model (1995) defining the organizational innovation process as consisting of two broad activities: initiation and implementation. Within the innovation literature, however, the focus on new product development (NPD) and new service development (NSD) has increased in the last couple of decades (e.g. Alam, 2002; Matthing et al., 2004; Nambisan, 2002; Kristensson et al., 2003). Alam and Perry (2002) have developed a stage model of NSD, taking into account the core elements in user involvement in NSD including objectives/purposes of involvement, the stages of involvement in the organizational innovation process, the intensity of involvement and the modes of involvement. They find involvement of users in idea generation and idea screening as the most important input to service innovation. User involvement in strategic planning, personal training and test marketing are of least importance.

In these innovation processes, customers or users may contribute in a number of ways including stating their needs, problems or solutions or criticizing existing services (Alam, 2002; Alam and Perry, 2002). They may also help in screening ideas by responding to concepts or alternative solutions with their thinking, dislikes or preferences. In order to get these insights customers may be involved through face-to-face meetings, user visits or meetings, workshops, user observations or direct types of communication (Alam, 2002). However, Alam and Perry (2002) argue that customers may not only contribute with ideas, but may also help screen these and may participate in the initial strategic planning. In addition recent research on user-driven innovation has also emphasized the important role of employees in involving users and interpreting their needs and wishes (e.g. Nicolajsen and Scupola, 2011; Sundbo, 2010). Previous research has also shown that it is important for organizations to harness the creativity of all employees, however, new ideas and innovation do not just materialize on their own, but require a special background and specific conditions for growth while also demanding nurturing and stimulation (Polewsky and Will, 1996). In this chapter I take an approach to the service innovation process as a process that can be strategically initiated and anchored, and, by drawing on Alam and Perry (2002), the chapter focuses on the idea-generation phase of such a process.

Given this background, the purpose of this chapter is to present, discuss and illustrate the use and application of Future Workshops in the idea-generation phase of service innovation processes in the context of research library services and specifically in the case of Roskilde University Library.

The chapter is structured as follows: The introduction above presents the background and purpose of the chapter. The second section introduces the method, while the third section presents an example of the application of the method in the specific case of Roskilde University Library. The fourth section provides a discussion of the method application, while the last section concludes the chapter and provides some learning points and discussion topics.

10.2   THE USE OF FUTURE WORKSHOPS IN INNOVATION RESEARCH

Future Workshops have been used since the 1950s and were first invented and applied by Robert Jungk and Norbert Müllert (1987) to involve people directly affected by political decisions in the decision-making process itself, which according to Jungk and Müllert (1987) often also fails to take the future into consideration (Dator, 1993). According to Vidal (2006), Future Workshops are around 50 years old and mostly used in practice, with little academic research and application. The method was originally used by local groups to deal with local problems. Later it was introduced in firms interested in practicing a more democratic and creative management style. During the last few years, Future Workshops have been used by firms and public institutions, and hierarchical and non-democratic organizations, in their planning activities. So there is evidence that companies are using Future Workshops in their innovation activities. Recently, Future Workshops have also been used in the design of new systems, processes and artifacts (e.g. Kensing and Madsen, 1992). However, to the best knowledge of the author, there is no academic literature investigating how Future Workshops have been used and can be used in service innovation research and especially in the idea-generation phase of library services. It can be argued therefore that this chapter makes a major contribution towards understanding the use and application of Future Workshops as a research method.

Future Workshops, as applied in this study in the context of engaged research (see section 3), are characterized by serving the double purpose of generating ideas useful for the service innovation process of the service organization, while also providing the researcher with data of relevance to research. In fact, an important academic discourse initiated in the last decade is the importance of conducting research that is also relevant to practice and that is conducted together with practice (Van de Ven, 2007). Van de Ven (2007) states that often practitioners find little value in academic and especially social science research and that often practitioner and academic knowledge are unrelated. Therefore, he identifies a dual challenge: academics need to put theories into practice and managers need to put practice into theory. This may be accomplished according to Van de Ven (2007) by studying complex problems *with* and/or *for* practitioners and other stakeholders, thus practicing what he defines as engaged scholarship. According to Van de Ven (2007) this form of scholarship should increase the likelihood of advancing knowledge for science and professions.

By following Van de Ven (2007) and the way Future Workshops are orchestrated in this study, it is argued here that such methods lay on the critical realist philosophy of science even though other approaches might be argued to be useful as well (please see Chapter 8 in this book for details about critical realism).

10.2.1 Phases of the Future Workshop

According to Jungk and Müllert (1987), a "classic" Future Workshop is typically divided into a "preparatory phase" and three workshop phases. The preparatory phase involves deciding on the topic of the workshop, making the practical arrangements such as selection and invitation of the participants, the timetable of the workshop, and the selection of the room and local facilities for the workshop. This preparatory phase is then followed by the workshop itself, which consists of three phases.

1. The critique phase
In this phase all the grievances and negative experiences related to the chosen topic are critically and thoroughly discussed and investigated. Brainstorming is the preferred creative technique used here, followed by a structuring and grouping of ideas in some main sub-themes.

2. The fantasy phase
Here the participants try to come up with ideas in response to the problems, and with their desires, fantasies and alternative views. A selection is made of the most interesting notions and small working groups develop these into solutions and outline projects.

3. The implementation phase
In this phase the participants critically assess the chances of getting their projects implemented, identify the obstacles and imagine ways to address them, thus coming up with a plan of action. Here the ideas found are evaluated by the workshop's participants in regards to their practicability and an action plan is elaborated.

These phases can last a few days, but normally they would last a few hours or just one hour each. According to Vidal (2006), the workshop phases are then followed by "The follow-up phase," where the action plan is monitored; eventually changes are performed and if needed, new Future Workshops are planned to come up with new ideas.

10.2.2   Future Workshops' Potential in Service Innovation Research

In service innovation research, the set-up and the potential research questions that could be investigated by using the Future Workshop method could, for example, focus on the different types of actors that can be involved in the innovation process: users for analyzing potentials of user-driven service innovation; employees for analyzing potentials of employee-driven service innovation; suppliers for supplier-driven innovation; researchers, expert-users, etc. Therefore Future Workshops as a research method could be beneficial and useful to: investigate various idea-generating potentials of different actors, such as managers, employees or users, in different service innovation contexts; investigate different types of workshop set-ups and their idea-generating potential; and generate collaborative and engaged research (with subsequent benefits for both researchers and practitioners).

In addition, it might be expected that Future Workshops are very useful in situations where a strategic or planned approach is taken to innovation and innovation processes but also in situations where it is important to get feedback from the customers on the service provided. As an example, if we take the NSD process as conceptualized by Alam (2002) and Alam and Perry (2002), Future Workshops might be very useful in the idea-generation phase of the innovation process, both to involve the users but also to involve the employees in the innovation process. However, other phases of the innovation process could also benefit from the application of Future Workshops. Finally, as most of the literature on customer involvement in innovation processes shows, it might also be expected that the ideas emerging from Future Workshops are mostly incremental in nature and that few radical innovations might be generated in such workshops. It might also be expected that some ideas generated in Future Workshops might be difficult to implement in practice.

To conclude, Future Workshops used in a research process are different from Future Workshops used only by practitioners in service companies. Research-based Future Workshops can, for instance, be informed by a preliminary case study and by most recent research knowledge to, say, determine issues that are to be dealt with in the Future Workshops, in addition to practice-based knowledge. "Traditional" Future Workshops instead will be based mainly on practice-based knowledge. Furthermore research-based Future Workshops will also include an analytical after-process, which is partly what makes it relevant to both practical and research interest. Thus Future Workshops qualify as a research method and result in research/practice collaboration in both practice and research relevant knowledge.

10.3 THE APPLICATION OF FUTURE WORKSHOPS IN THE IDEA GENERATION PROCESS AT ROSKILDE UNIVERSITY LIBRARY

10.3.1 The Study Context

In order to illustrate why and how Future Workshops have been applied and can be applied in practice to involve users in the idea-generation phase of the service innovation process, here the application of Future Workshops in the context of a case study (Yin, 1994) conducted at Roskilde University Library is presented. Roskilde University Library (RUB) was founded in 1971. It is a research library serving the students and staff at Roskilde University, accounting for about 9000 students, 650 teaching staff and about 430 technical and administrative staff. Roskilde University is named after the city where it is located in the Danish region called Zealand. The research, by reflecting and following the guidelines for engaged research, consisted of the following phases.

Phase 1
Uncovering current service innovation practices at RUB, with a particular focus on user involvement and tools for involvement and establishing agreements with RUB about the research problem to be investigated and frames for collaboration (see e.g. Scupola and Nicolajsen (2010) and Scupola and Zanfei (2016) for more information about user involvement at RUB).

Phase 2
Using Future Workshops to involve library users and employees to generate ideas to innovate the library services and self-services, which is the focus of this chapter.
  Please refer to Van de Ven (2007) and Chapter 8 in this book entitled "The role of social media data for research on user driven innovation" for detailed information about engaged research and Roskilde University Library.

10.3.2 Applying Future Workshops at Roskilde University Library

The main research purpose of using Future Workshops in this study was to understand how and why 1) users, 2) employees plus users together and 3) employees, can come up with relevant ideas for service innovation in the library context. This research purpose was guided by the case study conducted in Phase 1 in which it was concluded that RUB was not prepared for – or considered relevant to – the use of user and employee inputs in the innovation process. The Future Workshop was a way to scientifically illustrate/discuss if there were – even in such a "hostile" innovation context – a place for, and potential use of, user and employee inputs. Future Workshops were a face-to-face tool to generate ideas concerning service and self-service innovations that the library could use and implement to improve its service offerings, service satisfaction and position itself as an innovative library.

10.3.3   The Preparatory Phase to the Future Workshops

The preparatory phase involved several meetings and workshops (not Future Workshops) with the library management and employees to find out and agree upon the topics of the Future Workshops and the participants to invite. After several discussions and inputs from the researchers and their knowledge about service innovation and user involvement as well as the library's need for service innovation, it was decided that the best course of action was to organize three parallel Future Workshops. One workshop was organized with only library employees in order to find out what the library employees believed was needed concerning service innovations; one was organized with only library users to find out about their needs and wishes; and a third one was organized with mixed participants, made up of users and library employees to generate ideas that were enriched and discussed by both groups. An announcement was put on the library noticeboard, and on the reception counter, looking for potential users to participate in the Future Workshops. A ticket to a movie theater was promised to the participants to increase motivation and willingness to participate in the workshop. The library users participating in the Future Workshops were students and were selected randomly from all the students volunteering to participate, while the employees were strategically selected by RUB management from among those volunteering to participate (please refer to Table 10.1 below for details about the participants).

From an organizational point of view, it was decided that the workshops should take place simultaneously at the library premises and were facilitated by three researchers who acted as workshop facilitators. There were six participants in each workshop, which lasted two hours each.

10.3.4   Organization of the Future Workshops at RUB

In organizing the workshops, we adapted the format of the classic Future Workshops suggested by Jungk and Müllert (1987) by introducing a fourth phase that we named the "realistic suggestions phase." This phase

Table 10.1   Future Workshops' participants details

	Workshop type		
	User workshop	Employees workshop	Mixed workshop
Number of participants	6 students	5 employees	6 participants
Distribution of gender	2 men and 4 women	1 man and 4 women	3 female students 1 male employee 2 female employees
Age	Freshman – Masters level Average age: 24	2 younger ones and three elderly ones (close to pension) Average age: 52	Students from 1, 3 and 5 semester (one is student assistant at the library) Middle-aged employees Average age: 33 (students 23; employees 43)
Reward for participation	Ticket to the movie theater	Asked to participate, but provided with a bottle of wine at the end of the workshop session	Ticket to the movie theater to users asked to participate, but provided a bottle of wine to employees
Engagement during workshops	Very eager, high participation from all – Interested in the method itself and in generating solutions	Reluctant participation 2 very active, one middle active and 2 very limited	Variation in participation – Employees were more active than students in the mixed setting however also difference in engagement across the two groups

was introduced with the purpose of ranking the ideas generated in the fantasy phase and commenting on them to make them more realistic. The workshop participants were also encouraged to give suggestions on how to implement the ideas generated in the fantasy phase. This we found necessary in order to make a smoother transition from the fantasy phase to the implementation phase. The workshops were documented in a number of different ways. First, the participants were asked to fill in a questionnaire regarding their creative skills at the beginning of each workshop. Second, the ideas produced in the different phases of the Future Workshops were recorded on Post-It notes and pictures of them were taken by the researchers. Such ideas were then registered into three excel files, one for each Future Workshop. In addition the Future Workshop sessions were tape recorded in order to be able to go back and listen to details on the different ideas generated, as well as the process itself, in case it was necessary later on in the analysis process. At the end of each workshop, the participants were asked to fill in a questionnaire asking about what they personally saw as the most valuable ideas in relation to their own needs and wishes. The researchers/facilitators also took notes about the workshop process immediately after the workshops had ended. The ideas recorded in the excel files were then presented in a meeting to two managers of the library and discussed together with them. The library managers then further discussed the ideas among themselves in future meetings, ranked them in order of importance, and selected ideas were chosen for implementation and thus implemented. However, despite what was recommended by Vidal (2006), as researchers we only followed up on the implementation process in a limited way, so as to find out which ones were eventually implemented. Therefore we could say that the follow-up phase had not been fully implemented by the researchers, but mainly left in the hands of the library.

10.3.5　Future Workshops Implementation – Practical Guidelines

The topic of the Future Workshops was very broad after agreement with RUB management and was presented to the workshop participants as ideas for what Roskilde University Library could do to improve their service to the users. Both face-to-face and e-services were subjects of the workshop and ideas concerning the physical premises were also solicited. Box 10.1 presents the practical guidelines that were presented and handed out to the workshop participants, and followed by the Future Workshop organizers (the researchers) during the implementation of the workshops. These guidelines provide an idea of how the process was planned and implemented as well as the time allocated to each phase and in total.

From a practice-based point of view, the major findings of the Future Workshops were a number of innovation ideas that were summarized by the researchers in an excel file and presented to RUB managers in a workshop. Examples of ideas include the "branding" of the library and library services to the users, as many students lack the knowledge of existing services, and signs on the floor to make it easier to find their way around the library. The ideas were then discussed in further meetings by RUB management and RUB's coordination committee, rank ordered according

---

BOX 10.1   FUTURE WORKSHOP TOPIC: ROSKILDE UNIVERSITY LIBRARY SERVICES

Idea and Purpose

A future workshop is based on democratic principles that ensure that all participants are allowed to express their opinions and to ensure that through the community feeling and commitment created during the workshop, the participants can provide constructive ideas and solutions that can have a real impact on what is implemented.

The results from this future workshop are intended to provide Roskilde University Library with good ideas for the development of the library and its services, concerning library supervision, library courses, e-services, interior design, opening hours.

Future Workshop Phases

The Future Workshop is organized into four distinct phases, respectively: criticism, fantasy, realistic suggestions and the implementation phase.

1. Criticism phase
Establishment of a common approach to the theme through the formulation of criticism about the topic. Are there consumer needs that the library does not satisfy? Are there existing services that do not work as expected? etc.

- All participants express, in turn, critical attitudes (no argument or discussion). Write criticisms on a Post-It note. Give a brief oral explanation to the rest of the participants when placed on the criticism-poster (15 min)
- End phase by identifying the criticisms, you think most important (5 min)

2. Fantasy phase
Now focus on how you would like Roskilde University Library to best support students and staff. Are there any new or different services, equipment or anything else that could do it really well? Wishes do not need to be realistic – rather be very creative. Find as many ideas as possible.

- Express the wishes and wants, in turn. The wilder the ideas the better. Write wishes and ideas on Post-It notes and explain them when you put them on the fantasy poster (No argument or discussion) (25 min)
- Exit again the phase by prioritizing the wishes you think are most important (5 min)

3. Realistic suggestions phase
Focus on the wishes of the fantasy phase, starting with those important and "move down" to those less important. How can the wishes be reformulated so that they become more realistic? Formulate realistic proposals. In this phase you have permission to discuss and concretize the spirit and wording of the "realistic proposal".

● Discuss and write down suggestions on Post-It notes and place them on the poster for realistic ideas along with a brief oral explanation (20 min)
● End phase by prioritizing the most important proposals (5 min)

4. Implementation phase
Now look at the suggestions from the realistic suggestions phase and consider how they can be implemented. What will it take to get the ideas realized? What suggestions can easily be realized, which ones require a little more planning/ conversion to realize? Who is implied?

● Write back on Post-It notes what the findings are (15 min)

---

to the relevance for RUB's management and most of them implemented in the following years. From a research point of view, the Future Workshops showed that both users and employees can contribute with innovative ideas. However, our study corroborated previous research by showing that most ideas contributed by the users are incremental in nature and that the most radical ones are difficult to implement in practice. In addition, the Future Workshops also showed that, even though employees were able to come up with innovative ideas, they used much time discussing questions concerning internal organizational politics, thus showing that it was difficult for them to completely detach from their daily work and organizational politics and instead concentrate on innovation issues. Finally, the mixed workshop was mainly characterized by the fact that the interaction, dynamics and discussion were all mainly driven by the employees.

10.4   DISCUSSION

Based on the experience with conducting the three Future Workshops in collaboration with Roskilde University Library, a number of lessons have emerged. First of all, the case shows that Future Workshops can indeed be used to investigate the various idea-generating potential of different actors, in our case RUB's employees and users. In addition the case shows that Future Workshops are also strong in the context of engaged research, thus providing benefits for both researchers and practitioners.

However, there are also some issues with regards to the application of the method in an engaged research context. For instance, the findings of Future Workshops are generally very context dependent. This was also the case in RUB because there were internal disagreements that somehow affected the employees' ideas and lessened their interest in participating.

This can, however, be both a limitation and an advantage of the method as Future Workshops can teach us something about how different contexts may impact on the potential of, for example, user-based innovation. Also one could say that Future Workshops may support a quick and inexpensive type of engaged research, meaning that you can get results quickly but the level of collaboration perhaps does not necessarily need to reach the same level as in, say, action research.

Concerning the planning and implementation of the Future Workshops, several learning lessons have emerged. For example, it is very important that the subject of the workshop is neither too broad, nor too narrow. In our case, we found that the subjects of the workshop were too broad and the contributed ideas could have been better if they had been formulated in a more precise and concrete way. Finding the right balance between these two aspects might be a difficult task.

Allocating the right time to the whole workshop and its different phases is very important. This could be related to the number of participants. For example, the participants in the Future Workshops who comprised only library users were very eager to talk and discuss the ideas and more time could have been used for the whole workshop. However, finding the right balance between depth and length of discussion and focus on the subject/ phase is a challenge to be kept in mind. Adding a fourth phase, the *realistic suggestions phase* to the Future Workshop in addition to the three original phases proposed by Jungk and Müllert (1987) has kept the focus on reality and minimized the ideas that cannot be implemented at the end. In addition, it was a good idea to give time to the participants to explain their idea when they wrote it on the Post-It note. Finally it might be a very good idea to keep contact with the organization benefiting from the workshops and take time to closely follow the implementation phase within the organization. We did this only to a limited extent with a follow-up interview and we feel that our research results would have been stronger if we had also more closely followed this part of the innovation process.

10.5 CONCLUSIONS

The study shows that Future Workshops can be a useful tool for service innovation research as Future Workshops provide benefits for both research and practice. Companies and organizations can conduct Future Workshops to generate ideas from different sets of actors, such as users, employees and suppliers. Such ideas can be used to innovate their services and service offerings. On the other hand the researchers might get useful insights into the extent to which these diverse groups of actors can contribute to the service innovation process, thus collecting data that can potentially contribute to different theoretical debates within innovation research such as user-driven innovation, open innovation, etc. This is especially relevant in engaged research where collaboration between industry and academia is a prerequisite and it is important that the method is beneficial for both involved parties. The Future Workshops set-up and the data generated during the Future Workshops in this study have contributed to understanding user and employee-driven innovation in service industries and specifically, library services.

However, the application of Future Workshops as a research method requires also a stronger commitment from the collaborating organization than just practice-based Future Workshops. The collaborating organization, in fact, needs to provide data of relevance to the research of the collaborating research institution and together establish a common ground for conducting the workshops.

Finally, conducting Future Workshops requires some extra attention as the findings are often context dependent and the method might support a quick and inexpensive type of collaboration in respect to, for example, action research.

LEARNING POINTS

- It is important to select, motivate and involve the right people in the workshops as they are context dependent and their results depend on the participants and internal workshop dynamics.
- It is important to take time to follow up the implementation phase of the ideas generated in the workshops and eventually conduct new ones for further idea generation/refinement as suggested by Vidal (2006).
- Adding a fourth phase (the realistic suggestion phase) to the three standard phases of the Future Workshops might lead to ideas that are easier to implement at the end.

DISCUSSION TOPICS

- Are there contexts in which the method is a better choice than in others?
- Are there contexts and situations where the method should not be considered at all?

- What kind of aspects could the method illustrate in the specific context in which it is considered to be applied?

REFERENCES

Alam, I. (2002), "An exploratory investigation of user involvement in new service development," *Journal of the Academy of Marketing Science*, 30(3), 250–261.

Alam, I. and C. Perry (2002), "A customer-oriented new service development process," *Journal of Services Marketing*, 16(6), 515–534.

Chesbrough, H. W. (2003), *Open Innovation: The New Imperative for Creating and Profiting from Technology*. Boston: Harvard Business School Press.

Chesbrough, H. W. (2006), *Open Business Model: How to Thrive in the New Innovation Landscape*. Watertown: Harvard Business Press.

Dator, J. (1993), "From future workshops to envisioning alternative futures," *Futures Research Quarterly*, 9(3), 108–112.

Hennestad, B. W. (1999), "Infusing the organisation with customer knowledge," *Scandinavian Journal of Management*, 15(1), 17–41.

Jungk, R. and N. Müllert (1987), *Future Workshops: How to Create Desirable Futures*. London: Institute for Social Inventions.

Kensing, F. and K. H. Madsen (1992), "Generating visions: Future workshops and metaphorical design," in J. Greenbaum and M. Kyng (eds.), *Design at Work*. Hillsdale: Erlbaum Associates Inc.

Kristensson, P., A. Gustafsson and T. Archer (2003), "Harnessing the creative potential among users," *Product Innovation Management*, 21(1), 4–14.

Magnusson, P. (2003), "Benefits of involving users in service," *European Journal of Innovation Management*, 6(4), 228–238.

Magnusson, P., J. Matthing and P. Kristensson (2003), "Managing user involvement in service innovation," *Journal of Service Research*, 6(2), 111–124.

Matthing, J., B. Sandén and B. Edvardsson (2004), "New service development: Learning from and with customers," *International Journal of Service Industry Management*, 15(5), 479–498.

Nambisan, S. (2002), "Designing virtual customer environments for new product development: Toward a theory," *The Academy of Management Review*, 27(33), 392–413.

Nicolajsen, H.W. and A. Scupola (2011), "Investigating issues and challenges for customer involvement in business services innovation," *Journal of Business and Industrial Marketing*, 26(5), 368–376.

Piller, T. T. and D. Walcher (2006), "Toolkits for idea competitions: A novel method to integrate users in new product development", *R&D Management*, 36(3), 307–318.

Polewsky, S. and H. Will (1996), "Creativity workshops: Tools for innovation in organizations?," *European Journal of Work and Organizational Psychology*, 5(1), 43–51.

Rogers, E. M. (1995), *The Diffusion of Innovations*, 4th edition. New York: Free Press.

Scupola, A. and H. W. Nicolajsen (2010), "Service innovation in academic libraries: Is there a place for the customers?," *Library Management*, 31(4/5), 304–318.

Scupola, A. and A. Zanfei (2016), "Governance and innovation in public sector services: The case of digital library," *Government Information Quarterly*, In press.

Sundbo, J. (2010), *Medarbejder- og brugerbaseret innovation i service: Servicevirksomhedernes organisering af innovationsarbejdet*, Research Report No 8, Center for Servicestudies, Roskilde University.

Sundbo, J. and Toivonen, M. (eds.) (2011), *User-based Innovation in Services*. Cheltenham, UK and Northampton, MA, USA: Edward Elgar Publishing.

Van de Ven, A. H. (2007), *Engaged Scholarship: Creating Knowledge for Science and Practice*. Oxford: Oxford University Press.

Vidal, V. (2006), "The future workshop: Democratic problem solving," *Economic Analysis Working Papers*, 5(4), 21.

von Hippel, E. (1986), "Lead users: A source of novel product concepts." *Management Science*, 32(7), 791–805.

von Hippel, E. (1989), "New product ideas from 'Lead Users,'" *Research Technology Management*, 32(3), 24–27.

von Hippel, E. (2001), "User toolkits for innovation," *Journal of Product Innovation Management*, 18(4), 247–257.

von Hippel, E. and R. Katz (2002), "Shifting innovation to users via toolkits," *Management Science*, 48(7), 821–833.

Yin, R. K. (1994), *Case Study Research Design and Methods*, 2nd edition, Vol. 5. Thousand Oaks: Sage Publications.

11. Service innovation field experiments: developing and testing new innovation processes

Flemming Sørensen

11.1 INTRODUCTION

This chapter discusses the potential of field experiments in service innovation research. Experiments are rarely used in research on innovation and this also applies to service innovation research (however, see Magnusson et al., 2003; van Rijnsoever, Meeus, and Donders, 2012). However, Sørensen et al. (2010) have discussed the potentials of different experimental methods in innovation research. This chapter further develops their arguments by relating them to service innovation research, taking into consideration the specific characteristics of services, service innovation and service innovation processes. In particular the chapter will argue that *field* experiments have specific and strong potential in service innovation research.

Field experiments are carried out in real life (as opposed to laboratory experiments) (Harrison and List, 2004). In service innovation research, they can include experiments with innovation processes or with other aspects that may have an impact on service innovation, such as managerial and employee routines and practices, organisational and conceptual issues and value propositions. The settings for such experiments are service organisations where the experiments are carried out in close collaboration between researchers and the organisations' management and employees, and if relevant, their users. Service innovation field experiments are therefore integrated with real-life service innovation practices, and they sustain the development of service innovation processes that can increase service organisations' innovativeness. They are related to different types of interactive and engaged research methods that rely on close collaboration between researchers and practitioners. Thus, service innovation field experiments represent a typology of research methods that satisfy society's call for collaboration between academia and businesses and for the development of applicable knowledge (as discussed in the introductory chapter). Furthermore, service innovation field experiments can test prototypes of service innovation procedures. Thus, they can create knowledge that cannot be developed using other service innovation research methods, which mainly investigate characteristics and outcomes of already existing innovation procedures. In other words, in other service innovation research methods, researchers are mostly a step behind real-life initiatives, but in field experiments, researchers take the development initiative in collaboration with companies.

In this chapter, the potential of field experiments in service innovation research is illustrated by the example of an experiment in a hotel where the joint development of new practices led to immediate as well as derived service innovations (Sørensen and Jensen, 2015). The experiment was rooted in the theoretical argument that front-line employees are important actors, not only concerning the service experience (Bitner et al., 1990; Carlzon, 1989; Nickson et al., 2005), but also in relation to service innovation because of their interactions with users (Fuglsang and Sørensen, 2011; Sørensen, Sundbo, and Mattsson, 2013). The experiment aimed at developing and testing new practices among front-line employees that could enhance their role in service innovation. The findings of the experiment in relation to several theoretical arguments have been presented in Sørensen and Jensen (2015). In this chapter, the focus is put on the methodological aspects of the experiment, which are emphasised and discussed to illustrate the possible methodological set-ups and potential benefits of service innovation field experiments.

The chapter will first briefly discuss the nature and benefits of field experiments. This discussion will be followed by an introduction to the possible application of field experiments in service innovation research. Subsequently, the hotel experiment example is presented after which different learning points will be discussed. Finally, the conclusions about the potentials of service innovation field experiments are presented.

11.2 FIELD EXPERIMENTS

Social sciences often associate experiments with those of natural sciences, i.e. positivist experiments carried out in laboratories, which are entities disconnected from 'real life' (Neuman, 2000). In such social science laboratory experiments, researchers investigate how changes controlled by the researchers of one (independent) variable affect another (dependent) variable. Participants in the experiments are typically individuals who are randomly assigned to groups. These groups are treated differently, and the result of this differentiated treatment is measured in numbers (Sørensen et al., 2010; Willer and Harry, 2007). Laboratory experiments are considered to offer an objective, unbiased and scientific way to study social life (Neuman, 2000). Such laboratory experiments have benefits but also obvious limitations. Their advantages are, for example, that experimental conditions can be controlled so that no other interfering variables influence the results. This can ensure the internal validity of such experiments. The disadvantages are, for example, that laboratory experiments cannot easily measure more complex processes. Instead, to simulate and measure such complex processes in laboratory settings, variables must be manipulated and simple indicators of behaviours must be applied, which can limit the external validity of such experiments (Sørensen et al., 2010). Service innovation processes often belong to such complex processes and are therefore not directly suitable for laboratory experiments. However, experiments include a variety of studies, which have the common characteristic that they investigate how changes in a dependent variable are caused by planned/deliberate actions upon independent variables (Sørensen et al., 2010), and these experiments are not confined to positivist studies in isolated laboratory settings. Such methods include different techniques that are often referred to as 'quasi-experiments' (including, for example, laboratory experiments without control groups or without random assignment to groups) (Neuman, 2000). Importantly, these quasi-experiments also include field experiments, which are experiments situated in real-life contexts instead of in laboratories. They include studies that observe the effects induced by changes that are deliberately caused by an investigator in collaboration with other actors in real life. The settings in which such experiments can be carried out can include companies (Gibbs et al., 2014; Wang, Noe, and Wang, 2011), public entities, e.g. schools (Shadish, Cook, and Campbell, 2002), and elderly care (Fuglsang and Sørensen, 2011; Langer and Rodin, 1976), urban environments (Mattsson and Sørensen, 2015) or even broader social settings, for example, in studies of employment (Bertrand and Mullainathan, 2003).

As opposed to the traditional positivist laboratory experiment, field experiments may rely on quantitative *or* qualitative techniques (observations, interviews, etc.). Thus, they may belong to both positivist and more interpretivist, hermeneutical or constructivist research paradigms. A qualitative and interpretivist approach may be preferred if the complexities manipulated within experiments cannot be measured or understood through quantitative data analysis (Lee, 1989). Field experiments can also benefit from mixed methods (Johnson and Onwuegbuzie, 2011) and a pragmatic (Morgan, 2007) research approach. This can, for example, be the case when effects may be measured numerically but the process leading to the effects cannot.

11.3   FIELD EXPERIMENTS AND SERVICE INNOVATION RESEARCH

Laboratory experiments can hardly demonstrate the more complex aspects of innovation processes. Nevertheless, a few such laboratory experiment studies have been published. Darai et al. (2010), for example, investigated the impact of competition on innovation, and van Rijnsoever et al. (2012) measured the effects of economic status on innovative behaviour in a laboratory experiment. In the latter of the mentioned studies, measures included the relation between points representing money possessed by students and their willingness to risk their points in a card laying game (van Rijnsoever et al., 2012). Yet laboratory experiments cannot ensure that such variables represent real-life innovation variables nor that they affect each other in similar ways or are not affected by other variables in real-life settings (Green and Gerber, 2003). Thus the need for simplification of otherwise complex innovation processes and the use of artificial constructs to measure them and their potential outcomes make such processes less prone to laboratory experiments, and the construct as well as external validity of such innovation laboratory experiments can often be questioned.

Instead, service innovation experiments are more beneficially carried out in real life. While such field experiments have been almost absent from service innovation studies, a few articles about service innovation experiments have been published recently indicating an increasing interest in such experiments. These include studies of user and employee-driven innovation in mobile services (Magnusson et al., 2003), tourism (Sørensen, 2011; Sørensen and Jensen, 2015), attractions (Sørensen and Sundbo, 2014), libraries (Scupola and Nicolajsen, 2013), public home help services (Fuglsang and Sørensen, 2011) and in a high-tech company (Gibbs et al., 2014). The studies indicate the suitability of field experiments in service innovation research. A reason for this is, for example, that services are often easy and inexpensive to experiment with. Because services are often produced and consumed simultaneously through interactions in service encounters between users and employees (Nickson et al., 2005; Sørensen et al., 2013), it is, for example, easy to test new production methods, that is, changed practices in service encounters. Equally because service innovation processes mostly do not occur as laboratory R&D work but can be interwoven with daily practices (Fuglsang and Sørensen, 2011; Sørensen et al., 2013; Toivonen and Tuominen, 2009), it may be relatively low-cost and easy to develop and introduce new practices that may be assumed to sustain service innovation and develop the innovation capability of the participating service company. For the same reasons service firms often carry out their own 'experiments', for example, trying out and evaluating new ways of communicating with customers to develop the customer experience. However, service firms mostly do not carry out systematic experiments based on methodological and scientific considerations. Instead they are more like unplanned, trial-and-error, practical attempts (Sundbo, 2010). In comparison, research-based service innovation field experiments will often be informed by theory and be based on academic methodological and scientific considerations, which sustain the creation of both practical and scientific knowledge and learning.

While there is no strict general method to apply in service innovation field experiments, a typical experiment will be based on five and potentially six phases (Figure 11.1):

Relationship Building

This first phase is not part of the actual experiment as such but is nevertheless crucial for the following phases. Building relations with organisations is important in all research that involves some kind of collaboration between researchers and companies. However, because field experiments involve the intervention, development and application of new procedures in the organisation in close collaboration between researchers and the organisation, the development of trust, common knowledge, common interests and common goals is particularly relevant in this kind of research. This first phase may have a long duration and the possibility for carrying out an experiment often develops out of already existing knowledge and trust-based relations between researchers and organisations. This phase may partially overlap with the following phase.

Initial Case Study

The initial case study, which can be exploratory (inductive) or more theory-based (deductive) or abductive, has the purpose of detecting issues or illuminating already detected issues related to service innovation in the organisation that the experiment will attempt to solve. Such issues can be related to idea generation processes, user involvement in innovation, idea selection processes, creativity enhancing procedures, implementation processes and so forth.

Developing and Designing

The phase involves considerations about the specific actions that must be taken in order to attempt to solve the identified problem. Such actions will typically include changing existing or developing new innovation practices,

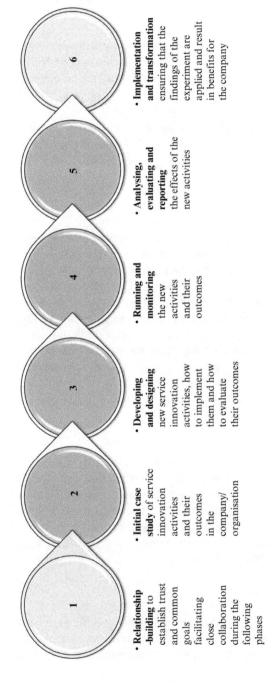

Figure 11.1   The phases of a typical service innovation field experiment

activities or procedures. The design will be guided by the case study findings and by some theoretical assumption or hypothesis. Importantly, it
should be designed in collaboration with the management of the company
and those employees who may be affected by and should implement the
experiment. This secures the anchoring of the experiment in the company
and ensures that it is accepted by its employees.

Running and Monitoring

The researchers' involvement in the experiment during its execution can
be more or less intense. In some service innovation field experiments, it
can make sense that the involved researchers participate in the experiments and even act as facilitators, for example, in short-term experiments
(such as workshops). In other cases this is not viable and data collection
may consist mainly of interviews carried out with participants during or
after the experiment has taken place. Participants may include employees,
management, users and so on, depending on the specific experimental
set-up and its context. One way or the other, some kind of monitoring
of the experiment is needed during its execution, for example, through
regular contact with the company and/or the involved employees. Such
monitoring is important and necessary, so as to avoid unforeseen negative
consequences of the experiment or other potential sticking points (see the
discussion section of this chapter).

Analysing, Reporting and Discussing Findings

Analysing and even reporting and discussing findings may occur during
the experiment, but the most important part of this phase will normally
take place after the experiment has been run. After collecting and analysing the data, the researcher should present the findings and possible suggestions to the experiment's participants and discuss these findings and
suggestions with them. This optimises the benefits of the collaboration for
the company, for example, in relation to organisational learning, but it will
also sustain the reliability of the research findings by ensuring intersubjec-
tive interpretations.

Implementation and Transformation

This potential phase will be focused on anchoring the relevant new procedures in the organisation and thereby ensuring that the benefits of the
experiment, for instance in terms of raising the innovation capability of
the company, are finally achieved. This may require various organisational

and managerial adjustments. From a research point of view this phase is interesting as it illuminates the adjustments needed for implementing the new procedures in the daily life of the organisation and in the wider organisational context.

As is suggested above, the service innovation field experiment method, including all its phases, may start out by applying an inductive or deductive logic. However, the experiment itself will predominantly be deductive in its logic as its nature is to test assumptions, propositions or hypotheses about how new procedures, activities or practices affect service innovation. Additionally, data collection can be qualitative, quantitative or mixed and can include various data collection methods. In this sense the service innovation field experiment can beneficially rely on a pragmatic approach to social science (Morgan, 2007) in which the choice of data-collection methods depends on considerations about what type of data help answer the research question in the best way, rather than on paradigmatic stances about what type of data is generally more valid. This pragmatic approach goes hand in hand with the general purpose of the service innovation field experiment which is, fundamentally, to find solutions to problems encountered in real life that are related to service innovation and simultaneously develop new theoretical insights.

Furthermore, following the above suggestions, soliciting responses from the participants and having prolonged collaboration with the service company can secure the trustworthiness of the findings (Lincoln and Guba, 2007; Morgan, 2007). This may also help researchers detect Hawthorne, reactivity and demand characteristics effects and help researchers consider these effects when analysing the experiment. Hawthorne effects may arise from experimental set-ups when participants act in particular ways simply because they know they are participating in an experiment (McCambridge et al., 2014; Neuman, 2000). Demand effects occur when participants attempt to create the effects they know (or think) the research is looking for (Boot et al., 2011; Klein et al., 2012). Service innovation field experiments will typically include activities of employees and managers with whom the experiment is developed and planned. Such experiments may therefore be particularly prone to bias caused by the above-mentioned effects. Thus, such effects and their importance should be taken into consideration and detected, for example, through qualitative interviews. When they are detected, acknowledged and considered as an aspect of the analysis, such effects are not necessarily problematic in service innovation field experiments. In that case they become, instead, part of the explanation of why the experiment failed or succeeded and how it did so.

In service innovation field experiments, researchers have less control over events than in laboratory experiments, given the real-life context.

However, this limitation is outweighed by other benefits and potentials of these experiments. They include the fact that results are based on investigations of real-world service innovation processes instead of manipulated processes in laboratory settings. This means that the construct validity is easier to establish. Furthermore, (as mentioned initially) qualitative field experiments are related to a wider field of interactive research methods carried out by researchers in interactions with practice (see also the introductory chapter of this book as well as Chapter 7 on blogs and Chapter 10 on future workshops). In such methods interpretations of results should be made by researchers together with representatives of those for whom results are relevant (Gummesson, 2000; McNiff and Whitehead, 2000). This increases the findings' reliability and means that service innovation field experiments can create new knowledge of direct relevance for innovation practitioners in service companies while they also solve their real-life problems, often related to how to enhance the innovativeness of their service organisation.

A possible limitation of the method is (like in other types of experiments) that it operates with a few variables, which must be of a relatively simple nature (though they can and must be more abstract than in a quantitative laboratory experiment). Nevertheless, this means that the service innovation field experiment method can sustain the analysis of relatively specific cause–effect service innovation relations in otherwise complex organisational set-ups and processes. Service innovation field experiments may focus on individual innovation processes in complex contexts, but they cannot ignore the role of the context. Therefore, findings of field experiments may not be generalised in a positivistic sense. They can, however, still be of general interest because they may be transferred and adapted in other contexts (cf. the transferability concept, Morgan, 2007).

In the next section the hotel experiment is presented as an example of a simple, yet powerful, service innovation field experiment. Based on the presentation, additional issues related to service innovation field experiments will subsequently be discussed.

11.4 EXAMPLE: DEVELOPING SERVICE ENCOUNTER-BASED INNOVATION IN A HOTEL

The example concerns a service innovation field experiment carried out in collaboration with a small design hotel in Copenhagen. Its aim was to develop knowledge-creating mechanisms of the hotel reception's service encounters, that is, the meetings between front-line employees of the reception desk and the guests of the hotel, to sustain innovation in the hotel.

Service encounters are important for users' evaluation of service quality (Bitner et al., 1990; Carlzon, 1989), but they can also result in knowledge and information about users and thereby sustain user-based innovation in service companies (Engen and Magnusson, 2015; Sørensen et al., 2013). However, in hotels most service encounters are highly standardised, one-way service deliveries that are focused on efficiency, so there is hardly any room for communication and knowledge creation in hotel service encounters (Sørensen and Jensen, 2012). While co-creation in service encounters can improve customer experiences and provide unique knowledge about unique customers (Boswijk et al., 2007; Prahalad and Ramaswamy, 2004), this potential is not generally or automatically utilised in hotel service encounters (Binkhorst and Den Dekker, 2009). Consequently service encounter-based innovation (Sørensen et al., 2013) is not widespread in hotels (Sørensen and Jensen, 2012, 2015). As described below this was also evident in the case hotel. The aim of the service innovation experiment was to test if and how this situation could be changed. The experiment consisted of six phases as outlined in Figure 11.2.

Phase 1

The relationship between one of the researchers involved in the experiment and the hotel went back a long time and was established while the hotel manager was studying a Masters degree. Later the manager and the researcher collaborated in various university-related events and in an expert group. The possibility for more intense and close development-oriented collaboration grew out of this relationship, and out of the common interests and trust between the researcher and the manager.

Phase 2

This phase consisted of a brief initial preliminary case study, including semi-structured interviews with managers and employees and observations of service encounters. The case study showed how the hotel's service encounters were traditional and highly standardised and did not support the idea that knowledge was created about users of the hotel. As a consequence the hotel had limited knowledge about the users, and front-line employees had little influence on innovation in the hotel. Knowledge about users was confined to such that could be derived from traditional hotel satisfaction questionnaires and from websites such as TripAdvisor. However,

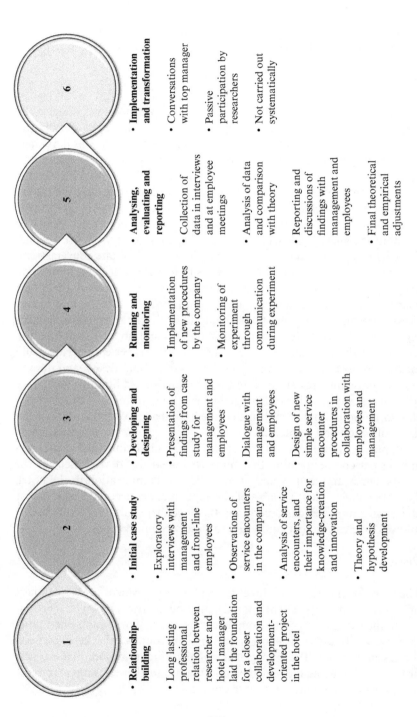

Figure 11.2   The six phases of the hotel service innovation field experiment

more profound knowledge, for example, about users' latent needs, was non-existent (for a detailed description see Sørensen and Jensen, 2015).

Phase 3

Based on the findings of the pilot study, the experiment was designed by the managers and researchers in collaboration with the receptionists in an employee meeting. Thus the service innovation experiment was developed in a relatively flat organisational mode and not dictated by the top management. New simple work practices that could easily be implemented by the front-line employees were developed at the employee meeting: First, allocation of rooms before the arrival of guests should be avoided to provide an opportunity to converse with the guests about the hotel's design as well as about the guests' (latent) needs when they arrived at the hotel. Second, front-line employees should use simple phrases to facilitate conversations, such as asking guests why they were visiting the city, to gain knowledge about what they wanted to experience during the course of their stay. Third, in the conversations resulting from the first and the second practices, front-line employees should apply their 'local' knowledge concerning the hotel and its rooms and their design, and about the destination to support the co-creation of the guests' tourist experiences. This could include, for example, the employees' knowledge about design and designers, art museums, restaurants and exhibitions. In addition to the above procedures, information about guests resulting from the conversations should be noted and stored in the hotel database to create a systematic data collection and a potential to use this for development activities. These small practices should lead to more flexible and individualised encounters and deeper communication that supports knowledge development of the guests' needs and desires and, in turn, supports innovation in the hotel. Thus, the independent variable of the experiment concerned a new way of communicating with customers, and the dependent variables concerned 1) knowledge creation that could lead to 2) service innovations.

Phase 4

The experiment ran for three months during which the researchers 'monitored' the experiment by participating in two employee meetings where the experiences of the employees using the newly established practices were discussed. Furthermore, regular contact was kept between the researchers and the management of the hotel to ensure that the new processes were being implemented and that no further assistance from the researchers was required during the process.

Phase 5

The analysis of the experiment was based on the information retrieved from the employee meetings, frequent contact with the managers during the experiment, and from a more formal interview with the top manager shortly after the experiment. The findings were presented during a final employee meeting, and feedback from the employees was retrieved to ensure that the analytical findings matched the employees' perceptions.

Phase 6

The five phases were followed by later conversations between researchers and the hotel's top manager, which supplied important information about the experiment's results and about how the results transformed organisational, managerial and employee practices in the company. However, in this sixth phase the researchers only participated passively.

Condensing the findings of the experiment in a brief summary, the results can be divided into two groups: 1) new knowledge creation and 2) bricolage and innovation (see Sørensen and Jensen (2015) for a full and theoretically based analysis).

1. New knowledge
Due to the new approach, it was quickly discovered, through personal communication, what guests desired from their visit to the city. For example, not allocating rooms to the guests before their arrival resulted in new conversations with guests, which led to new insights about them. This concerned, for example, knowledge about individual guests' preferences – guests who showed interest in the Danish design were allocated rooms decorated with that particular design (thus resulting in upselling). It also included knowledge about the more general characteristics of the guests (e.g. that the guests generally preferred rooms facing the street in spite of its noise). Also, the conversations resulting from the practice of asking guests about their reasons for choosing to stay at the hotel and in the city resulted in new information about what the guests desired from their visit. When the employees used their individual knowledge to help the guests create more valuable experiences, this resulted in further conversations and the co-creation of value. For example, from knowing what activities or trips the guests were planning during their stay, the employees could provide insider knowledge and tips that could enhance the guests' experiences, giving them the feeling that they had received unique and personalised attention.

2. Bricolage and innovation

The information gained from the new conversations with the guests resulted in a new knowledge-base in the company. Because information about guests (gained from the flexible encounters) was now noted in the booking system, the knowledge could be used strategically to innovate. Noting down information also resulted in a better distribution of guest information between the employees as well as between employees and the management. While some knowledge derived from the new encounters was of immediate use for creating improved guest experiences for individual guests (in a sort of bricolage) (Fuglsang and Sørensen, 2011; Salunke, Weerawardena, and McColl-Kennedy, 2013), some knowledge also led to ideas for innovations of new features that could enhance guests' experiences more generally. For example, connections between the changing desires of tourists and the changing offerings at destination were identified. This, for example, led to knowledge about the popularity of different restaurants and art exhibitions among the hotel's typical guests. This gave rise to the idea of making an information utility and finally of developing an iPhone and smartphone application ('Design CPH by Hotel Alexandra'). This application provides continually updated information about sights, exhibitions, restaurants, etc., which are observed to be of particular relevance to the guests of the hotel at any time.

Thus, the experiment illustrated and confirmed the assumption that by substituting standardised service encounters with flexible and interactive encounters through simple practices, valuable new knowledge about customers could be gained that can support service innovation.

11.5   DISCUSSION

The experiment illustrates the possible benefits of service innovation field experiments. For example, the experiment utilised the nature of services, including the close relation between production and consumption, and thus the central role of the service encounter, and the fact that service innovation processes are often rooted in service practices.

However, the example also results in a discussion about other issues related to such experiments. These include issues regarding 1) which phases of the innovation process can be experimented with; 2) if and to what degree experiments result in 'true' innovations (leading to economic benefits) or just good ideas; 3) the potentially positive or negative side effects and the research ethics of experiments; and 4) the generalised and combined practical and research relevance of service innovation field experiments.

11.5.1   Experimentation with Different Phases of Service Innovation Processes

The described experiment focused mainly on the knowledge and idea-generating part of the service innovation process and on improving the conditions for this 'fuzzy front-end innovation process' (Alam, 2006). This has also been the case for other recently reported service innovation experiments (Fuglsang and Sørensen, 2011; Scupola and Nicolajsen, 2013; Sørensen, 2011; Sørensen and Sundbo, 2014). Reasons for this may be rooted in the ease with which such processes can be experimented with and because this is the natural first step of the innovation process. Stepping into the innovation process at a later point and doing experiments in such innovation phases may be more complicated. Furthermore, the costs of experiments may be an issue in some contexts. The described experiment had a simple and inexpensive set-up (for researchers and the company) partly because it focused on the knowledge-creating and idea-generating process. Nevertheless, it still had a significant effect on innovation in the hotel as it fed ideas into the later stages of the innovation process. Also in other types of experiments with the so-called fuzzy front-end service innovation process, such experiments may have low implementation costs. Because most services are produced in interactions between users and producers (and often mediated by front-line employees) (Bitner, 1990; Kallio, 2015; Sørensen et al., 2013), service innovation is often rooted in practice and occurs as bricolage (Fuglsang, 2010; Salunke et al., 2013) under the right conditions (Fuglsang and Sørensen, 2011), and experiments with service innovation can also often be rooted in practice and therefore be inexpensive. However, while the fuzzy front-end is perhaps particularly prone to being experimented with, experimenting with, for example, processes of development and implementation are also possible. This has been done recently in experiments in the Danish NICE Project (NICE: New Innovative Customer Experiences; see Chapter 12 in this book) in which new tourist experiences have been developed in companies, for example, in a hotel and a zoo, by intervening in the development and design phase of the innovation process. Furthermore, innovation processes in service companies do not always follow sequential processes neatly, but may jump back and forth between phases in a more reflexive process of idea generation, and the development and implementation of new innovations may occur more or less simultaneously, and idea generation may become integrated with the later phases of innovation, which also unintentionally happened in the experiment.

11.5.2   Innovations or Just Good Ideas?

Especially when the focus of service innovation field experiments is on the fuzzy front-end of innovation, the question is whether the experiment leads to real (i.e. economically beneficial) innovations and not just good (or bad) ideas. The experiment reported above resulted in improved guest experiences immediately as a result of the adjusted encounter procedures (which were small innovations themselves) and in innovations in the longer term, which were based on the new knowledge derived from the changed encounters. The new procedures and the innovations led to more satisfied guests. Increased customer satisfaction was observed in practice by front-line employees as well as by the manager who systematically audited guest evaluations and recommendations on various websites (e.g. booking.com and TripAdvisor.com) as well as in traditional customer surveys. Improved customer satisfaction, customer loyalty, increased sales, etc. can be considered final aims of service innovations and, thus also of service innovation field experiments. Identifying such values of innovations ensures that the new or improved services or service processes resulting from a service innovation field experiment have an economic value for the company and, thus, can be considered true innovations according to definitions, which emphasise that innovations are only innovations if they have an economic impact (e.g. Schumpeter, 1969). Chapter 2 in this book discusses how to measure the value of inputs to and outputs from service innovation processes. Such methods can be beneficially integrated with service innovation field experiments to estimate their success.

11.5.3   Side Effects and Research Ethics

The above described experiment induced a number of positive side effects, some of which the researchers had expected and others which they had not thought of when designing the experiment. The first group of side effects is related to organisational learning and the professional development of individual employees. Such organisational learning and individual development should be taken into consideration when planning service innovation field experiments to enhance their benefits. In the described experiment such learning and development included a new perspective on services and experiences and of value creation in the hotel. To the second group of side effects belonged improved satisfaction with working conditions and enthusiasm among the employees, which resulted in a reduced employee turnover in the hotel. For example, the employees no longer felt they were only service-facilitators but also co-creators of experiences, which they felt gave their jobs a new interesting dimension. Conversely, for some employees the experiment resulted in certain insecurity. For example, some of the employees' professionalism and habits initially posed a barrier for integrating the new procedures in the service encounter. These issues were not severe but they indicate the danger of poorly planned experiments because they may have a number of less positive side effects. The potential harm to individuals, unreasonable demands or pressure on participants must, according to general research ethics, be avoided and handled carefully (Ritchie et al., 2013; Webster and Sell, 2014). This raises ethical questions about the use and proper planning of field experiments as a research strategy because, by introducing change in real-life conditions, field experiments may easily come into conflict with such ethical demands. Whereas in service innovation field experiments, the underlying interest is to facilitate development of favourable service innovation procedures and when doing so to avoid any negative effects, the complex context dependence of the manipulated and investigated processes may easily result in unthought-of negative effects in other places or processes of the system. However, when service innovation field experiments are carefully planned and developed and, not least, carried out in close collaboration with companies, it can be possible to avoid most negative impacts in the design phase because the company will have knowledge about potential negative impacts and will (normally) be interested in avoiding these. Furthermore, monitoring (by researchers as well as managers) of the experiment will make sure that most negative impacts will be observed and detected quickly, and the experiment may be adjusted or stopped in case of such negative impacts.

11.5.4 Generalised Relevance for Research and Practice of Findings

Findings of service innovation field experiments can be relevant at the practical level for other companies because the experiment is practice-based and related to real-life problems. While the hotel described in this chapter can be considered unique due to its design, it may on the other hand be considered typical in terms of its service encounters and its lack of service encounter-based innovation and when considering the potential to develop such service encounter-based innovation. Thus at a more general level, it is not a unique characteristic that the hotel produced standardised service encounters. This is a more general characteristic of most hotels of a certain quality (Sørensen and Jensen, 2012). Thus though the hotel is unique in terms of its design, other companies may develop similar procedures as those tested in the experiment and may derive similar benefits. Consequently in service innovation field experiments, the concept of transferability (Morgan, 2007) becomes relevant and even more so because service innovation experiment set-ups can be relatively inexpensive and simple and, therefore, also relatively easy and inexpensive to copy and adapt by other companies.

11.6   CONCLUSION

This chapter has presented the field experiment and argued that it is an important but largely ignored method for doing service innovation research. Service innovation field experiments are an alternative to traditional service innovation research methods, and they provide a number of benefits. The findings of service innovation field experiments have an important research interest, as well as practical importance. In particular two characteristics of field experiments make them specifically interesting for developing research knowledge as well as knowledge that is relevant for practitioners. First, service innovation field experiments are integrated with practice and involve close collaboration between researchers and practitioners, and they attempt to provide solutions to real-life problems. Second, service innovation field experiments do not simply investigate existing innovation procedures but can develop new innovation procedures and test their potential importance. Thus, service innovation field experiments can test how to solve real-life service innovation problems in close collaboration with practitioners by developing new previously non-existent innovation processes or practices, and they can provide research as well as practical knowledge that other service innovation research methods cannot provide. Consequently, both researchers and companies learn from the method, which can result in new service innovations, organisational development, new service innovation capabilities and in new research knowledge and theories about service innovation.

While loaded with such benefits, the method also has some limitations. One such limitation concerns the limited generalisability of results (in a positivist sense) due to the context dependence of the experiments and their results. However, because the method is highly practice-oriented and practice-based there is a strong possibility for transferability of results, that is, the possibility of applying results in other settings, taking into consideration the new context (Morgan, 2007). Thus, knowledge provided by specific service innovation field experiments may be adapted to and applied in the contexts of other service companies.While field experiments have not been used much in service innovation research, this chapter has indicated how they can be a valuable complement to other service innovation research methods. Service innovation field experiments are tied to service practices and result from interactions between practitioners and researchers. Thus, service innovation field experiments create scientific results while solving practical problems. Whereas other methods typically collect and analyse data on already existing applied service innovation initiatives, service innovation field experiments join researchers and companies at the frontier of development of new service innovation processes. Consequently, the service innovation field experiment should have a more important and central role in future service innovation research.

LEARNING POINTS

- Service innovation field experiments can develop and test new service innovation procedures in collaboration with companies.
- A service innovation field experiment consists of six different phases: relationship building, initial case study, developing and designing, running and monitoring, analysing and reporting and, finally, implementation and transformation.
- Service innovation field experiments develop knowledge that can mostly not be provided by other methods. Furthermore, the knowledge is highly relevant for research as well as for practitioners.
- The results of service innovation field experiments are often easy to transfer to other service contexts.

DISCUSSION TOPICS

- Are there situations where the service innovation field experiment method is a less fortunate choice because of ethical concerns?
- What are the differences and similarities between service innovation field experiments, action research and engaged research?
- How and when can different data-collection techniques be relevant in service innovation field experiments?

REFERENCES

Alam, I. (2006), 'Removing the fuzziness from the fuzzy front-end of service innovations through customer interactions', *Industrial Marketing Management*, 35(4), 468–480.

Bertrand, M., and S. Mullainathan (2003), 'Are Emily and Greg more employable than Lakisha and Jamal? A field experiment on labor market discrimination', No. w9873. National Bureau of Economic Research.

Binkhorst, E., and T. Den Dekker (2009), 'Agenda for co-creation tourism experience research', *Journal of Hospitality Marketing & Management*, 18(2–3), 311–327.

Bitner, M. (1990), 'Evaluating service encounters: The effects of physical surroundings and employee responses', *Journal of Marketing*, 54(2), 69–82.

Bitner, M.J., B.H. Booms, and M.S. Tetreault (1990), 'The service encounter: Diagnosing favorable and unfavorable incidents', *Journal of Marketing*, 54(1), 71–84.

Boot, W.R., D.P. Blakely, and D.J. Simons (2011), 'Do action video games improve perception and cognition?', *Frontiers in Psychology*, 2, Art. 226.

Boswijk, A., T. Thijssen, and E. Peelen (2007), *The Experience Economy: A New Perspective*. New York: Pearson Education.

Carlzon, J. (1989), *Moments of Truth*. New York: HarperCollins.

Darai, D., D. Sacco, and A. Schmutzler (2010), 'Competition and innovation: An experimental investigation', *Experimental Economics*, 13, 439–460.

Engen, M., and P. Magnusson (2015), 'Exploring the role of front-line employees as innovators', *The Service Industries Journal*, 35(6), 303–324.

Fuglsang, L. (2010), 'Bricolage and invisible innovation in public service innovation', *Journal of Innovation Economics*, (1), 67–87.

Fuglsang, L., and F. Sørensen (2011), 'The balance between bricolage and innovation: Management dilemmas in sustainable public innovation', *The Service Industries Journal*, 31(4), 581–595.

Gibbs, M., S. Neckermann, and C. Siemroth (2014), 'A field experiment in motivating employee ideas', IZA Discussion Paper No. 8096, Institute for the Study of Labor.

Green, D.D.P., and A.A.S. Gerber (2003), 'The underprovision of experiments in political science', *The Annals of the American Academy of Political and Social Science*, 589(1), 94–112.

Gummesson, E. (2000), *Qualitative Methods in Management Research*. London: Sage.

Harrison, G., and J. List (2004), 'Field experiments', *Journal of Economic Literature*, XLII, December, 1009–1055.

Johnson, R.B., and A.J. Onwuegbuzie (2011), 'Mixed methods research: A research paradigm whose time has come', *Educational Researcher*, 33(7), 14–26.

Kallio, K. (2015), 'Collaborative learning with users as an enabler of service innovation', PhD Thesis. Espoo: VTT.

Klein, O., S. Doyen, C. Leys, P.A. Magalhaes de Saldanha da Gama, S. Miller, L. Questienne, and A. Cleeremans (2012), 'Low hopes, high expectations: Expectancy effects and the replicability of behavioral experiments', *Perspectives on Psychological Science*, 7(6), 572–584.

Langer, E.J., and J. Rodin (1976), 'The effects of choice and enhanced personal responsibility for the aged: A field experiment in an institutional setting', *Journal of Personality and Social Psychology*, 34(2), 191–198.

Lee, A. (1989), 'Case studies as natural experiments', *Human Relations*, 42(2), 117–137.

Lincoln, Y.S., and E.G. Guba (2007), 'But is it rigorous? Trustworthiness and authenticity in naturalistic evaluation', *New Directions for Evaluation*, 1986, 107–114.

Magnusson, P.R.P., J. Matthing, and P. Kristensson (2003), 'Managing user involvement in service innovation: Experiments with innovating end users', *Journal of Service Research*, 6(2), 111–124.

Mattsson, J., and F. Sørensen (2015), 'City renewal as open innovation', *Journal of Innovation Economics and Management*, 16(1), 195–215.

McCambridge, J., J. Witton, and D.R. Elbourne (2014), 'Systematic review of the Hawthorne effect: New concepts are needed to study research participation effects', *Journal of Clinical Epidemiology*, 67(3), 267–277.

McNiff, J., and J. Whitehead (2000), *Action Research in Organisations*. London: Routledge.

Morgan, D.L. (2007), 'Paradigms lost and pragmatism regained: Methodological implications of combining qualitative and quantitative methods', *Journal of Mixed Methods Research*, 1(1), 48–76.

Neuman, W. (2000), *Social Research Methods: Qualitative and Quantitative Approaches*. Bosten: Allyn and Bacon.

Nickson, D., C. Warhurst, and E. Dutton (2005), 'The importance of attitude and appearance in the service encounter in retail and hospitality', *Managing Service Quality*, 15(2), 195–208.

Prahalad, C.K., and V. Ramaswamy (2004), 'Co-creation experiences: The next practice in value creation', *Journal of Interactive Marketing*, 18(3), 5–14.

Ritchie, J., J. Lewis, C. Nicholls, and R. Ormston (2013), *Qualitative Research Practice: A Guide for Social Science Students and Researchers*. Thousand Oaks: Sage.

Salunke, S., J. Weerawardena, and J.R. McColl-Kennedy (2013), 'Competing through service innovation: The role of bricolage and entrepreneurship in project-oriented firms', *Journal of Business Research*, 66(8), 1085–1097.

Schumpeter, J. (1969), *The Theory of Economic Development. An Inquiry Into Profits, Capital, Credit, Interest and the Business Cycle*. Oxford: Oxford University Press.

Scupola, A., and H.W. Nicolajsen (2013), 'Library perceptions of using social software such as blogs in the idea generation phase of service innovations: Lessons from an experiment', in *Organizational Change and Information Systems*, Vol. 2. Berlin and New York: Springer, pp. 137–144.

Shadish, W.R., T.D. Cook, and D.T. Campbell (2002), *Experimental and Quasi-experimental Designs for Generalized Causal Inference*. Boston: Houghton Mifflin Company.

Sørensen, F. (2011), 'Inducing user-driven innovation in tourism: An experimental approach', in J. Sundbo and M. Toivonen (eds.), *User-Based Innovation in Services*, Cheltenham, UK and Northampton, MA, USA: Edward Elgar Publishing, pp. 303–322.

Sørensen, F., and J.F. Jensen (2012), 'Service encounter-based innovation and tourism', in E. Fayos-Solá, J.A.M. Silva, and J. Jafari (eds.), *Knowledge Management in Tourism: Policy and Governance Applications*. Bingley: Emerald Publishing, pp. 129–152.

Sørensen, F., and J.F. Jensen (2015), 'Value creation and knowledge development in tourism experience encounters', *Tourism Management*, 46, 336–346.

Sørensen, F., and J. Sundbo (2014), 'Potentials for user-based innovation in tourism: The example of GPS tracking of attraction visitors', in G. Alsos, D. Eide, and E. Madsen (eds.), *Handbook of Research on Innovation in Tourism Industries*. Cheltenham, UK and Northampton, MA, USA: Edward Elgar Publishing, pp. 132–154.

Sørensen, F., J. Mattsson, and J. Sundbo (2010), 'Experimental methods in innovation research', *Research Policy*, 39(3), 313–322.

Sørensen, F., J. Sundbo, and J. Mattsson (2013), 'Organisational conditions for service encounter-based innovation', *Research Policy*, 42(8), 1446–1456.
Sundbo, J. (2010), *The Toilsome Path of Service Innovation*. Cheltenham, UK and Northampton, MA, USA: Edward Elgar Publishing.
Toivonen, M., and T. Tuominen (2009), 'Emergence of innovations in services', *The Service Industries Journal*, 29(7), 887–902.
Van Rijnsoever, F.J., M.T.H. Meeus, and A.R.T. Donders (2012), 'The effects of economic status and recent experience on innovative behavior under environmental variability: An experimental approach', *Research Policy*, 41(5), 833–847.
Wang, S., Noe, R.A., and Z.M. Wang (2011), 'Motivating knowledge-sharing in knowledge management systems: A quasi-field experiment', *Journal of Management*, 40(4), 978–1009.
Webster, M., and J. Sell (2014), *Laboratory Experiments in the Social Sciences*. Philadelphia: Elsevier.
Willer, D., and A. Harry (2007), *Building Experiments: Testing Social Theory*. Palo Alto: Stanford University Press.

12. Service innovation in complex research projects: learnings from working within a triple helix framework

Claire Esther Staddon Forder

12.1 INTRODUCTION

A growing body of research into triple helix projects underlines the increasing interest in these frameworks. The triple helix focuses on the process of interaction between the three societal helices of government, industry and academia. According to Leydesdorff (2012), changes in society are creating driving forces towards a knowledge-based economy, resulting in a need for stronger interactions between the helices which offer potentials for synergy and innovation. When cooperation between the three helices becomes locked into a particular framework resulting in innovation potential, this framework becomes known as a triple helix project. However, there seems to be very little research that investigates the process of developing triple helix projects, how they function, what innovation they foster, what role their differences play in service innovation and what implications these types of projects have for service innovation and service innovation research. This chapter is an attempt to fill these epistemological gaps. The development of a triple helix project entitled the 'New Innovative Customer Experiences (NICE) Project' is examined as a case example of a triple helix project. The mandate of the NICE Project was to lift general tourism service quality in a Danish city, which was reported to be lower than other similar European cities (Horesta, 2015a). The NICE Project will be used to exemplify the synergetic potential of a triple helix project in order to showcase embedded helical synergies and differences to further understand how and why these project frameworks can facilitate and/or hinder service innovation and service innovation research. The focus of the NICE Project was on tourists' perceptions of service quality, which explains why tourism and hospitality services are highlighted in this chapter. The emphasis of this chapter is on service logics emphasising service innovation and research trends highlighting tourism and hospitality services.

The wide variety of terminology used to define the triple helix model can be confusing as they have been alternatively dubbed; 'helixes or helices' (Björk, 2014), 'spheres' (Etzkowitz et al., 2000), 'systems' (Etzkowitz and Leydesdorff, 2000), 'institutions' (Leydesdorff, 2000), 'institutional spheres' (Etzkowitz and Leydesdorff, 2000) or 'domains' (Leydesdorff, 2010b). Yet none of these terms adequately captures the complex individual natures of policy–industry–academia. The characteristics of the helices inform their members' understandings of the worlds they work in which combines to create a helix 'worldview'. The meaning of a helix 'worldview' is adapted from Cobern (1991), who defines a worldview as one that 'inclines one to a particular way of thinking' (p. 3) and 'is a communally shared, epistemological framework essential for daily life' (p. 4). A worldview can also be used to describe a 'philosophy' (Vidal, 2008), or a 'mindset' (Vargo et al., 2008). The terms worldview, philosophy and mindset will be used interchangeably throughout this chapter. The contention is that the different worldviews of the three helixes can facilitate or hinder service innovation and service innovation research.

Service innovation is a complex and challenging process due to two intertwined aspects of services and service innovation; firstly, the inherent multifarious nature of services as intangible, temporal, individually experienced, insubstantially differentiated between production and consumption, involving both technological and human interaction (Grönroos, 2001; Lovelock and Gummesson, 2004; Sørensen et al., 2013). The very intangibility, individuality and co-created characteristics of services make it challenging to know where and how to initiate measurable innovation (Ford et al., 2012). Additional complexity is also due to the blurred boundaries between consumer and provider (Gorman and Kevin, 2006). Second, service innovation can occur at fundamentally different layers of the service organisation ranging from both top-down to bottom-up, and from strategically planned to on-the-floor bricolage-type improvements (Fuglsang and Sørensen, 2011). These often-disconnected attempts at innovation make results difficult to coordinate and track, causing fuzziness around the concrete outcomes of improvement initiatives. This chapter adds an extra dimension to the complexities of service innovation and research by examining the benefits and challenges embedded in a complex service innovation and research project. The purpose of this chapter is not to discuss the methodologies and findings of the NICE Project. The aim is to analyse the process and development of a triple helix configured project, to deliberate on the worldview differences of the helices, and discuss what impact these differences might have on service innovation and research.

In order to achieve these aims, the chapter is structured in the following manner: first, a brief introduction to the contextual framework (the knowledge economy) of the triple helix model and the model itself is given, followed by a discussion of the relevance of triple helix projects for service innovation and research. Then a theoretical analysis of the different worldviews of the three helixes is undertaken. This is followed by a brief introduction to the NICE Project, which is then showcased to exemplify the variances of the different worldviews highlighted in the theoretical debate of the triple helix configuration. Finally, a discussion of the implications these worldview differences have for service innovation and research is undertaken and suggestions about how to bridge seemingly unbridgeable worldview gaps are offered.

The chapter is written on the basis of various sources. Three project founders from each of the helices were questioned, using semi-structured interviews. The interviews were conducted face-to-face or by telephone and the participants were asked to describe the development of the projects and the advantages and disadvantages they perceived while working within a triple helix configuration. They provided valuable inside knowledge of the project, and explained some of the benefits and difficulties they experienced while working with actors from different worldviews. Other stakeholders' knowledge was garnered by the author's two-year participative observations of NICE Project forums, workgroups and evaluation meetings. Finally, a broad selection of relevant theory on triple helix projects, the knowledge economy, worldviews, etc. was employed.

12.2   THE KNOWLEDGE ECONOMY AND THE TRIPLE HELIX MODEL

Etzkowitz (2002) and Leydesdorff (2000) argue that the emergence of the 'knowledge economy' is driving a closer triadic interaction between the three societal spheres of industry, government and universities (knowledge) (Leydesdorff, 2012; Ranga and Etzkowitz, 2013) which they call a triple helix model (Leydesdorff, 2012). Although a precise definition of the knowledge economy remains elusive (Brinkley, 2006), and considerable debate remains whether advanced societies have moved from an industrial-based economy to a knowledge economy (Powell and Snellman, 2004), certain changes in society are highlighted to signify the increased importance of, and reliance on, services and knowledge (Powell and Snellman, 2004). Key drivers of these changes are:

- increasing recognition of services as the key driver of modern economies as manufacturing activities are increasingly outsourced to developing economies (Hirsch-Kreinsen, 2003);
- increased levels of continual innovation (Brinkley, 2006);
- the ubiquitousness of (communication) technology (Bastalich, 2010);
- the increased significance and codification of knowledge (Leydesdorff, 2010b, 2012);
- the importance of 'knowledge workers' (Bastalich, 2010); and
- innovations in work practices towards flexible work places, broad job descriptions, the use of teams etc. (Powell and Snellman, 2004).

Historically, innovation in industrial societies was considered to be driven by the dyadic relationship between industry (R&D[1]) and policymakers, even though much of this innovation was scientifically developed (Ranga and Etzkowitz, 2013). Educational institutions appeared to play a less important role in industry-relevant innovation. Although universities are recognised as key players in the development of the future work force, little attention has been paid as to how they encourage and apply innovation (Turpin et al., 2009). With growing focus on the societal importance of knowledge and services, universities are becoming progressively attractive partners for industry and policymakers. Recognition is being given to the powerful role universities and other post-secondary educational colleges can play in societal development as 'cost effective and creative inventor[s] and transfer agent[s]' (Etzkowitz et al., 2000). Leydesdorff (2012) argues that the triple helix model provides a framework for developing complex sector level research projects through industry, policy and research interfaces. These interfaces result in the development of innovative synergies and the application of discovery (Leydesdorff, 2012). In other words, research projects in which actors from all three spheres are embedded, can create a context in which innovation, knowledge transfer and application can be achieved on a national level.

According to Lawton Smith and Leydesdorff (2012), triple helix configurations with negative overlaps are those where the three helixes have common touchpoints but do not overlap each other. They have different types of communications and therefore do not create combined synergies leading to innovation. Triple helix projects with positive overlaps between the subsystems are those where exploration of knowledge and innovation potential is made possible (Lawton Smith and Leydesdorff, 2012). Additionally, the active overlap of the three helixes drives the emergence of new innovation facilitating structures (Rodrigues and Melo, 2013) such as an innovation project.

12.2.1   Relevance of Triple Helix Model for Service Innovation Research

In the context of the knowledge economy, the service sector is considered to play an increasingly important economic role in developed societies, yet influential sub-sectors such as tourism and hospitality are not typically included in the current definition of the knowledge economy (Brinkley, 2008). These sectors are considered to be low-tech and low-skilled industries, and thus do not fall in line with the high skilled high-tech definitions of the knowledge economy (OECD, 1996). If triple helix projects are an outcome of the knowledge economy, it might be difficult to present reasons why this configuration would be a relevant framework for service innovation and research. However, proponents of the knowledge economy recognise fundamental weaknesses embedded within its definition (Brinkley, 2006; Powell and Snellman, 2004), and the OECD acknowledges that 'human capital indicators, particularly those relating to education and employment are central measures for the knowledge-based economy' (OECD, 1996, p. 43). Powell and Snellman (2004) contend that knowledge production is not necessarily an accurate measure of the knowledge economy, but it is when 'new technologies are married to complementary organisational practices' (p. 215) that substantial gains can be made. Furthermore, strong arguments have been made for the wide adaption and importance of information technologies in both the hospitality and tourism sectors (Morais et al., 2013), belying the notion that they are low-tech sectors and arguing for their inclusion in the knowledge economy (Sommer-Ulrich and Scholz, 2012). Furthermore, the heterogeneous and fragmented yet overlapping nature of these sectors with a predominance of small- and medium-sized businesses (Nickson, 2007), make them ideal candidates for service innovation and research through triple helix frameworks, such as the NICE Project, as a mechanism for binding the fragments together.

Although much has been written about service innovation through triple helix projects, there seems to be very little research aimed at understanding the process of triple helix development. There is also limited investigation into the implications that the differing worldviews of the helices have for actual service innovation and service innovation research. Most research on triple helix models appears to focus on measuring the success of triple helix projects, at regional or national policy levels. However, some concrete micro-level cases can be found. Ranga et al. (2008) studied the knowledge transfer capacity of small financial services firms from the triple helix perspective and found poor knowledge transfer due to a range of problems, most significantly due to communication deficiencies between helixes. Hagen (2002) examined the impact of a strategic alliance between public–university–private sectors and established that a triple helix configuration has a significant impact if university knowledge and expertise was disseminated through industry-linked partnerships. Breakey et al. (2009) investigated the results of a successful tourism knowledge exchange partnership, developed through student internships and discovered that triadic partnerships facilitated knowledge transfer. Beesley (2004) examined an Australian triple helix tourism project and determined that expectations to triple helix project results needed to be 'of immediate use to the industry' (p. 22). However, Bienkowska (2010) argues that this seldom occurs because of fundamental differences between the three helixes. Even these studies of triple helix partnerships provided no evidence of actual service innovation, and it is difficult to find concrete empirical evidence of implemented service innovation facilitated by the triple helix configuration. Moreover, there is little evidence of how triple helix service innovation projects evolve, and what factors facilitate or hinder service innovation and research. The aim of the following sections is to fill some of these epistemological gaps by examining the worldview differences of triple helix projects, and bring to light the implications they have for service innovation and research.

12.3 THEORETICAL WORLDVIEW DIFFERENCES OF TRIPLE HELIX CONFIGURATIONS

Creating overlapping and effective innovative spheres of the triple helix configuration is a challenging process as each sphere has its own embedded worldview. Vidal (2008) argues for the necessity of having a worldview/philosophy to make sense of the world and that a worldview 'encompasses everything that is important to an individual' (p. 7). Given the diverse objectives, purposes, cultures and knowledge domains of the different helices, there is a strong argument for a worldview of academia, policy or industry encompassing different mindsets. 'Mindset' could be interpreted as concepts of knowledge or as Ferguson (2005) terms it 'differing epistemological views' (p. 50). Collective mindsets reflect the construction, knowledge stocks and orientations of societies, cultures or economies (Pohlmann et al., 2014). Based on Luhmann's theory of social systems, Leydesdorff (2010a) argues for contrarily coded discourses in the political, industrial and academic helices. According to Bracken (2010), 'epistemology is about [. . .] the creation and dissemination of knowledge' (p. 2) thus epistemology can also be the symbolic representation of knowledge, in other words, its discourse. It can therefore be argued that different helixes have different discourses and thereby different 'languages' and different worldviews. The following section presents the variant triadic worldviews, and discusses the consequences of joining three helixes with different worldviews in relation to service innovation and research.

12.3.1 Government Worldview

The penultimate political institution operates at the macro-level and its structure is found in mezzo-level institutionalism. Hodgson (2006) defines institutions as 'systems of established and prevalent social rules that structure social interactions' (p. 2). A multitude of different institutions can be found under the umbrella of 'state institutionalism'. These bodies could be characterised as political due to the direct or indirect influence of state policy and/or funding, which subsequently plays a significant role in the shaping of these organisations and their strategies. The characteristics of political institutions are embedded in historical and political thought, replicated in sets of customs and practices informed by habits and norms (Rhodes et al., 2006). In the public sphere, macro-level institutions initiate changes, creating ripple effects among other actors and impacting on mezzo-level public institutions (Amenta and Ramsey, 2010).

A stereotypical governmental/political institutional worldview is epitomised by public accountability, rules, hierarchy, professionalism and bureaucracy with an element of resilient longitudinal temporality (Scartascini et al., 2013). Strategies and goal setting have long-term perspectives. The operative economic activity of political institutions is budget maintenance, as opposed to profit-generation. Public accountability is ensured by a vast array of different stakeholders with varying interests. When considerations about strategy, structure and budget have to be decided, different stakeholders carefully monitor the actions of policymakers to ensure public funding is used appropriately. These interests have to be taken into consideration (Christensen et al., 2009) thus increasing the institutional complexity of policy. Institutionally inherent hierarchical structures and multifarious bureaucratic coordination can result in lengthy top-down decision-making processes as bureaucracy, regulation and varying internal and external interests are negotiated (Christensen et al., 2009). Thus, negotiation and compromise within the organisation and their often conflicting goals and interests are key factors to its existence (Christensen et al., 2009). Finally, macro- and mezzo-level political actors are habitually considered to be distanced from the public (Stivers, 2009). Because policymakers simultaneously have to be accountable and negotiate institutional constraints (Amenta and Ramsey, 2010), they are typically viewed as over bureaucratic, inflexible and at worst, even tyrannical (Hall, 2010).

Political worldviews could be argued to be embedded in the necessity for accountability, ensured through regulation and control coordinated by bureaucratic procedures managed by specialised experts distanced from civilians or industry. The final objective being appropriately managed public funds through negotiating and balancing the interests of a vast array of stakeholders. Their discourse is composed of complex language dominated by legal and regulatory terminology directed towards compromise.

In helix configurations, political institutions contribute not only from a fiscal point of view through governmental funding, but also represent a force of stability, regulation and control (Stivers, 2009). Policy and legislation can be passed, which actively encourages and facilitates innovation and research activities through strategic alliances between the helixes of industry and academia. Thus political institutions can have a positive influence on service innovation and research by allocating funding and implementing regulation that positively influences conditions for bottom-up innovation involving a varied array of actors.

12.3.2 Service Sector Industry Worldview

It is debatable whether the service sector can be considered to have a worldview as it is so fragmented and heterogeneous (Becker et al., 2015). However, Lemey and Poels (1973) argue for a worldview of service systems as a commitment between service provider and customer, with interaction being the defining paradigm of service. On the other hand, Vargo and Lusch (2004) propose a new service worldview called 'service-dominant logic' as a 'collective mindset' (p. 2) built on many abstractions which 'create language that enables people to communicate and create shared worldviews' (Maglio et al., 2009, p. 396). According to Vargo and Lusch (2004), the worldview of service-dominant logic is constructed of concepts such as 'specialised competencies' 'deeds', 'performances', 'processes' and 'benefits' to others (p. 2).

A generic worldview of service encapsulates a shared comprehension of the diversity and complexity of services (Lemey and Poels, 1973) their simultaneous production and consumption causing their perishability, their intangible nature (Shostack, 1977; Zeithaml, 1988) and high levels of human involvement (Nickson, 2007) making their standardisation difficult. Many firms operating in the service/tourism/hospitality sector are profit-making, have relatively flat and simple hierarchies compared to political institutions particularly because of the predominance of small- and medium-sized businesses in the tourism and hospitality sectors (Stigler, 1956). The temporal aspect of business is short-term goal setting, against a competitive background in a rapidly changing, dynamic environment. As a result of these challenges, there is a predominantly short-term-oriented, problem-solving mindset. Furthermore, high dependency on a large seasonal and/or temporary low-paid, low-skilled peripheral work force, with a relatively small core of permanent employees (Watson, 2008) demands internal flexibility and rapid reaction and adaption to changes. Sector players and strategy can be constrained by policymaking on areas such as hygiene, standards, employment rules, taxes and other regulations (Watson, 2008). Price-setting and profit-making strategy is influenced by competitor action and consumer choice, and the time frame for decision-making is often very short. The pace is fast and operational problem-solving is often done from a pragmatic fire-fighting perspective (Ferguson, 2005). Added to the service worldview are the subtly different yet integral worldviews of the tourism and hospitality sub-sectors.

The tourism and hospitality sectors reflect the fragmented and hetero-geneous state of the service sector, with organisational sizes varying from small, family-run bed and breakfasts, hotels, restaurants and camping grounds, large national and international hostels, hotels and restaurants, to large privately owned or state owned amusement parks, museums, art galleries and entertainment facilities. However, Franklin (2004) claims a worldview of tourism because it is an ordered activity in its own right, with its own culture, tradition and shared connectivity. The tourism worldview embraces the concepts of difference, experience and movement. The hospi-tality sector worldview is embedded in the very word 'hospitality', includ-ing Heidegger's ontology of 'dwelling' – man's relationship to place and thereby being, and Levinas' ethos of 'hospitality', that humans 'maintain a proper relationship to place when it welcomes the Other' (Eubanks and Gauthier, 2011, p. 4). Thus, the service sector worldview can be considered a conglomeration of commitment and interaction, embracing tourism's mindset of movement, experience and difference and hospitality's philoso-phy of home and welcome. However, these worldviews are also obligated to operate within the industry/business worldview.

The following characteristics of the service industry worldview, para-doxically different from the policy sphere, are:

- The 'service' worldview of close and personal interaction with the user versus the acknowledged 'distance' of government;
- The 'tourism' mindset of 'movement and difference', dichotomous to the policy ontology of long-term stability; and
- The 'home and welcome' philosophy of hospitality versus the distant 'tyrannical' nature of the political mindset. Thus the service industry helix represents a complex mix of differing worldviews.

The overarching worldview of the service industry might be considered to be the social interaction of humans in an economic relationship supported by the application of resources to solve, pragmatically and flexibly, complex real-life business challenges. Their dialogue would typically be grounded in common sense and problem-solving embedded in goal and profit-oriented terms.

The multifaceted interface of many actors in the service ontology provides a strong network for pragmatic service innovation, through idea generation, experimentation, knowledge sharing and access to resources. It also provides an environment conducive to practice-led research, as research ends should be tightly linked to business goals and/or solutions to practical problems (Mohrman et al., 2001).

12.3.3 The Academic Worldview

Academic institutions offering long-term educational programmes typically have future-oriented goals and are designed to endure in a fairly stable environment with little/slow change. A predominant characteristic of the academic sphere is that of adding to or creating or developing knowledge through the application of scientific methods during the investigation of a particular phenomenon in order to model the world (Vidal, 2008). This, as well as knowledge dissemination, can be understood as the primary goals of the research community (Battaglio and Scicchitano, 2013). An important aim of the academic worldview is status, defined by recognition, in particular, through publication in renowned/influential journals or other arenas. Research efforts by academics are not necessarily driven by the utility of the research outcomes, but by curiosity and the drive to understand and explain the world. Research projects characteristically have medium-to long-term time frames, and results are typically published after lengthy review processes. Success in an academic institution could be defined as 'a flourishing research community', achieved by the development of formal knowledge (Ferguson, 2005). Research validity, from an academic perspective, is important to the construction of knowledge, thus the relatively slower the pace of academic research, the better to legitimise outcomes. Knowledge is bound to theory and the practical relevance of knowledge is subordinate to its legitimacy.

Despite different scientific ontological stances occupying the academic sphere, the overarching worldview of the academic helix can be said to be that of the search for explanatory knowledge to explain the world theoretically through the application of scientific principles and the dissemination of knowledge. Their worldview is typically symbolised by curiosity of the unknown, articulated through abstract, complex language. The academic helix creates legitimacy for new knowledge and contributes to the helix configuration with time and expert resources to examine relevant areas of investigation with appropriate methods.

Considering the varied mindsets of the three helixes, tensions and gaps in new triple helix structures are unavoidable. The following section examines these tensions and gaps.

12.3.4 Worldview Tensions and Gaps Inherent in the Triple Helix

Essentially, the tensions between the three helixes can be grouped into three main areas: the temporal, contextual and schema cognitive landscape (Spiro et al., 1988). These tensions and the worldview attitudes towards innovation are visualised in Table 12.1 below.

Compared with the service industry helix, the temporal outlook of policy and academia is longer and more future-oriented. For example, goal setting outcomes in the service sector are typically set against short-term deadlines (Hayes and Fitzgerald, 2009), whereas academia and policy typically operate with longer planning time frames (Hayes and Fitzgerald, 2007). The policy and academic spheres can be imagined as large ships changing course; it is a lengthy and time-consuming process seemingly lacking a sense of urgency with long-term outcomes. Industry can be compared to a small yacht, reacting quickly to changes resulting in fast results but with a limited future orientation. Due to rapidly changing environments and daily fire-fighting, decision-making needs to occur rapidly and produce immediate results.

Contextually, government and academia share similar environments in terms of stability, although policy exists in a more complex environment due to its extensive range of interests. The competitive arena for these helixes is traditionally almost non-existent (although for academia this is changing); therefore competitive innovation and change are usually not high on their agendas. The fundamental difference between policy and academia can be seen in their internal focus. Policy relies on regulation to control innovation outcomes, whereas academia searches for understanding through the production of tested knowledge which may lead to innovation (Leydesdorff, 2012). Ultimately, the end goals of research are academic journals, which may influence policy (depending on the nature of the research) but may be of little practical use for practitioners. Tenure, the definition of academic success, promotes individual achievement as opposed to the collaboration required in the policy sphere. Knowledge supersedes regulations. Innovation is conducted only after theory is verified, tested and proven true.

The industry sphere, represented by the service sector, faces a fundamentally different external and internal environment. The external environment can be characterised as having a medium level of complexity, but is unstable with high uncertainty (OECD, 2000). Economic, technological,

Table 12.1 Visual depiction of worldview differences of three helixes

Helical worldviews	Temporal	Contextual		Cognitive landscape	Attitude to innovation
		Internal	External		
Policy	• Long term • Future-oriented • Deliberate top-down decision-making • Lack of urgency	• Public accountability • Budget maintenance • Multiple hierarchies • Bureaucracy • Rules and regulation • Balance interests	• High complexity • Stable • Low competition • Slow change	• Interaction with policy and regulation • Complex regulatory and legal • Control • Negotiation	• Low priority – not essential for survival • Slow • Top-down
Service Industry	• Short-term oriented • Fast decision-making • Immediate results	• Profit • Customer focus • Goal-oriented • Problem–solution • Flexible standards	• Middle complexity • Fast change • High competition • High uncertainty	• Interaction with customers • Pragmatic • Problem-solving • Goal-oriented	• Fast • Pragmatic • High reliance on customer • Necessary for survival
Academia	• Medium long term • Future-oriented • Slow consensus decision-making process	• Hierarchy • Truth • New knowledge • Appropriate methods • Valid and verified • Curiosity • Knowledge dissemination	• Simple/low complexity • Low competition • Stable • Slow change	• Interaction with theory and empirical • Truth • Abstract • Complex	• High outcome of new knowledge • Tried and tested • Reviewed • Final result

regulatory and competitive changes can have unpredictable and unforeseen consequences. A key performance indicator for service sector players is profit. Innovation and change are essential for survival and valuable knowledge must be pragmatic (Battaglio and Scicchitano, 2013). Theory bound academic knowledge is not considered relevant (Ferguson, 2005). Innovation can take place on an individual day-to-day basis or as strategically planned initiatives and must have profit-oriented outcomes.

Finally, the last domain of difference can be seen in the schemata of the different worldviews. The policy schemata operates in an extremely complex environment with a multitude of actors who potentially can have an influential impact (LaPalombara, 2003), but where policymaking and legislation create the framework for action. Slow change and adherence to legislation result in lengthy decision-making processes (LaPalombara, 2003) leading to risk-averse, rigid approaches to knowledge and innovation. The academic mindset can be characterised by complex language, unfamiliar methods and slower approaches to achieving valid results (Battaglio and Scicchitano, 2013) in the creation of 'true' theoretical knowledge. Often, in the interests of knowledge creation, it is frequently perceived to be removed from the regulatory and/or industry sphere (Ferguson, 2005). The industry mindset is characterised by strategic thinking, based on dynamic changes requiring quick decision-making and practical knowledge for problem-solving as opposed to academia's focus on explanatory knowledge (Vidal, 2008) or policy's regulatory knowledge (Battaglio and Scicchitano, 2013). Resource constraints such as the dilemma of the trade-offs between time, costs and quality also require rapid judgements. Day-to-day problem-solving of urgent situations does not allow for keeping abreast with new research often communicated in complex academic language (Ferguson, 2005). For the industry mindset, research should be tightly connected to 'real' organisational problems, backed up by evidence and conducive to solving problems (Battaglio and Scicchitano, 2013). Furthermore, concrete outcomes of innovation research must be timely, as shifting conditions make results quickly obsolete and thus irrelevant to immediate problem-solving needs (Battaglio and Scicchitano, 2013).

To summarise, different worldview agendas, strategies, contexts and even languages cause tension between the different spheres. Communication is constrained, collaboration difficult and knowledge transference problematic (Bansal et al., 2012). These complexities pose challenges for communication, knowledge dispersal and ultimately service innovation and research (Beesley, 2004). Furthermore, practitioners are often incognizant of the findings of academic research (Battaglio and Scicchitano, 2013). The question is: can these differences be sufficiently bridged so as to facilitate service innovation and research? The following sections attempt to answer this question through a triple helix project in practice, as exemplified by the NICE Project.

12.4   NICE PROJECT BACKGROUND

This section introduces the NICE Project, the key drivers of its development and the actors of the triple helix and demonstrates the different worldviews of the triple helix through the NICE Project. The section concludes with a discussion of the gaps in worldviews the NICE Project has managed to bridge, which gaps to date still exist, and what implications these worldview differences in the triple helix project have for current and future service innovation and research.

12.4.1   Contextual Background and Development of the NICE Project

The negative impact of the economic crises of 2008 on the world tourism sector (Jones, 2009; Ritchie et al., 2010), resulted in increased awareness of perceived poor quality of service delivered by the Danish tourism sector (Hall, 2013) and declining numbers of tourists (Blanke and Chiesa, 2011). Consequently, political efforts to bolster the competitive strength of the Danish tourism sector were increased (Østergaard, 2013; Danish Government, 2014). These interconnected events created a fertile field for various successful initiatives aimed at improving the level of service in the service and tourism sector, involving the typical dyad of government and private sector players.[2] However, failure to improve sector service quality catalysed the formation of the NICE Project. The project, developed by influential actors in the industry and policy helices who agreed to broaden the field of service innovation by involving the academic helix,[3] was mandated to improve the perceived low quality of tourism services (Horesta, 2015a). In 2014 a triple helix project structure was formed as visualised in Figure 12.1 below.

As Figure 12.1 demonstrates, the triple helix NICE Project structure overlaps the three helixes of policy–industry–academia, but it is also a unique configuration due to the sheer multitude and variety of actors, including the representation of two academic institutions. Another unique feature of the NICE Project, is the presence of stakeholders who operate between policy and industry (DMO, Trade Union and Transport Organisations). They do not make policy, but have the wherewithal to influence policy while at the same time representing industry. Thus these stakeholders played a unique role by bridging policy and industry.

In order to structure and maximise on helix overlaps, the NICE Project

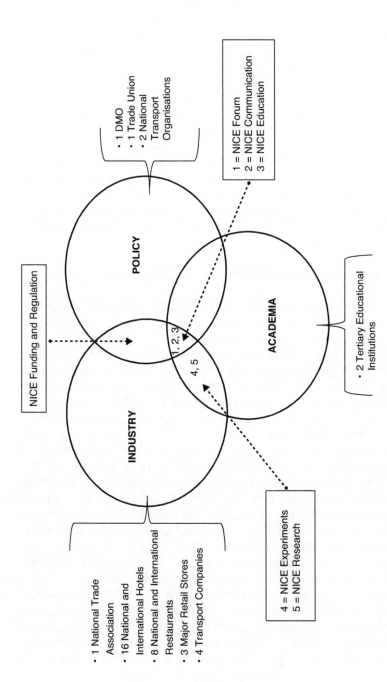

Figure 12.1   The triple helix configuration of the NICE Project – representation of stakeholders and their innovation overlaps

was subdivided into five innovation activities: 1) NICE Forum – a network and knowledge-disseminating activity aimed at lifting the sector's service level through shared experiences; 2) NICE Communication – which disseminated project results to all stakeholders; 3) NICE Education – aimed, in cooperation with policy, at innovating sector-relevant competency-lifting courses; 4) NICE Experiments – where firms and academia tested service innovation in field experiments; and 5) NICE Research – aimed at researching, developing and documenting service innovation (WOCO, 2014). With 38 different actors representing the three helixes, the NICE Project began to find a way to collectively lift the service level across the service sector. As each of the helixes operates in their own contexts with differing characteristics, synergies and barriers to service innovation and research were inevitable. The following sections examine the synergies the NICE Project enabled by bridging worldview gaps facilitating service innovation and research, and which worldview differences the NICE Project found challenging to bridge.

12.4.2   Bridging Worldview Differences in the NICE Project

The most significant worldview gap successfully bridged by the NICE Project was the characteristic academic–industry cognitive landscape difference of useful knowledge (as shown in Figure 12.1). Mohrman et al. (2001) documented that research conducted in academic/industry collaborative research projects was perceived to be more relevant if the opinions of participants were included, thus facilitating ownership. This was achieved through the varied activities of the NICE Project, in particular the NICE Forum which offered triadic stakeholders the spatial and temporal opportunity to contribute to the direction of the NICE Project through exchanging ideas for practice-led research, leading to service innovation and research. Specific industry issues (e.g. the lack of a top class service and hospitality educational programmes, and the desire to know more about guests' motivations and needs) were expressed and addressed. NICE Education undertook a successful analysis of available sector-relevant educational programmes resulting in the innovation of the digital platform of these programmes. NICE Research, in collaboration with the service sector, collected evidence of tourists' service quality perceptions, covering the entire tourist value chain and resulting in a report with important, and surprising, findings for the sector (Horesta, 2015a). Furthermore, NICE Research and NICE Experiments successfully joined researchers and practitioners in concentrated service innovation through field experiments. Although the financial outcomes of these experiments remain undocumented, optimistic accounts of their positive impact on employee motivation have been reported. These organised activities satisfied industry's need for timely research results tightly tied to organisational goals. The activities also tied academia's natural curiosity for new knowledge to industry-relevant problems, while ensuring the legitimacy of the new knowledge through the application of appropriate scientific methodologies. Policy's agenda – raising the general standard of service to bolster its competitive advantage – is yet to be met. However, the establishment of a service manifesto (Horesta, 2015b), specifying general service quality principles across the service sector, could be regarded as a considerable step towards achieving policy's long-term agenda.

12.4.3   Unbridged Gaps: Goals, Communication, Knowledge Transference and Epistemologies

Despite the successes depicted in the previous section, significant worldview differences between the helixes still remain unbridged. These variances are embedded in the temporal and cognitive landscapes explained in Table 12.1, and they have significant implications for service innovation and research. Goal setting in the different worldviews is related to temporal differences. The overarching long-term goal of the NICE Project, that of a national service quality lift, managed to bridge some helical differences, yet time-based differences unintentionally hindered bridge-building. Academia's temporal attitudes towards goal setting delayed the production of research outcomes, frustrating industry's desire for immediate knowledge to meet short-term goals. Moreover, the combined contextual mindsets of policy (interest-balancing) and academia (consensus-building decision-making) may have played a significant role in the way NICE Forum set up project goals which, while encouraging participative direction-setting of the NICE Project, never addressed worldview temporal differences. Without specific short-term goals and milestones, expectations remained implicitly embedded in the temporally differential worldviews, causing frustration and, in some cases, disillusion.

Through the various activities of NICE Research and NICE Experiments, rich data was collected and various innovation activities were accomplished. However, again, the temporal differences of the worldviews became problematic. From industry's perspective, usable results from research were too slow to be useful. Furthermore, actual service innovation was embedded in voluntary partnerships between academia and industry, leading to company-entrenched experiments solely benefiting the participating firms. Innovation activities did not meet policy's goal of a general service quality lift, or industry's need for pragmatic answers to solve real-time problems. Thus, as reported by Beesley (2004), the issue of results from a temporal and cognitive landscape point of view was problematic, revealing an unbridged gap between the helices. These differences may have left some industry stakeholders with the impression that, although the initial objective of the NICE Project was attractive, its goals and results remained unclear, which effectively widened the gap. Additionally, from an academic viewpoint, pressure to produce quick, pragmatic results compromised scientific principles. Finally, expectations towards communication and dissemination of the effectiveness and results of the different service innovation initiatives and research had not been solidified at the beginning of the project. Which results, to whom, how and when had never been addressed, further adding to frustrations, which were explicated when some industry partners declared NICE Forum dialogues as being 'too academic'.

From the discussion above, it is clear that the academic helix still struggles to meet the short-term time frame of the industry helix. Service innovation and research based on empirical data needs to be addressed appropriately if it is to meet the needs of the scientific community. Industry wants results as soon as possible in an understandable language, uncomplicated by sophisticated academic linguistics and methodologies. Policy needs to be able to show accountability by communicating positive results.

12.5 DISCUSSION AND CONCLUSIONS

Given the challenges discussed in the previous section, two fundamental questions can be asked, and partially answered:

1. Can worldview differences between policy, industry and academia be successfully bridged in the NICE Project?
2. How can current worldview gaps possibly be bridged in future triple helix projects?

The answer to the first question is both yes and no: bringing the triad into a neutral space and facilitating stakeholder participation enabled a positive overlap of the three helices. This resulted in some service innovation and research satisfying most worldviews. Moreover, actual innovation and research efforts involving industry and academia were tied to industry-relevant problems.

On the other hand, the temporal worldview differences were more challenging to overcome. The long-, medium- and short-term worldviews appear to be insurmountable obstacles. Unless industry is willing to accept slower, but valid results, or unless academia is prepared to deliver quicker, but less valid scientific outcomes, and policy is able to mediate between the two, acceptable and utilitarian results seem to require a bridge between the earth and the moon. Furthermore, worldview cognitive landscapes differences also remain unbridged. Academia's dialogue was too complex and abstract for the pragmatically oriented industry, whereas industry's rhetoric was too focused on problem solution rather than finding explanations for difficulties.

Lessons learnt while working in the triple helix project may provide answers to the second question of how to bridge these gaps. It would have been advisable to break down the overarching goal of a service quality lift into a series of medium- and short-term goals. Clear goal setting would have revealed different worldview expectations and may have been a means to bridging temporal and communicative differences. Additionally, knowing the industry helix desire for fast problem-solving results, academia could learn to work at two different tempos: 1) a fast tempo allowing rapid data processing through the application of less complicated analytical methodologies. This would facilitate the timely output of relevant results for industry, which policy could also utilise to communicate to relevant stakeholders; and 2) a slower tempo allowing for more complicated analytical techniques designed to uphold scientific principles. Industry could also upgrade decision-makers' skills to better understand the theoretical and abstract mindset of academia. Finally, although the NICE Project resulted in some tangible service innovations, these efforts were limited to specific organisations. Without a clear plan as to how to transfer this knowledge to other industry stakeholders, it will be difficult to accomplish policy's long-term goal of a sector-wide service quality lift. Useful results, the dissemination of knowledge, techniques used and lessons learnt need to be successfully shared in the triple helix configuration in order to facilitate effective service innovation and research.

LEARNING POINTS

- Differing helical worldviews bring synergy to service innovation and research but can also present significant barriers.
- Three characteristic worldview differences can be categorised into the temporal, contextual and cognitive landscape.
- Triple helix configurations can facilitate service innovation and research if temporal and cognitive landscape differences are systematically addressed at the beginning of the helix structure formation.

DISCUSSION TOPICS

- What techniques can academia employ to satisfy industry's need for immediate research outcomes to solve pragmatic problems?
- What efforts can industry make to try to meet academia?
- What role (how and why) does policy play in this triadic relationship?

NOTES

1. Research and Development.
2. Examples of pilot innovation initiatives are, for example (but not limited to), 'Den Gode Værstskab' (self-translated to 'The Good Hostess' (2013–2015). The 'Good Hostess' project consisted of cooperation between five North Zealand municipalities aimed at improving service employees' hostess competencies (http://www.visitnordsjael-land.dk/nordsjaelland/fem-kommuner-indgaar-partnerskab-med-det-gode-vaertsskab, retrieved 10 November 2015). Another example is the 'Open Arms' project (2012), in cooperation with various companies, aimed at improving employees' service competencies through innovative and exceptional means. Key players cooperating in the 'Open Arms' project were Open Copenhagen, HORESTA, The Municipality of Copenhagen, Meng & Company and Fucking Flink (http://www.horesta.dk/da-DK/Nyheder%20 og%20Politik/Nyheder/Nyhedsarkiv/2012/05/Open%20Arms, retrieved 10 November 2015).
3. '*Vækstforum*' or 'The Forum of Growth' is a collection of partners from policy, industry and academia dedicated to achieving growth in the capital region of Denmark through EU funding (Vækstforum Hovedstaden, 2015).

REFERENCES

Amenta, E., and K.M. Ramsey (2010), 'Institutional theory', in K.T. Leicht and J.C. Jenkens (eds.), *Handbook of Politics: State and Society in Global Perspectives*. New York: Springer Science+Business Media, pp. 5–39.

Bansal, P., S. Bertels, T. Ewart, P. MacConnachie, and J. O'Brien (2012), 'Bridging the research–practice gap', *The Academy of Management Perspectives (AMP)*, 26(1), 73–92.

Bastalich, W. (2010), 'Knowledge economy and research innovation', *Studies in Higher Education*, 35(7), 845–857.

Battaglio, R.P., and M.J. Scicchitano (2013), 'Building bridges? An assessment of academic and practitioner perceptions with observations for the public administration classroom', *Journal of Public Affairs Education*, 19(4), 749–772.

Becker, M., M. Böttcher, and S. Klingner (2015), 'Systemising service classifications', in J. Sundbo, L. Fuglsang, F. Sørensen, and N. Balsby (eds.), *RESER2015 – Innovative Services in the 21st Century*, RESER – European Association for Research on Services, pp. 1–17.

Beesley, L. (2004), 'Multi-level complexity in the management of collaborative tourism research settings', in C. Cooper, C. Arcadia, D. Solnet, and M. Whitford (eds.), *Creating Tourism Knowledge: A Selection of Papers from CAUTHE 2004*.

Council For Australian University Tourism and Hospitality Education Inc, pp. 19–36.

Bienkowska, D. (2010), 'The Triple Helix balancing act: Industrial research institutes as knowledge intermediaries', in Tariq Durrani (ed.), *Proceedings from the 8th International Triple Helix Conference*. Bandung, Indonesia: Triple Helix Association, pp. 1–6.

Björk, P. (2014), 'The DNA of tourism service innovation: A Quadruple Helix approach', *Journal of the Knowledge Economy*, 5(1), 181–202.

Blanke, J., and T. Chiesa (2011), *The Travel & Tourism Competitiveness Report 2011 – Beyond the Downturn*. Geneva: World Economic Forum.

Bracken, S. (2010), 'Discussing the importance of ontology and epistemology awareness in practitioner research', *Worcester Journal of Learning and Teaching*, 4(4), 1–9.

Breakey, N.M., R.N.S. Robinson, and L.G. Beesley (2009). 'Students go a "Waltzing Matilda" – A regional tourism knowledge exchange through innovative internships', *Journal of Teaching in Travel & Tourism*, 8(2–3), 223–240.

Brinkley, I. (2006), 'Defining the knowledge economy: Knowledge economy programme report', *Knowledge Creation Diffusion Utilization*, pp. 1–31.

Brinkley, I. (2008), *The Knowledge Economy: How Knowledge is Reshaping the Economic Life of Nations*. London: The Work Foundation.

Christensen, T., P. Lægreid, P.G. Roness, and K.A. Røvik, (2009), 'Organization theory and the public sector: Instrument, culture and myth', *Public Administration*, 87(1), 156–157.

Cobern, W. (1991), 'Worldview theory and science education research', *National Association for Research in Science Teaching*, 1–25.

Danish Government (2014), *Denmark at Work: Plan for Growth in Danish Tourism*. Copenhagen.

Etzkowitz, H., and L. Leydesdorff (2000), 'The dynamics of innovation: From National Systems and "Mode 2" to a Triple Helix of university–industry–government relations', *Research Policy*, 29(2), 109–123.

Etzkowitz, H., A. Webster, C. Gebhardt, and B.R.C. Terra (2000), 'The future of the university and the university of the future: Evolution of ivory tower to entrepreneurial paradigm', *Research Policy*, 29, 313–330.

Eubanks, C., and D.J. Gauthier (2011), 'The politics of the homeless spirit: Heidegger and Levinas on dwelling and hospitality', *History of Political Thought*, 32(1), 125–146.

Ferguson, J.E. (2005), 'Bridging the gap between research and practice', *Knowledge Management for Development*, 1(3), 46–54.

Ford, R.C., B. Edvardsson, D. Dickson, and B. Enquist (2012), 'Managing the innovation co-creation challenge: Lessons from service exemplars Disney and IKEA', *Organizational Dynamics*, 41(4), 281–290.

Franklin, A. (2004), 'Tourism as an ordering: Towards a new ontology of tourism', *Tourist Studies*, 4(3), 277–301.

Fuglsang, L., and F. Sørensen (2011), 'The balance between bricolage and innovation: Management dilemmas in sustainable public innovation', *The Service Industries Journal*, 31(4), 581–595.

Gorman, O., and D. Kevin (2006), *Jacques Derrida's Philosophy of Hospitality*. Retrieved 5 November 2014, from https://pureapps2.hw.ac.uk/portal/files/4162817/Jacques_Derrida_s_philosophy_of_hospitality.pdf.

Grönroos, C. (2001), 'The perceived service quality concept – a mistake?', *Managing Service Quality*, 11, 150–152.

Hagen, R. (2002), 'Globalization, university transformation and economic regeneration: A UK case study of public/private sector partnership', *International Journal of Public Sector Management*, 15(3), 204–218.

Hall, E. (2010), 'Live bureaucrats and dead public servants: How people in government are discussed on the floor of the house', *Public Administration*, 62(2), 242–251.

Hall, O. (2013), *Dansk service skraber bunden*. Retrieved 3 September 2015, from http://www.business.dk/detailhandel/dansk-service-skraber-bunden.

Hayes, K.J., and J.A. Fitzgerald (2007), *Herding Cats: Practical and Theoretical Perspectives on Inter-Organisational Knowledge Transfer Across Research-Industry Boundaries*. Centre for Industry and Innovation Studies, University of Western Sydney.

Hayes, K.J., and J.A. Fitzgerald (2009), 'Managing occupational boundaries to improve innovation outcomes in industry-research organisations', *Journal of Management and Organization*, 15(4), 423–437.

Hirsch-Kreinsen, E.A. (2003), 'Low-tech industries and the knowledge economy: State of the art and research challenges', *STEP-Centre for Innovation Research*, Norway.

Hodgson, G.M. (2006), 'What are institutions?', *Journal of Economic Issues*, XL(1), 1–25.

Horesta (2015a), 'København er dyr men gæstfri', in *NICE Live Magasine*, Hotel-, Restaurant- og Turisterhvervets Arbejdsgiverforening, January 2015.

Horesta (2015b), 'Kommende manifest for service-oplevelser i særklasse', in *NICE Live Magasine*, Hotel-, Restaurant- og Turisterhvervets Arbejdsgiverforening, January 2015, 22–23.

Jones, P. (2009), 'Impact of the global recession on the hospitality and tourism industry', *Tourism and Hospitality Research*, 9(4), 363–367.

LaPalombara, J. (2003), 'Power and politics in organisations: Public and private sector comparisons', in M. Dierkes, A.B. Antal, J. Child, and I. Nonaka (eds.), *Handbook of Organizational Learning & Knowledge*. Oxford: Oxford University Press, pp. 557–599.

Lawton Smith, H., and L. Leydesdorff (2012), 'The Triple Helix in the context of global change: Dynamics and challenges', *SSRN Electronic Journal*, 32(4), 1–13.

Lemey, E., and G. Poels (1973), 'Towards a service system ontology for service science', in G. Groos, J. Hartmanis, and J. van Leeuwen (eds.), *Service-Oriented Computing*. Berlin: Springer, pp. 250–264.

Leydesdorff, L. (2000), 'The triple helix: An evolutionary model of innovations', *Research Policy*, 29(2), 243–255.

Leydesdorff, L. (2010a), 'The communication of meaning and the structuration of expectations: Giddens' "Structuration Theory" and Luhmann's "Self-Organisation"', *Journal of the American Society for Information and Technology*, 61(10), 2138–2150.

Leydesdorff, L. (2010b), 'The knowledge-based economy and the triple helix model', *Annual Review of Information Science and Technology*, 44, 365–417.

Leydesdorff, L. (2012), *The Triple Helix of University–Industry–Government Relations*. Amsterdam: Kluwer.

Lovelock, C., and E. Gummesson (2004), 'Whither services marketing? In search of a new paradigm and fresh perspectives', *Journal of Service Research*, 7(1), 20–41.

Maglio, P.P., S.L. Vargo, N. Caswell, and J. Spohrer (2009), 'The service system is the basic abstraction of service science', *Information Systems and E-Business Management*, 7(4), 395–406.

Mohrman, S., C. Gibson, and A. Mohrman (2001), 'Doing research that is useful to practice: A model and empirical exploration', *Academy of Management Journal*, 44(2), 357–375.

Morais, E.P., C.R. Cunha, and J.P. Gomes (2013), *The Information and Communication Technologies in Tourism Degree Courses: The Reality of the Iberian Peninsula*. Retrieved 17 March 2016, from https://bibliotecadigital.ipb. pt/bitstream/10198/8504/3/beta_crc_jp_resumo.pdf.

Nickson, D. (2007), *Human Resource Management for the Hospitality and Tourism Industries*. Oxford: Elsevier Ltd.

OECD (1996), *The Knowledge-Based Economy. Development*, Vol. 96. Paris: OECD.

OECD (2000), *The Service Economy. Business and Industry Policy Forum Series*. Paris: OECD.

Østergaard, M.Z. (2013), *Forecast Turismen i Danmark 2013–2016*. Copenhagen: VisitDenmark.

Pohlmann, M., S. Bär, and E. Valarini (2014), 'The analysis of collective mindsets: Introducing a new method of institutional analysis in comparative research', *Revista de Sociologia e Política*, 22(52), 7–25.

Powell, W.W., and K. Snellman (2004), 'The knowledge economy', *Annual Review of Sociology*, 30(1), 199–220.

Ranga, M., and H. Etzkowitz (2013), 'Triple helix systems: An analytical framework for innovation policy and practice in the knowledge society', *Industry and Higher Education*, 27(4), 237–262.

Ranga, L.M., J. Miedema, and R. Jorna (2008), 'Enhancing the innovative capacity of small firms through triple helix interactions: Challenges and opportunities', *Technology Analysis & Strategic Management*, 20(6), 697–716.

Rhodes, R.A.W., S.A. Binder, and B.A. Rockman (2006), 'Old Institutionalisms', in R.A.W. Rhodes, S.A. Binder, and B.A. Rockman (eds.), *The Oxford Handbook of Political Institutions*. Oxford: Oxford University Press, pp. 90–108.

Ritchie, J.R.B., C.M. Amaya Molinar, and D.C. Frechtling (2010), 'Impacts of the world recession and economic crisis on tourism: North America', *Journal of Travel Research*, 49(1), 5–15.

Rodrigues, C., and A.I. Melo (2013), 'The triple helix model as inspiration for local development policies: An experience-based perspective', *International Journal of Urban and Regional Research*, 37(5), 1675–1687.

Scartascini, C., E. Stein, and M. Tommasi (2013), 'Political institutions, intertemporal cooperation, and the quality of public policies', *Journal of Applied Economics*, 16(1), 1–32.

Shostack, L. (1977), 'Breaking free from product marketing', *The Journal of Marketing*, 41(2), 73–80.

Sommer-Ulrich, J., and R. Scholz (2012), 'The Serbian Knowledge Economy Market Report', Working Paper 2012, The Serbian Knowledge Economy. London: European Bank for Reconstruction and Development.

Sørensen, F., J. Sundbo, and J. Mattsson (2013), 'Organisational conditions for service encounter-based innovation', *Research Policy*, 42(8), 1446–1456.

Spiro, R.J., R.L. Coulson, P.J. Feltovich, and D.K. Anderson (1988), *Cognitive Flexibility Theory: Advanced Knowledge Acquisition in Ill-Structured Domains*. Technical Report No. 441, University of Illinois Urbana-Champaign, Illinois.

Stigler, G.J. (1956), *The Classification and Characteristics of Services Industries*. Princeton, NJ: Princeton University Press, pp. 1–15.

Stivers, C. (2009), 'The ontology of public space: Grounding governance in social reality', *American Behavioral Scientist*, 52(7), 1095–1108.

Turpin, D.H., E. Sager, L. Tait, and L. De Decker (2009), *Universities and the Knowledge Economy*. Business Council of British Columbia, Canada, 1–24.

Vækstforum Hovedstaden (2015), *Om Vækstforum*. Retrieved 28 September 2015, from https://www.regionh.dk/Vaekstforum/om-vaekstforum/Sider/default.aspx.

Vargo, S.L., and R.F. Lusch (2004), 'Evolving to a new dominant logic for marketing', *Journal of Marketing*, 68(January), 1–17.

Vargo, S.L., P.P. Maglio, and M.A. Akaka (2008), 'On value and value co-creation: A service systems and service logic perspective', *European Management Journal*, 26(3), 145–152.

Vidal, C. (2008), 'What is a worldview?', in H. Van Belle and J. Van der Veken (eds.), *De wetenschappen en het creatieve aspect van de werkelijkheid*. Leuven: Acco, pp. 1–13.

Watson, S. (2008), 'Conceptual model for analysing management development in the hospitality industry: A UK perspective', *International Journal of Hospitality Management*, 27(3), 414–425.

WOCO (2014), *NICE Project – It's a Nice Project We Have Here*. Retrieved 3 September 2015, from http://niceproject.dk.

Zeithaml, V.A. (1988), 'Consumer perceptions of price, quality, and value', *Journal of Marketing*, 52, 2–22.

Index